PASHA OF JERUSALEM

If I forget thee, O Jerusalem,
Let my right hand forget her cunning.

(Psalm 137, v.5)

Contents

List of Illustrations viii
Glossary ix
Acknowledgements xiii
General Foreword to the Series xiv
Foreword xvii

1. A Safe Job with a Pension at Sixty? 1
2. Trooper, Bombay Light Horse 16
3. The Open Desert 30
4. 'Received, One Palestine' 52
5. Is Great Britain Honest? 73
6. Pasha of Jerusalem 98
7. The District Commissioner 108
8. The Naked Sword 114
9. Dr Jekyll and Mr Hyde 130
10. Retrospect 147
11. The Christian Holy Places 152
12. Religious Services 158
13. Funeral Rites 164
14. The Giant Turtle 175
15. The Storm 183
16. No Common Ground 205
17. Farewell 225

Index 229

Illustrations

Frontispiece   Portrait of Edward Keith-Roach, 1943

Plate 1   Portrait of Edward Keith-Roach at 17
Plate 2   Edward Keith-Roach with his mother, sisters and brothers
Plate 3   Edward and Violet Keith-Roach before their presentation at
             Buckingham Palace, 1922
Plate 4   With the 2nd Battalion, 7th Lancashire Fusiliers, in 1916
Plate 5   Annual spring gathering of Jews, Muslims and Christians
             outside Jerusalem
Plate 6   Jews on their way to the Wailing Wall
Plate 7   King Ali of the Hedjaz and the author, 1933
Plate 8   Ready for the coronation parade at Haifa, 1937
Plate 9   Edward and Philippa Keith-Roach on their wedding day,
             4 October 1939, with Sir Harold MacMichael, the high
             commissioner
Plate 10   Presentation to the Muslims of the Nebi Musa Banner for
             the annual pilgrimage to Jericho
Plate 11   Edward and Philippa Keith-Roach with Bishop Graham-
             Brown and the Patriarchs
Plate 12   The Armenian ceremony of the washing of the feet
Plate 13   Greek Orthodox Easter morning procession to the Church
             of the Holy Sepulchre
Plate 14   The Latin Patriarch's Easter Sunday procession in the
             Church of the Holy Sepulchre
Plate 15   Edward and Philippa Keith-Roach at a village gathering
             near Quebebe
Plate 16   Edward Keith-Roach with the Sephardic chief rabbi, early
             1940s

Glossary

abaya	dark cloak
Abu Gelda	Father of Lashes
Agudat Israel	Union (or Association) of Israel
Al Neby	the Prophet
Ashraf	Sherifian Party
atwa	tribal or feudal truce
ayat	illuminated scroll
baksheesh	money given as a tip, present or alms
bamiyah	okra
berat	document bestowing powers on a patriarch
berseem	Egyptian clover
bimbashi	a military rank
bism'illah	in the name of God
buraq	the pavement in front of the Wailing Wall in Jerusalem
burka	material covering face, veil
burra sahib	chief
chummeries	boarding houses
custos	head of the Franciscans
dervish	holy man, sufi
dhow	lateen-rigged coastal Arab sailing vessel
dhurra	maize
diwan	Oriental council of state or court of justice
diya	blood money
dukhn	kind of millet of the birdseed variety
durbar	court of a native ruler or governor in India
effendi	title of respect in the Ottoman Empire
ekka	carriage

Eretz Israel	Land of Israel
fakir	religious beggar
fantass	water container
fellah	peasant
felucca	narrow lateen-rigged vessel of the Mediterranean
frangi	foreigner
galabieh	long loose robe worn by Arab men
gharry	horse-drawn vehicle used in India
haboob	sandstorm
Hadassah	women's Zionist fundraising organization
Haganah	underground military Jewish organization
hadj	Muslim pilgrimage to Mecca
halukka	financial support for inhabitants of biblical Israel from Jews of the Diaspora
Haram al-Sherif	holy sanctuary (enclosure around mosque)
Ha-Tikvah	The Hope (Jewish national anthem)
heskaneet	variety of coarse grass
ighal	black goat-hair cord on head to hold *keffiyeh* in place
imam	Islamic religious teacher
janizary	Turkish soldier
jibbah	a long loose coat worn by Muslims and Parsees
Kaddish	Jewish equivalent of the Lord's Prayer
kavass	Turkish armed attendant
keffiyeh	Arab headdress
Keren Hayesod	Jewish Foundation Fund
Keren Kayemeth	Jewish National Fund
Khalil	the Friend of God
khatib	preacher
kismet	the will of Allah
kombaz	Turkish trousers
kusa	marrows, often stuffed with rice
Kyrie Eleison	Lord, have mercy upon us
Lag Ba'Omer	Jewish festival at which fires are lit and four-year-old Jewish boys are given their first haircut
maidan	open space in or near a town
marissa	fermented grain
mihraj	celestial journey of the Prophet Mohammed

minbar	platform in mosque where imam or speaker stands
mohur	tree named after the British Indian gold coin of the same name
muezzin	the official from the mosque who calls the faithful to prayer
mufti	Muslim religious authority, legal expert and adviser on the law of the Koran
mujahideen	those who struggle — the resistance
mukhtar	headman, local chief
nabout	wooden club
pasha	high official of the Ottoman Empire or Egypt
patrona	owner or manageress
Purim	Jewish holiday in February or March to commemorate the deliverance of the Jews from the massacre planned by Haman (Esther 9)
sadhu	holy man
sakiya	water wheel
schekhinah	divine spirit
schloss	castle
schnorring	securing money from the rich
Seder	Passover service
Sharia	the body of doctrines that regulate the lives of those who profess Islam
sheikh	religious leader or head of an Arab tribe or village
shekhita	ritual slaughter boards
sherif	Muslim leader
shroff	banker or money-changer in the East
sirdar	commander-in-chief
subhana 'llah	praise God
tallith	prayer shawl
tarboosh	cap of cloth or felt with a tassel attached at the top worn by Muslims, either by itself or as part of a turban
tebeldi	baobab tree
thobe	long garment worn by men
thowar	rebels
tikka	very small
tric-trac	backgammon

Va'ad Le'ummi	Jewish National Council
wadi	dried-up watercourse
waler	horse imported from Australia, especially New South Wales
waqf	property dedicated to charitable uses and to the service of God
yeshivah	religious school
yishuv	ingathering or settlement
zawiya	place where sufis meet
zikr	Muslim religious dance

Acknowledgements

For 40 years, since my husband's death, it has been my constant wish to see the publication of his memoirs. I am, therefore, most grateful to all who have contributed to the realization of this aim. My thanks go to the Master and Fellows of Pembroke College, Cambridge, for their generous support, and especially to Professor Malcolm Lyons, who recognized the value of the memoirs and whose vision and determination were essential to ensure publication.

I am grateful to the Master, Sir Roger Tomkys, for his perceptive Foreword with its introduction to my husband's life, the outline of the complexities he faced in Palestine, and the generous appreciation of his achievement. Particular thanks go to Paul Eedle for his informed and sensitive editing of the text. I am also indebted to Dr Lester Crook and the Radcliffe Press for the considerate and appreciative way in which they have guided the process of publication.

I am grateful to my son, Philip Keith-Roach, himself a former student of Pembroke College, for the part he has played on my behalf in arranging publication and to my daughter Christabel Ames-Lewis, who together with her husband Francis Ames-Lewis gave invaluable advice and assistance on the details of the manuscript and for their willing and meticulous reading of the proofs.

Philippa Keith-Roach
Cirencester, 1994

General Foreword
to the Series

Anthony Kirk-Greene MBE

Emeritus Fellow of St Antony's College, Oxford University, and
formerly of the Colonial Administrative Service, Nigeria

A whole generation has passed, nearer two in the case of the
Asian sub-continent, since Britain's colonial territories in
South-East Asia, Africa and the Caribbean achieved independence. In the Pacific the transfer of power came about a decade later.
There was little interest in recording the official or the personal experience of empire either in the inter-war years — viewed by some, often
among those personally involved, as the apogee of the British
empire — or in the immediate aftermath of empire. And in this latter
period attitudes were largely critical, largely condemnatory and even
positively hostile. This is not surprising: such a reaction is usual at the
end of a remarkable period of history.

With the passing of time and with longer historical perspective it was
possible to see events in a better and more objective light and the trend
was gradually reversed. In due course there came about a more sympathetic interest in the colonial period, both in Britain and in the countries
of the former empire, among those who were intrigued to know how
colonial government operated — in local, everyday practice, as well as
at the policy level of the Colonial Office and Government House. Fur-
thermore, those who had themselves been an integral part of the process

wanted to record the experience before, in the nature of things, it was too late. Here was a potentially rich vein of knowledge and personal experience for specialist academic historians as well as the general reader.

Leaving aside the extensive academic analysis of the end of empire, the revival of interest in the colonial period in this country may be said to have been stimulated by creative literature. In the late 1960s there were novels, films and radio and TV programmes, now and again tinged with a touch of nineteenth-century romance and with just a whiff of nostalgia to soften the sharp realism of the colonial encounter. The focus was primarily on India and the post-1947 imagery of the 'Raj': there were outstanding novels by Paul Scott — surely destined to be one of the greatest twentieth-century novelists — J. G. Farrell and John Masters; epic films like *A Passage to India* and *Gandhi*, the charming and moving vignette of *Staying On*, and, for Africa, *Out of Africa* and *Mister Johnson*.

In the second half of the 1970s there emerged a highly successful genre of collective 'colonial' memoirs in the *Tales of ...* format: Charles Allen's splendid trilogy *Plain Tales from the Raj* (1975), *Tales from the Dark Continent* (1979) and *Tales from the South China Seas* (1983), followed by others like *Tales of Paradise: Memories of the British in the South Pacific* (1986), all good history and good reading.

Throughout the period from India's independence until that of the last crown colony there had, of course, been those splendid works which combined both academic history and creative literature: for example, Philip Woodruff's *Men who Ruled India: The Founders* (1953) and *The Guardians* (1954); and Jan Morris's *Heaven's Command, Pax Britannica* and *Farewell the Trumpets* (1973–8).

Finally, as the 1970s gave way to the 1980s, those voices which had remained largely silent since the end of empire now wanted to be heard. The one-time colonial officials, be they district officers, agriculturalists, veterinary, medical or forestry officers, policemen or magistrates, and just as often their wives, began to write about their experiences. They wrote with relish and enthusiasm, with a touch of adventure and few personal regrets. There was a common feeling of a practical and useful task well done, although some thought that more could have been achieved had independence come about more slowly.

These memoirs often began as little more than a private record for the family, children and grandchildren, some of whom had never seen a colonial governor in full fig, shaken hands with an emir or paramount chief, discussed plans with a peasant or local politician, or known at first hand the difference between an *askari* and an *alkali*, an *amah* and an *ayah*. By 1990, the colonial memoir had begun to establish itself as a literary genre in its own right.

The initiative of the Radcliffe Press in harnessing and promoting this talent, primarily autobiographical but also biographical, promises to be a positive addition to both the historical and the literary scenes. Here are voices from the last Colonial Service generation, relating from personal experience the lives and careers involved in the exercise of latter-day empire. They were part of what was arguably the most influential and far-reaching international event of the second half of the twentieth century, namely the end of empire and the consequent emergence of the independent nations of the Third World. It could also perhaps be argued that this is part of an even greater process — decolonization 'writ large', a sea-change in world affairs affecting greater and lesser powers into the late twentieth century.

It may well be that by 2066, the centenary of the closing down of the Colonial Office, great-great-grandchildren will find the most telling image of Britain's third and final empire in these authentic memoirs and biographical studies, rather than in the weightier imperial archives at the Public Record Office at Kew or in Rhodes House Library, Oxford.

Foreword

E dward Keith-Roach's memoirs are a very English document and his was an essentially English life. His first memories were of early childhood in provincial England and in the countryside in the golden age at the end of the century. Educated at home by his father, he was the youngest surviving child of a large clergy family. At 17 he went into banking in London, then, to seek his fortune, he joined the Mercantile Bank of India, first in Bombay, then in Karachi, before returning to England to marry the girl he left behind. Swept up in the First World War he served first in Egypt and then for three lonely years in administration in the remote western desert Darfur district of the Anglo-Egyptian Sudan. This set his life's pattern as he moved after the war at his request to Palestine, first as public custodian of enemy property in Palestine, then to succeed Sir Ronald Storrs as governor of Jerusalem. He made the remainder of his career in Palestine, with a year's secondment to the Colonial Office in 1925 and with intervals in northern Palestine, but always returning to Jerusalem, until his retirement in 1943.

The memoirs evoke other impressions. The England of Keith-Roach's childhood is the England of Sassoon's *Memoirs of a Fox-Hunting Man*. The bank clerk in London steps out of the pages of H. G. Wells. In India it is a very personal account of life in the business community of Kipling's Raj. In the Sudan and in Palestine Keith-Roach records the world of T. E. Lawrence and of Ronald Storrs's *Orientations*. The comparisons are literary because these are personal memoirs, not didactic history written for publication, and because it is the people who emerge clearly on his pages, warts and all, rather than precise dates and the sequence of events. The author's own personality is of his time and country and his part of its society; it is singularly attractive, dedicated to public service, modest and enduring, but full of physical and moral courage.

His record of the history of the British Mandate in Palestine is balanced and judicious, but not bland. For the general reader it may be worth recalling briefly the background to, and history of, that Mandate. It was awarded to Britain at the 1920 San Remo Conference to put into effect, under the League of Nations, the commitment made in the 1917 Balfour Declaration in favour of the establishment in Palestine of a national home for the Jewish people, it being clearly understood that nothing should be done which might prejudice the civil and religious rights of existing non-Jewish communities in Palestine, or the rights and political status enjoyed by Jews in any other country.

This commitment was opposed from the outset by the Palestinian Arabs, who then composed the overwhelming majority of the population. Throughout the inter-war years British attempts to strike an acceptable balance between Zionist aspirations and Arab fears that they would lose their land failed to satisfy either party. Pressure increased after Hitler came to power in 1933, with the new wave of persecution of the Jews of Central Europe. The British White Paper of May 1939 effectively froze Jewish immigration at a level of 75,000 over a five-year period, with immigration thereafter to be subject to Arab approval. Only after the war was Britain to relinquish a mandatory responsibility she could no longer carry, and the State of Israel was founded in the resulting conflict.

When Keith-Roach left Jerusalem in 1943, therefore, he had lived through a quarter of a century of great bitterness and political turmoil. His account of the period is essentially about people. The high commissioners and many others who appear in the memoirs were greater public men than Keith-Roach. He records their strengths and their shortcomings fairly and with human understanding. He also records the structural weakness by which Britain administered a Mandate in Palestine through a Colonial Service staffed largely by officials for whom, whatever their devotion to duty, Palestine was but an untypical episode in a career likely to be spent shuttling between postings throughout a far-flung empire largely made up of territories far less sophisticated than the Holy Land. Many had little Arabic and less Hebrew and no time to absorb the deep historic intricacies of an irreconcilable conflict. For those who, like myself, have tried to help forward, in the post-

Mandate, post-colonial period, some partially satisfactory reconciliation of opposing interests in Palestine, it has always been difficult to suppress the conviction that an inherently difficult, perhaps insoluble, problem has been made worse time and again by amateurs; the intervention of well-intentioned outsiders who, however great they might be in their own fields, were inadequately prepared for this most complex of issues has rarely had positive results. The reader of Keith-Roach's memoirs may find this conviction reinforced, but with the proviso that Keith-Roach himself is exempt. Would that there had been more like him. He devoted the greater part of his working life to Palestine and to his service there.

The memoirs are therefore the record of one Englishman's career, albeit an unusual one. The author himself, in his style and in his dedication to public service, exemplifies many of the qualities on which the English most pride themselves, and his writings are illuminating, sometimes instructive, and often entertaining. The responsibilities Keith-Roach carried with such distinction in Palestine were indeed considerable. His predecessor in Jerusalem, Sir Ronald Storrs, never one to hide his light under a bushel, who had played a major part during the First World War in shaping the modern history of Palestine, wrote of his transfer to be governor of Cyprus that 'for me Jerusalem stood and stands alone among the cities of the world. There are many positions of greater authority and renown within and without the British Empire, but in a sense that I cannot explain there is no promotion after Jerusalem.' Readers of this book will understand why Keith-Roach must have shared that feeling and why he was worthy to be Pasha of Jerusalem.

Sir Roger Tomkys
Master, Pembroke College, Cambridge
March 1994

1

A Safe Job with a Pension at Sixty?

A very small boy, dressed in skirts that came well below the knees, swung himself down by the curving mahogany banisters, ran across the hall and thumped against a door, from behind which came the roar of talk and laughter. The door was opened and he was greeted by shouts of 'many happy returns' from his nine brothers and sisters seated round the long breakfast table. There was a hushed expectancy as he climbed onto his highchair and discovered the large brown paper parcel on his plate. At first he did not quite know what to do, but helped by an elder brother he was soon pulling off the string and paper and there lay exposed a shining scarlet watering can with a long spout and a golden rose.

At that moment the door opened and his mother came in. The child scrambled down and ran across the room towards her, when suddenly there was a crash, he slipped and fell flat on his face. The blood spurted from his forehead to fall on the shining but now slightly dented watering can by his side.

Swept up into nurse's arms, he was soon being taken off to the doctor two doors away. There followed the sharp pains and hurts of two stitches, but after it the triumphal return home, still in nurse's arms, with a sweet in his mouth for having been a brave boy.

That is my only recollection of what happened on 31 March 1888, the day when I was three years old; I remember it perhaps because of the marks above my nose I bear to this day.

There is a string of later memories.

My parents were Gloucestershire people. I can just remember my grandfather, who was brought up by Canon Cockin, Rector of Minchin-hampton, his own father being in the service of the East India Company. He lived to spend his days as a parson in Gloucestershire and Wiltshire.

My father was sent to Marlborough when he took one of the foundation scholarships; he went on to St John's, Cambridge, to a double first in mathematics and an honours degree in moral science. He was then ordained and became mathematics master successively at Wellington, Repton and finally Clifton. But the 1870s to the 1890s were the hey-days of the 'crammer' and some years before I was born my father left Clifton to set up successfully as a coach for the army and the Indian Civil Service examinations; and it was in the rather gaunt house of 23 bedrooms on the outskirts of Bristol, already occupied by nine children and perhaps a dozen pupils, as well as by my mother and father, that I was born.

My mother was the daughter of Thomas Clutterbuck Croome, lord of the manor of Painswick, that picturesque Cotswold village that has still kept its beauty; the Croomes, like the Daubeneys with whom they had intermarried for generations, had been long rooted to the lands of Gloucestershire.

The succeeding years are a medley of the comings and goings of elder brothers and sisters, catechism by a kind white-haired clergyman in church on Sunday afternoons, and walks with nurses on Clifton Downs. Often a policeman with white knitted gloves would accompany nurse and let us play with his gloves.

Once four of us came back from a party in a Bath chair. As it was raining the chairman pulled up the window and we were shut in. There was a dreadful feeling of being trapped in an airless prison from which there was no escape. This torture culminated in a further tragedy because when we were decanted at our door, in the misery and the excitement, a tiny flag that I had been given was lost.

Father took some of us to the docks to see a cattle boat come in from Ireland. What gorgeous smells! Warm and heavy! What thwackings and noise as cattle and squealing pigs were forced up the gangways and prodded and pushed ashore, accompanied by shouts in an unknown language.

Just before I was eight years old my father retired and, feeling that the country rather than the town would give better scope to his lusty family, announced that we were to move to Owlesbury House near Winchester.

Every minute of the great day is still crystal clear.

Three enormous bright-red vans arrived outside the house, 12 huge and patient dray horses were taken out of the shafts and given their nosebags, green-aproned men bustled in and out with the well-known pieces of furniture. How we children enjoyed it, and how surprised we were when a few days later the same vans and the same horses and the same men appeared with the same furniture outside our new house in Hampshire when we got there.

We had spent a long day, for me my first journey in a train, with frequent changes before we reached Shawford station. Tired and rather cross, we tumbled down some wooden steps and found a carrier's cart awaiting us. The younger of us got into it and the elder ones set off to walk under the dripping trees of Shawford Park, through the rain-soaked yet lovely village of Twyford, by the side of Hazely Down where there were rabbits, yes, real wild rabbits, running off at the sight of us. We rode on to Morestead. There most of the family got out of the cart to ease the horse as our road passed between churchyard and village pond and up a steep hill. There was the warm rich smell of animals across the water, and in the hedges some curious white objects. We pounced on them and came back holding lumps of chalk. At the top of the hill stood a windmill with its majestic sails and we were told that this was Owlesbury village. A little way further on through great wooden doors lay our house.

In a few minutes all 12 of us were sitting down to tea. In our household, tea had never varied from huge slices of bread and butter and large jugs of milk, and on occasions seed cake, but on this day of days there was a large brown egg on each plate and strawberry jam as well. How well I remember the dilemma. Should I gobble up the egg and get to the jam, or should I eat the egg slowly and really enjoy it? It was all too exciting; to my everlasting regret I gobbled the egg as fast as I could to start on the jam!

Next morning we got up early and looked out across the hills. Far, far away we saw some small objects with long tails moving slowly backwards and forwards. We decided that they were foxes. We called our elder brothers and they revealed that the objects were men and horses ploughing. Such was the impact of country and distance on the town-bred child.

Owlesbury was a tiny village on the Hampshire Downs. Besides our house there were the church and vicarage, a farm house, a blacksmith's, a wheelwright's, a baker's, three or four labourer's cottages and at each of the four corners of the village a public house. The only connection with the outside world was the carrier's cart to Winchester, five miles away. Twice a week Bunney left Owlesbury at nine o'clock in the morning in this barrel-roofed vehicle and winter and summer he returned at six.

Passengers and parcels were all mixed up together and in the winter evenings were lighted by a candle lamp. It was Bunney who bought the bootlaces or the extra joint, or the needles and cotton, and who matched the pieces of stuff. However obscure or however many the things we wanted he was never known to fail.

My mother's advance order for bread had so amazed the local baker that he had said it could not be possible and he came to church on the first Sunday morning especially to count us.

Our penny a week pocket money we spent at Fanny Hooker's cottage. A grey-haired woman, she sold only one sweet; Fanny Hooker's humbugs, lemon or peppermint flavour, 20 for one penny. With judicious sucking they would last all Saturday afternoon and into Sunday. For years Fanny had made one boiling a week. After our arrival she made two.

My six elder brothers and a sister were now either at work or at boarding school and as our old governess had not come with us from Bristol, my father took over the task of educating the four youngest: two sisters, a brother and myself. Eventually I, the youngest, alone remained.

The day started with morning prayers. When anyone was going away Father always had a special prayer that he or she 'who leaves this house this day, may be preserved in his going out and in his going in', and incidentally both my parents wrote weekly to all their children who were away from home and continued this practice until their deaths.

Immediately after breakfast, promptly at nine o'clock, the cloth was removed from the dining room table and school started. My father taught us Latin, elementary Greek, French, mathematics, geography, history and Shakespeare. It took me several years to get into the full course. He gave us a good deal of 'rep' (repetition) and twice a week I had to write an essay. Curiously enough he left religious instruction to my mother. When I knew all the Collects by heart she started on the Epistles. Somehow I thought this unfair.

For us children Owlesbury was enough. There was a farm attached to our house and we rode the carthorses to and from their work in the fields, kept a lamb or two and quantities of rabbits, which we exercised on the lawn on Sunday afternoons.

But for my parents it was a very different matter. The vicar, an elderly bachelor, had long forsaken even parish visiting for the more solid comforts of his study. My father took over this pastoral work and soon knew all the villagers. He continued to write one sermon a week whether he went off for Sunday duty or not. But of social life there was none whatsoever. We kept no horses and the only means of transport other than the carrier was 'Troad's pony'. Troad the blacksmith owned a high dogcart and a brown almost unbroken pony. With Troad hanging onto the plunging animal, my mother would mount the box seat and the children chosen for that particular day would jump in and hold on as best they could. My mother would call out 'Right!' and we would dash forward down the hill. My mother, who had been a fine horsewoman, had not jumped the Cotswold stone walls in her youth for nothing. She kept the pony going and was imperturbable, however fast he went. As soon as the pace slackened she kept him at it with a flick of the whip. In Winchester the pony was put up and baited at the Black Swan and we came home at a more sober pace.

Wherever we were living, on Wednesday and Saturday afternoons Father walked to the nearest public library and came back to tea, high tea for him. Bringing out of his pocket an envelope covered with notes he would repeat to Mother the salient articles in the *Spectator*, the *Fortnightly* and the *Nineteenth Century*. The cartoons in *Punch* were graphically described.

I understood little but in those days small boys were 'seen and not heard' at table and we must have absorbed far more than we knew. My father also belonged to some learned society and once a fortnight he posted to another member a problem that he had set. The following week he received a similar problem to solve sent to him by a very learned woman, a Miss Markham. They never met.

Because of this virtual isolation we later moved to Chandlers Ford, midway between Winchester and Southampton and not far from East-leigh. A shrewd house agent had had the tip that the London and South Western Railway proposed to site their workshops at Eastleigh and bought up all the land he could get there. With the resulting profits he invested in land at Chandlers Ford, where he started a building estate. Wallis, for that was his name, built a clubhouse, laid out cement tennis courts and built his own house there as well. The house we took was a somewhat pretentious three-storeyed villa on the main road, called Kingsmead after Wallis's grander Kingscourt. The ford through which the mythical chandler had taken his flocks had long ere this disappeared beneath the road, but there were other streams and compensations. The woods were a marvellous source of pleasure and we roamed for hours, climbed trees, fought across sandpits, played in the pond and picked hazelnuts, blackberries and mushrooms. Every spring the nightingales came to the nut woods opposite our house. My brother and I would get up night after night to listen. They would sing and sing until it seemed as though their throats would burst.

Twice a week a coach and four plying between Winchester and Southampton drove past our house. As the red-coated, top-hatted guard got to know us he gave the children a special toot on his horn.

Safety bicycles had come in but a few people still rode penny-farthings. My brother and I acquired one in exchange for five shillings and two rabbits. We learned to go downhill with our feet and legs over the handlebars, and it gave us a lot of fun until my brother had an accident and it disappeared.

When I was 14 Barnum and Bailey's Circus came to Southampton. My brother and I walked in to see the show. In a darkened tent we saw moving pictures on a white cloth. Incredible! A man wheeling a barrow down the street was being chased by small boys. The people were moving very quickly and jerkily and the flickers hurt our eyes, so we left the tent and went to see the bearded lady.

But wonders did not cease there. One day Father came home and told us that he had seen going along a street in Southampton a horseless carriage!

After a few years we moved to Twyford, nearer Winchester. Here there was an excellent village cricket team. Our best batsman was a platelayer on the railway. I played regularly with them and developed as a fast bowler. I also played football with the village and got my place

6

as outside left. A tough little Lancashire mechanic from the waterworks was the dour captain. He saw that I had developed a habit of jumping when I was charged, and in a practice game he laid into me. He won all right!

At 16 I was confirmed, knowing little of what it was all about. I liked the bishop, Randall Davidson.[1] He had a lovely voice and bushy eyebrows and he called me 'This thy child'. I had not seen him again for 20 years, when, as Archbishop of Canterbury, he invited me to stay with him at Lambeth Palace.

My next recollection is extremely vivid. One day I had a very bad toothache and walked into Eastleigh to a dentist. After looking inside my mouth he told me to sit down in his smart new operating chair made of cast iron. Without attempting to give me anything to deaden the pain, he began to pull out the tooth. In my agony I clung onto the chair arms for all I was worth. The dentist gave a final tug; with a convulsive heave I fell off the chair, the cast-iron arm broken off and lying beside me.

At this time the trains running past the village were full of troops going to South Africa to the war. Sometimes they stopped for an hour or two in a siding. The men sang 'Good-bye Dolly I must leave you' and the girls would wave to them. My eldest brother had gone as a chaplain leaving his wife and two children behind.

Puberty found me interested but very confused. Life began to change.

My father died at the age of 62, but my mother lived until 1937 and the age of 92. She had successfully brought up 10 out of 12 children. She had kept house for all the students in my father's educational establishment, as well as for her own family, and yet she found time to do a good deal of district visiting and to write a novel, *Dick Chichester*, a tale of the political wooing of the county. In fact she kept her interest in politics to the end. When women first got the vote she wrote to me an account of her experience at the polling booth. 'As I cast my vote into the box I did not feel any the less a woman for doing so,' and she added in the same letter a description of her new summer hat.

In the last years of her life, although nearly blind, she continued to

---

1. Randall Davidson, who served as Queen Victoria's domestic chaplain early in his career, became Archbishop of Canterbury in 1903 and held the post for 25 years.

help my sisters tackle *The Times* crossword puzzle and, told the letters, would do the anagrams in her head.

I was 17 years old. What was to be done? I had no qualifications. A friend of my father's, an old private banker, was consulted. It was decided that I was to go into a bank. Up to that date I had never been inside one. An examination in London followed, during which I was set to write an essay on 'The Advantages and Disadvantages of Free Libraries'. I summed up the advantages and visualized few disadvantages. I was accepted and offered a salary of £4 3s 4d a month. The salary sounded generous; before long I was to learn it was particularly small in the months when there were five Saturdays, and my landlady had to be paid five times. My parents helped me.

In June 1902, very, very shy and frightened, dressed in a navy-blue suit, straw hat, black boots and gloves, with five golden sovereigns in my pocket, I set out for Richmond, Surrey, to join the London and County Bank. It was my third journey in a train. Leaving my Gladstone bag at the station I went off to search for lodgings. The roads seemed stifling, full of noise and the smell of horses' dung. At one house a flashy young woman called me dearie, so I ran away. At last I found a room in a house in a side street near the Lion Gate, Kew Gardens. For 17s a week the landlady offered to 'do' for me and give me three meals a day. It was a small room on an upstairs floor with a bed in it and numerous little tables covered by white crocheted doilies that were always slipping off the polished tops.

Next morning, Sunday, I went into a church. There was incense; it seemed sensuous and unreal, and I slipped out. That evening I went up Richmond Hill, even ventured inside the park gates. A woman called to me, I went towards her, then was frightened and ran away and got to my lodgings as quickly as possible.

Monday morning dawned. I was still so young and so fair that I had never shaved, so getting up was a simple affair. I walked to the bank, which was situated next to the Greyhound Hotel in the narrowest part of the High Street. The big door was flanked on either side by heavy Gothic windows, the lower halves covered inside with dark gauze. It gave me the same impression as the entrance to the dentist's surgery in Eastleigh.

The bank was panelled with mahogany and divided by a long counter. A man, clothed in seemingly full evening dress of green melton cloth adorned with gilt buttons and a black tie, met me — he turned out to be the office messenger — and escorted me to a personage referred to as the chief clerk, who lived in a kind of raised glass rabbit hutch. He was a thin-lipped, crabbed little man with a beard, whose job was apparently to find fault in icy tones all day.

A dozen people made up the staff. One senior man was very nice. He looked a misfit, as though he had stepped into the wrong surroundings. The English of some of the clerks sounded clipped and strange. I was to learn it was a cockney accent.

I was then taken into a private office to be presented to the manager, Mr Terry, who arrived at ten o'clock. He was a man of about 60, who had formerly been a private banker. A white-haired, distinguished-looking man, he talked to me for quite a long time about my parents and my home before I was dismissed to my work.

My duties were chiefly concerned with filling up forms with particulars of cheques, squeezing out copies of letters, written in copying ink, in the letter press — a cumbersome affair — addressing envelopes, entering letters into the stamp register and keeping the stamp account. Then, last thing at night, before it was possible to go home, I had to take all the cheques that had been passed in the current accounts ledger, and enter them into books called the check ledgers, which I had to add up and make agree with the cashier's account books and the general ledger. All very strange and to me most tedious, especially as I was always last in the office, despite being there the first in the morning. Of course I was hopeless at the job; my fingers were always covered with ink; I could rarely balance the check ledgers, due to my making mistakes, and I was invariably short in the stamp account.

As the two most often alone, the office messenger and I became friends. A man of decided character, he used to supplement his income by going out waiting at nights at private houses and at public banquets. One day I received an invitation from the manager's wife to go to dinner at her house. I had but one anxiety, what was I to wear? The messenger saved the situation. It was true he was going to wait there at table, but he would lend me his best evening clothes and would wear his old ones. So, for three shillings I was smartly apparelled and went to dine and found a pleasant family with grown up daughters.

I longed to play tennis, but I had means for neither racquet nor club. So, after tea, I used to hang over the railings of a club near the Lion Gate and watch the players.

Once I saved up half-a-crown and asked a nice girl to come out on the river for an hour and have tea afterwards. It cost 18d the first hour and tea would be sixpence each. We got tied up in a jam owing to my inexperience with oars and were quarter of an hour over the hour. And oh, the agony of mind with which I approached the boatman — he must have read it in my eyes, because he only charged 18d.

I hated Saturdays. Everybody was in a hurry to get away, but the tradesmen would only send in their cheques at about one o'clock. These then had to be cleared through the books, the various forms made out and all the final statements of accounts sent to the London Office. The junior could not leave until all this had been done. In addition, the check ledgers had to be written up and the letters posted, so it was nearly half-past three before I got away to my dinner. I roamed about Richmond Park on Sundays. The deer and squirrels were very tame. One day some friends of my family wrote and asked me to their flat at Kensington. With them I went to theatres and to Earls Court.

In the late winter I was transferred to Horsham, an uninteresting market town in Sussex. There was no bank messenger there and in consequence I had to open the doors, clean the inkpots, take the shutters off the lockers containing the passbooks, fetch the books and money up from the safe and put them back again at night. All this offended me greatly, as well as the custom of people entering the bank and keeping their hats on. The manager was a dried-up, mean-looking man who, I was told, preached every Sunday at some chapel. He certainly did not bring into the week what he talked about on Sundays. He used to open a sub-branch once a week in a neighbouring town and I drove with him there in his dilapidated dogcart. Those were uncomfortable days in close proximity to this peevish individual, and when we got back to Horsham in the evening I had to close up the main office.

My lodgings were in a poor part of the town. I got to know few people, entered nobody's house and the only interesting person I met was Shrubb, the world's record long-distance runner, who kept a tobacconist's shop.

A Safe Job with a Pension at Sixty?

Then, oh brightest of days, I was moved to Eastbourne to the main office. Life became a different thing in this lovely, clean, sweet-smelling town, where the writ of the Duke of Devonshire held good and beauty had not been sacrificed for so-called commercial benefit. I was no longer 'the junior' and had more interesting work, taking what was termed 'the waste' from one of the cashiers. This consisted of taking all the paying-in-slips received by the cashier, entering particulars of the cheques, notes and drafts, classifying them into their own columns and balancing up with the cashier at night.

Later I was transferred to the branch at Meads, on the hill. I was the only clerk in addition to the manager; we had a handful of accounts, chiefly with schools. I helped with everything and really took an interest in what I was doing and, still more important, tried to learn what the rudiments of banking meant.

I rapidly made lots of friends. I joined the local dramatic club and played in Pinero's[2] play *The Liars*, produced by Nugent Monck, who eventually created the Madda Theatre Norwich Players. The Devonshire Park was then in full swing. Roller-skating in the winter, Norfolk Megone's largely augmented band in the summer.

An old man, Colonel Howard-Williams, took me up and let me drive his tandem, perched high on the box seat. Life assumed its highest pitch when, on Sundays, I drove along the Grand Parade past the Lawns, the wheeler trotting, the leader cantering.

But all things come to an end. I went to the Brighton main branch and realized what work means. It was an exceptionally large office in a modern building, near the Pavilion. I was attached to a cashier — there were seven of them — to take his waste; and also I had to keep up to date eight rows of passbooks. Some of them belonging to drapers would often have 200 or 300 entries a day. It was one continuous slog and I was too busy to be miserable. The only time recreation was possible was on Saturdays, when I blossomed as outside left at football. Many months of this and then once again I was transferred, to Halstead in Essex. A bleak, uninspiring, ugly little town with no redeeming interest at all. Nothing can be chillier than Essex.

However, after six weeks of this I was again moved and I went to Basingstoke in Hampshire. Basingstoke was then just developing from

2. Sir Arthur Wing Pinero (1855–1934), distinguished author of 54 plays.

a market town into an industrial centre, for Burberrys was already established and Thornycrofts had recently started a branch of its works and was beginning to manufacture motor trucks.

Typhoid fever was raging when I arrived; actually I was sent to replace two men who had gone down with it. No steps were taken by the manager to find me lodgings, or to warn me what to eat or drink, or what precautions I should take. Indeed, the first systematic sterilization of a public water supply was not carried out in England until the following year — to check an epidemic that threatened Lincoln city. In a few weeks the fever started to abate, but many had died and there was much distress, so a relief fund was opened. It struck me that we might put on a theatrical show for the sufferers. The idea was taken up and I plunged into organizing it; and eventually we had a performance in the local drill hall. It was presented as a kind of thanksgiving gala. I played the hero with a rather heavily built young heroine. To my amazement and consternation I received an ovation. We netted a profit of £123. I still possess an elaborate letter of thanks from the mayor on behalf of the town council.

A week or two later I attended a dance at the same hall. I arrived late and saw at the end of the hall a vivacious-looking girl of about 26, dressed in a low-cut black evening dress. She was surrounded by men, all of whom were laughing heartily. She was about middle height with big bones, a plump figure, hair done up high on her head, thick eyebrows, very short upper lip, straight nose and prominent eyes. She had a keen look of intelligence, a ready wit and an air of bursting energy. She was easily the centre of attraction in that rather sombre drill hall. She gave all around her a keen sense of being alive. Something said 'that is the woman for me' — so I went straight up, asked for a dance, and monopolized her against all comers for the rest of the evening. Thus began my association with one of the most brilliant women I have ever met. She came from Gloucestershire, as I did, and eight years later Violet Oliva Barnard and I were married.

The Basingstoke branch had a staff of six. The manager was a dark-skinned, heavy-looking man who had married a woman of means. He wrote all his letters himself in a splendid clear handwriting — most important in those days when all letters were handwritten and had to be put through the copying book. He was, however, a bully and his particular secret vice was consuming brandy neat.

Once a week he and I drove over in an old brougham to open a sub-branch at Hartley Wintney, where he spent much of the day quietly drinking from a large silver flask, his complexion getting darker and his nose deeper red as the long day passed. We did not have many customers; there were a few tradesmen, the preparatory school, Sir Anthony Cope, a grand old man who always took his hat off, and Lord Calthrop, who was usually represented by his butler, a man of most imposing mien.

The journey back was trying, my chief very morose and the cab filled with alcoholic fumes. But he was a fine banker and rarely made bad debts, for he had great agricultural knowledge and was an expert valuer of land and timber.

I acted as cashier for an hour a day. On market days the office was kept open an extra hour so that the farmers and dealers could bring in their day's takings, and they always chose the last hour. I generally liked my daily hour at the counter. There were no notes smaller than a fiver and the touch of gold, as one rapidly counted the sovereigns and checked them by weight before shovelling them into a bag, was exhilarating.

But the money on market days — and there was always a large amount of it — was dreadful. Much of it was covered with fish scales, or blood from the butchers' stalls, or had fallen in the muck of the cattle pens. In that last hour, three of us, working hard, used to take in many hundreds of pounds in specie, as well as countless cheques and five-pound notes. Farmers always expected us to fill out the paying-in slips for them. When the door had slammed on the last customer, we would put all the coins into a bucket of water and permanganate of potash, so that we could clean them before sorting them away into bags. We then had to deal with all the accounts and it was very late before we got away for the night.

The day came when inevitably I had a row with the manager. I admired his knowledge but despised him as a person. He accused me of wasting my time outside the bank, so I flared up. He reported me to the head office and I was called up to London before the country manager. I rather enjoyed the experience; I listened to what he had to say and then did a little exposing of my superior's habits, so I felt we parted even. But of course I could not stay in Basingstoke. After a few weeks at the Brighton West branch, I joined the 'relieving staff for holidays' and spent many months relieving people on leave. I went to nearly all the little south-coast towns — Littlehampton, Worthing, Shoreham, Bexhill, Hastings, St Leonards, and Rye in Sussex, before coming back to roost at the Brighton branch in Hove.

Three glorious weeks were spent at Rye. It was a tiny branch, the manager was away and the only clerk, who had been there for 30 years, was running the office. There was little to do; we closed down at three o'clock in the afternoon and the rest of the day was mine in which to enjoy the beauty of the country and the village.

At the end of four years I was getting bored. I asked myself the question, 'Whither goest thou?' Except at Eastbourne, I never remember speaking to a minister of religion. There I took up some social work for boys and became a lieutenant in the Church Lads' Brigade. My church-going was intermittent but liberal. Brought up in a rigid religious atmosphere, it came as a shock to me to discover that Roman Catholics and 'Dissenters' might possibly find places in heaven. At Brighton I divided my attendance on Sundays between a Roman Catholic church (the Revd R. J. Campbell's chapel — he had not yet gone over to the Church of England) and the Anglican church of Saint Bartholomew, where ritual and passionate sermons were the order of the day. The height of religious fervour was surely reached in Passion Week, when at a snap of the fingers from the master of ceremonies, the entire body of clergy fell down flat on their faces before the altar and formed a living cross.

I had lived in every type of lodging and with every type of landlady, from the prude who held her left hand before her face when she brought my hot water lest she should see me in bed — she rejoiced in the delicious name of Miss Heinnemier — to the elderly virgin in a French household at Hove, where I had gone to learn French, who tried to seduce me while I was reading to her. At Brighton I lived in a cheap boarding house kept, I think, by South African Jews, but I never penetrated into their domestic lives. In the summer time the boarding house was forever being emptied and refilled with constant relays of visitors, mainly from the north of England. Looked at from the distance of time, it was a funny agitated life, which might have been expressed in the

14

immortal words of Mrs Patrick Campbell,[3] who, when asked after her marriage what it was like, replied, 'Oh the peace: the peace of the double bed, after the hurly-burly of the chaise longue.'

I gradually learned to tot up figures until the task became automatic and I could do it at lightning speed, and can even to this day. But there was no system of training and little interest was taken by either the bank or its managers in the Banker's Institute examinations. On quarter days at the bigger branches, when all the books, including the customers' passbooks, had to be made up to date and balanced, the clerks were frequently called upon to work all night until five or six in the morning; they were then let out for breakfast, but had to be back at work by nine o'clock. For this service, a generous board of directors awarded us a gift of two shillings.

I noticed that all real power was concentrated in London with the country manager and the Loan Advance Department and that the average manager had to ask permission to grant a loan for £100. Branch managers could do little on their own initiative. I thought that if I did not make a move, a long vista of dull monotony lay ahead, so I decided to look for a wider field. I got an interview with Sir Charles Addis, London manager of the Hong Kong and Shanghai Bank, but he had no vacancy available. Then Mr James Campbell, chief manager of the Mercantile Bank of India took me on the staff of the London office for training.

Before I sent in my resignation to the London and County Bank I was warned by the manager and the entire staff of the Hove branch of the risk that I was taking in throwing up a safe job with a pension at 60.

---

3. Beatrice Stella Campbell (1865–1940) soared to fame as an actress in Arthur Wing Pinero's play *The Second Mrs Tanqueray* in 1893. She was a dark, Italian beauty with a gift for portraying passionate, complex women. One of her last successes was as Eliza Doolittle in George Bernard Shaw's *Pygmalion* in 1914.

2

Trooper, Bombay Light Horse

As the doors of the bank swung behind me I entered a different world, a world inhabited mainly by Scotsmen. The London office was in an alley lying between Threadneedle and Throgmorton Streets. The bank was lit by two windows looking into a small court made out of the backs of other buildings. It was so dark that everybody worked by electric light of poor quality. In an odd-shaped room of many corners 50 men worked with their desks placed so near each other that there was little room to move one's elbows. The chief manager had a small wooden room dumped down in the middle of the office with the staff milling round him all day.

But if the ground floor was crowded and airless, the conditions in the basement, where the lavatories, cloakrooms, correspondence and bill ledger departments were accommodated, were far worse. It amazed me to think that any board of directors could let its staff work in such conditions. Today the Bank Clerks' Union, or should I say Bank Officers' Guild, would have called its members out on strike until conditions were altered. As a result of those unhygienic years, I developed catarrh of the nose and throat and despite two operations and every kind of 'cure', it has never left me. By now the bank has long since given up the old premises and has acquired decent working space in Gracechurch Street. Despite such bad conditions, because the little Scotsman who now controlled us was almost huggermugger in our midst, separated only by a partition, it seemed as though we were one family. Everyone appeared anxious to help and, what is of more importance, to teach the newcomer. It was a world in which current accounts, formerly the limit of my outlook, took a back seat.

The foreign staff under training comprised 15 young men, all with three or four years' previous experience in Scottish or English banks. From them appointments as assistant accountants would be made and future managers eventually selected. During their training they served some months in every section of the bank — Current Account Ledgers, Cash Book, Journal, Inward Bills, Outward Bills, Exchange Operations, Discounts, Local Loans, Bullion, Stocks and Shares, General Ledger, Shareholders' Dividends and the Checking Department. Each of these departments was controlled by an expert whose job it was, and who indeed was only too willing, to teach the pupil.

I threw my energies into the tasks, attended Gilbart lectures on banking and went in for examinations.

Fridays, mail days, brought the smell of the sea and the smells of the East. The great exporting houses used to send in their bills drawn on their agents at 30, 60, 90 or 120 days' sight, along with the invoices and shipping documents, which had to be delivered to the agents on acceptance of the bills or else upon payment. Upon these the London office gave advances to the drawers. The mail closed at five o'clock. By paying double rates we could get packets accepted up to six o'clock, and by paying triple rates up to seven o'clock. Obviously the thing to do was to get as many packages as possible off by five o'clock, and so we worked at top speed.

Some days we received gold sovereigns for shipment. The Indians paid a higher rate for Victorian shield sovereigns than for others because their jewellers considered that the gold was finer.

To adjust its balances between the branches and head office, the bank bid for and bought Indian treasury bills; and once a week one of us would rush to the Bank of England to bring back news of the percentage of the application that had been awarded and at what rate.

But big fleas have little fleas upon them. We, in our turn, often wanted money and the bank discounted bills with the discount houses; one of us in that section would visit them carrying bundles of bills popularly known as 'floaters'. This business was mainly in the hands of Jewish firms, such as the Montagues and the Samuels.

Interest in my work spurred me on to fresh energies. I joined the London Scottish Volunteers and on the average put in two evenings a week at Buckingham Gate. The rest of my spare time I spent in amateur acting. I joined no less than three societies and played with them all.

One of them made a speciality of playing at lunatic asylums and we had amusing experiences. Lunatics make attentive audiences, but occasionally one of them would be led out of the hall laughing hysterically.

But these activities were not enough. My energy was enormous. I joined a rowing club and on summer evenings would dash off to Putney to gain some proficiency in an eight. But I had to give it up. For the first 15 days of the month I could afford a good lunch at the old Crosbie Hall, which was then serving as a restaurant, or at a City chophouse where for 1s 3d the customers could have a steak grilled in front of them, followed by an excellent plum duff. As the end of the month drew near I was reduced — like many other people — to a bun and two bananas and a walk looking at the mural paintings in the Royal Exchange. One cannot row on this diet.

Then for some months I rode a bicycle daily from Clapham to the City, dodging the trams, horse-drawn buses, drays, traps, growlers and hansoms that filled the streets.

In winter I would come to Waterloo on an astonishing underground electric railway. It was always airless and overcrowded — a child's idea of Hades. The trains made terrific noises. They rattled and swayed and bumped. This had the effect of making all those passengers who had been lucky enough to secure seats sit absolutely silent. Bangs and noise made conversation impossible.

In the summer, on Saturday mornings an ordinary horse bus, but with four horses, was provided for those prepared to pay double fares, sixpence each, to the City. The seats were generally filled with 'regulars', but on occasion I got one and rode in enviable state to my office.

My greatest inspiration was Miss Barnard, who was now living in London, working at her profession of teaching. She had a keen appreciation of the theatre, but decidedly not of amateur theatricals. She had read widely, sewed beautifully and was an absolute genius with children. She had a keen appreciation of a really witty or subtle story, but woe betide the individual who tried to pass off a second-rater. She could not simulate or lie. She loathed petty gossip and scandals concerning men's and women's lives. This virtue was to prove a tremendous asset to the community in which she lived in later life.

Starting at £100 a year, from £80 in my old bank, I found that at Christmas time our generous board of directors gave us a bonus of an extra month's salary. And, at the annual meetings of the shareholders, one of them got up and thanked, yes, actually thanked, the staff for their past year's services.

One day, when I was still ninth from the top of the list of those due for foreign service, I was informed by the secretary that I was to be examined by the doctor and, if found fit, was to be sent to Bombay.

It was a bombshell. The thought of leaving Violet was overwhelming. I had never felt so miserable in my life. What did prospects mean compared with the bitter pangs of separation? Diabolo was the game of the moment. Utterly cast down I sat dazed in a London park on a bright winter's day and watched children and their nurses doing incredible things with the shuttle, running it up and down the string.

From £50 granted me as an outfit allowance, I spent £12 on a ring and handed it over to Violet silently. I could not speak.

Sailing day came all too soon and, in the company of the Bombay manager who was returning from furlough, I set off in the P & O Special for Marseilles.

The wagon-lit from Calais to Marseilles was an experience. It was a cold March day and, not content with swaddling the carriage with heavy felt across the windows, the management had turned the heating full on and the place became unbearable. Claustrophobia gripped me like a vice and I thought, if this is travel, give me home. However, next morning we reached Marseilles without mishap and, with gesticulating porters each fighting to obtain his prize, we were safely put on board the P & O ship, *Arabia*.

In those days the P & O looked upon passengers as a nuisance. Did they not carry His Majesty's mail? The ship's officers kept apart and had to feed alone at one end of the dining saloon. Ridicule, chiefly from travellers used to the comforts offered by Cunard's North Atlantic service, killed the feeding arrangements.

In 1909, the different courses were served to the stroke of a gong that reverberated through the first-class saloon. When everyone was seated, a gong was sounded and Goanese stewards, coming in procession from the serving-hatch, handed round the soup, which had already been poured into the plates. Whether an individual passenger wanted soup or was a quick or slow eater made not the slightest difference. At the

19

second sound of a gong his plate was removed and the next course was not handed round until a third stroke had been struck. And so it continued until the end of the meal. If anyone had the misfortune to be late, he or she never recovered the lost time or course.

A squat, fat tumbler, the hero of many a monsoon, was the standard glass for the ship; one found the same model for one's teeth in the cabin as upon the dining table. Fans were considered a necessity only for those passengers, the wily ones, who had ordered them before the voyage and paid the charge of a couple of pounds. But for 10s one could get a deck chair allotted for the fortnight's trip. Curtains over the portholes were thought to be unnecessary, but woe betide the luckless individual who omitted to dress for dinner at 7.30. He was made to feel his shame from the head steward downwards. So effective was their disapproval that recourse to the captain was unnecessary to make him change his habits.

I met a member of the Indian Civil Service on board. He was kind to me, lent me Dubois's *Hindoo Manners and Customs* and persuaded me to learn Urdu, at which I became mildly proficient over the next couple of years. Port Said had not then had the advantage of the Great War clean-up and when we arrived at night and went ashore to get some cigarettes from Simon Artz, the most filthy postcards and photographs were openly pressed upon us and we were urged to visit a brothel or watch the belly dancer.

The tour down the Suez Canal was fascinating. The camels on the banks, loaded to the limit with every kind of merchandise or bundles of fresh-cut clover, and the black-robed natives prodding them from behind, gave one a brief glimpse into the lives of the most enslaved and docile people in the world — a people who, since the oldest dynasty and probably even before that, had never known real freedom from debt, usury, bribery and land sharks.

At Suez I understood the truth of Kipling's poetic request to 'ship me somewhere east of Suez', for the smells were truly awful and when one was not coping with the shattering blow to one's olfactory nerves a plague of flies added to the business of trying to keep reasonably sane.

At Aden, where we coaled, we had a glimpse of our future *citoyens*, as the port seemed alive with Parsee bumboat men. At least, the Parsees seemed to be in charge of the boats, but Arabs did the rowing and vied with the sharks for their next victim.

Trooper, Bombay Light Horse

On 31 March, my twenty-fourth birthday, in the mist of early dawn our ship sailed into Bombay harbour and we cast anchor off Apollo Bunder. My chief carried me off to his house on Malabar Hill.

Early next morning I went into the garden. Kites wheeled and screamed overhead. Grey and rusty black crows cawed cantankerously as they flew from rooftop to verandah, or hopped from verandah to lawn. Ponderous vultures with drooping wings and straddling gait moved across the lawns, or squatted on the palm trees preening their dirty plumage, or sat with their heavy heads sunk into their breasts.

A lizard was lying along the dusty wall gazing at a bright bluebottle fly. The reptile blinked. It crept forward so stealthily that motion was almost imperceptible. Its claws contracted and its long tail was raised a fraction; the tongue flashed and the fly disappeared. A bird, its head bitten off, lay at the foot of the wall. At breakfast I read in the *Times of India* that 43 people had died in Bombay the day before of bubonic plague.

Accompanied by a Parsee clerk, sent to show me the way, I walked down the hill to the bank. He talked loquaciously of his people and especially of their funeral customs. We stopped at a gate giving entrance to a garden of exotic shrubs and plants. In the midst were five towers rather like half-filled gasometers. Along the edges vultures were sitting motionless, watching the road. There was a ripple of movement and their cruel piercing eyes were more intent as they craned their bald necks and peered expectantly. A white-robed funeral procession entered the gate carrying a body on an iron stretcher. The mourners, all men, followed, each pair holding a white handkerchief as a symbol of unity, their black shiny cow-heeled headdresses a sharp contrast to their robes. At the rear a nondescript dog was led. He had, I was told, in accordance with Zoroastrian tradition, been made to look upon the naked corpse. Overhead there was the beat of vultures' wings.

The kinsmen retired to a temple nearby where the sacred fire burned. A tower door was unlocked and the body was borne inside by the Untouchable bearers. The gaze of the vultures had never wavered but now, in a united movement, they turned their heads inwards. The bearers reappeared with stretcher and winding sheets; simultaneously the birds flopped in and those overhead plunged down to their meal. Unseen they burrowed into the flesh and vulture fought against vulture. In a few minutes the birds rose heavily, belching prodigiously.

21

We proceeded on our way. An emaciated bull, so thin that its hump had disappeared, lay dying beside the road. There was a smell of musk, of spices and of smouldering sandalwood. I heard pattering footsteps behind me. Looking round I found myself mixed up with the head of a procession of Hindus bearing their brother to the Burning Ghats, the sharp outline of the corpse hardly hidden by the meagre cotton wrappings. They were coming at a jog trot. I stepped aside as the cortège swung through some gates. Smoke was drifting over the walls and the acrid smell of burning flesh smote the nostrils. Similar processions passed us before we reached the centre of Bombay's business life. That morning death seemed very near.

The bank paid its assistants well, but it certainly had its pound of flesh. During my first year I got to the office at eight in the morning and, after a short break for luncheon (which my servant brought to the office in a little pyramid of tin bowls to keep it hot), started to work again immediately and rarely got away before seven o'clock in the evening.

The cashiers' department was kept entirely separate from the rest of the bank and was staffed by a Parsee *shroff* who provided his own clerks, mostly poor relations, and was paid so much a year for the service. Every entry in every book had to be checked and initialled by a British assistant and no cheque could be cashed until the entry had been so checked and initialled in the ledger.

The chief clerk was a Parsee and we had Muslims, Goanese, Eurasian and every caste of Hindu from high-caste Brahmins to Untouchable porters. Many of the clerks were very able men. One of them, a Parsee, could multiply six figures by six figures in a single line; another, a Goanese, could solve the most intricate exchange problems in a few minutes.

By every weekly mail bundles of bills accepted for payment by our London office would arrive, which had to be presented and accepted by the Indian merchants before the bills of lading for the goods being imported could be handed over. On many mail days, 5000, 10,000 or 15,000 sovereigns would arrive by ship, and it was my lot to go and collect them and bring them up to the safe. On outward mail days we were busy sending off documents for Indian goods, chiefly bales of cotton being exported to London. Once a week I had to go and visit stores, called godowns, and check the numbers of bales, running into thousands, upon which advances had been given, and also the piles of British goods for which the bills of acceptance had not yet been either signed or paid for.

These activities were routine jobs, which had to be learned before the real business of exchange banking could be mastered. My chief, the *burra sahib*, was an extremely busy man with heavy responsibilities for buying and selling 'forward', that is estimating what the rates would be when buying pounds in London in six months' time and recuperating himself by selling dollars in Hong Kong, or exchanging rupees in Ceylon for local currency in Penang. At first it was all a complete mystery to me, but gradually the tangled skein unravelled itself. The manager was given freedom of action by his London board within certain monetary limits, and, during the three years I worked under him, I never knew him to make a bad debt, except for that never-to-be-forgotten day when one of our British staff was found to have embezzled a large amount of money.

The Indian merchants, I found, were scrupulously honest. Indeed it would not have paid them to be otherwise because the European exchange bankers had an association and we all passed information freely between ourselves on the financial standing and repute of our customers. If a merchant got a bad name among us he might just as well shut up shop, for he was doomed.

The Bombay Port Trust was issuing a loan while I was there and we tendered successfully for the amount, buying it at a discount and selling the bonds in London. That transaction was enough to provide us with profits for the year. Deals that would have caused any of the managers I had met in my old country branches in England a sleepless night were dealt with as shrewdly and casually as buying a railway ticket. Banking had become a real romance at last and my work became my vocation.

Three months after my arrival the monsoon broke. The climate had been oppressively heavy and damp. One morning the heavens opened and the rain began. It was an astonishing sight. It was like a mammoth watering can pouring down its contents upon the earth. For hour after hour it poured down. By afternoon it was impossible to distinguish between railway line and station platform. Traffic was at a standstill and the whole city was flooded; thousands of disconsolate people wandered about, unable to get home. By nightfall ten inches of rain had fallen in 12 hours.

As I got more senior in the office I was able to get to the office later, so, having been a private in the London Scottish Volunteers in London, I joined the Bombay Light Horse as a trooper and went to a standing camp at Bandra outside Bombay for three winter months. There we had three mornings doing military exercises, two mornings hunting and two Europe mornings, when we stayed in bed late. We were on the train by half-past nine and in our offices by ten. The bank encouraged all this, gave me an allowance to keep a horse and loaned me £70 with which to buy one. I took up riding seriously and had 15 months in the riding school under a roughriding sergeant major of the Hussars, whose favourite expression, if he thought one was getting cocky, was 'You are comin' off this morning,' and one generally did, especially when we were riding newly imported Australian horses from Baldock's stables.

For those who could afford the cost, Bombay was a paradise for games. During the monsoons there were rugby matches, mounted sports and pony scurries. The triangular cricket matches on the great *maidan* were attended by thousands. I thought that I would take up racquets soon after my arrival. The marker was loafing about, a pair of sandals on his feet. He stayed in the centre of the court and never seemed to shift his feet. 'Who are you?' I gasped. 'Oh, I am Pestonjee, the champion of the world.' He was.

The bullock cart dominated the city. This ubiquitous two-wheeled cart was used for every purpose. The drivers sat upon the end of the single shaft that was fastened at the forward end to the yoke. Every driver kept his great toe nails abnormally long so that he could continuously prod the genitals of the beast he was driving. With the exception of the animals that drew the municipal carts, every beast had had its tail mercilessly twisted and the bones broken at some time or another to spur it on to greater efforts.

Cows wandered at will. *Tikka gharries*, or diminutive victorias, rushed about drawn by ponies. *Ekkas*, with curtains drawn to hide the ladies, were drawn by trotting bullocks. European businessmen drove to their offices in high dogcarts with spanking Australian horses. Younger men did likewise, or else drove in *gharries*, or rode on bicycles. The horse-drawn skeleton trams were not used by Europeans.

The blue-uniformed and yellow-turbaned police were models of smartness and cleanliness.

Every type of headdress was seen, from Afridi to Madrasi, from Bengali to Parsee. Men carried umbrellas and in the mornings, when the trains emptied, the roads looked as though they were filled with black mushrooms.

Scores of maimed, starving and scrofulous dogs roamed the streets. From the slimy waters of temple tanks crowds of mosquitoes swarmed. In the purely Indian quarters beggars were legion. Holy men covered with ashes or sores, the halt, the dumb, the blind and the deliberately maimed held out their handless arms for alms, or whined piteously.

I could not but be distressed by the obvious fact that hundreds, if not thousands, did not have enough to eat. It was equally apparent that no nation could afford to maintain such a large percentage of holy men and beggars producing so little towards the common good. The fantastic ochre-habited or ash-besmeared ascetics, Hindu *sadhu*s and Muslim *fakir*s, were repulsive to look upon, yet fascinating to watch with their disciples holding begging bowls beside them.

There were of course many sights of rare beauty: the grace and suppleness of a Parsee's wrists and fingers when he talked, literally with his hands; the swing of a Pathan striding through the bazaar; the curve of the arm of a Hindu woman steadying a brazen pot upon her head, as with effortless grace she walked along the highway. And then there were the flaming blossoms of the gold *mohur* tree looking from a distance as though crowds of crimson butterflies were alighting.

The promenade along Back Bay was a gorgeous sight during the hour before sunset, when the merchants and their families came out to take the air. The colouring of the clothes arrayed along the sea wall was extravagantly chaotic. Wine-coloured waves broke over lotus pink; eddies of jade green bubbled with flowered designs of apricot, oyster, purple or scarlet; light blue glowed against buttercup yellow, and iridescent silver gleamed alongside vivid emerald.

The men wore many types of dress made from cotton, silk or velvet. Occasionally a prince stood there garbed in velvet, with diamonds or other precious stones shining from his turban, and pearls around his neck.

Muslim ladies were robed in white, dark blue or brown, with *burka*s hiding their heads and faces. Parsee and Hindu ladies were draped in

saris of every colour, showing off their heads beneath in exquisite outline. The saris were bordered with fringes of superb needlework, or
with silver and gold thread. Right or left arms were bare, according to
the religion of the wearer, and bangles of glass, gold or silver orna-
mented with precious stones shone from them.

At sunset, the sun would sink swiftly and suddenly. The sky would
change into fiery glory, turning the sea into molten gold; then all the
colour would die away into the brief moments of acrid green that form
the twilight. In 1910 Halley's comet came, 99 years after its last
appearance. For many nights its brilliant head and fiery tail flooded the
bay with mysterious splendour.

There were other manifestations that were not so lovely. The swelter-
ing nights of May and June, followed by the clammy heat of the
monsoon, were almost unbearable and there was a pungent, fetid smell
like an overheated hothouse. Within a few weeks every European
woman who could go was wafted off to the hills and the young men
were left to sweat alone. The majority lived in chummeries or boarding
houses, where a man's only privacy was his bedroom. They got tired of
dicing for drinks at the club bar. There were many bachelor dinner
parties with not much to do afterwards. Talk would become aimless.
Then someone would say, 'Let's go down the Grant Road,' and off
would go *gharry*-loads of young men. I went there only once. I had
made friends with the Indian medical service doctor in charge of the
Gokaldas Tejpal Hospital, and one evening after dinner he took me
down. 'It's not nice,' he said, 'but you ought to see it and then
tomorrow I'll show you the aftermath in my hospital.'

In the side streets were hovels, the doorposts of which were splashed
with lime and excretion from noses and spittle. There, behind iron bars
thick enough to imprison ferocious monkeys, sat women displaying
their wares — Eurasians, Hindus and Muslims dressed in every gaudy
colour, flaunting their overworked persons and calling on passers-by to
'come up and have a good time'. They did not confine their activities to
their cages, but came out into the street and pulled prospective customers by the sleeve. In the more 'aristocratic' Grant Road were situated
the 'first-class' brothels containing the dregs of Europe. They were
generally controlled by an Italian *padrona*, who marshalled her troupe
of half-naked, sweating women, mincing about on backless shoes with
inordinately high heels and clothed in abbreviated tunics of red, green

or yellow transparent muslin. Their first duties were to sell to the customers as much poor champagne as they could be persuaded to buy at ten times the cost price. These transactions satisfactorily concluded, the *padrona* went on to display the women's other attractions. In the *gharry* going home I was violently sick.

Next morning the doctor took me round his hospital. In one of the wards there were about 30 beds, each of which was occupied by what was once a man. Some faces were so eaten away by syphilis that all features had been destroyed. These voiceless, deaf and blind organisms had to be kept alive and be fed and watered three times daily. A monstrous sum of human misery and suffering.

After nearly three years in Bombay I was picked as one of the men to represent the Bombay Light Horse at the Delhi *durbar*, so I went 'bust' and bought a magnificent *waler* from Baldock's stables and set about purchasing full dress. But within a few days I was promoted by the bank and sent off to Karachi as an accountant. My hopes of going to Delhi had been scotched.

Karachi was more primitive than Bombay. Donkeys pattered up and down the dusty streets. Dogs skulked in the shade. The goats picked their ways with their heads hanging low, always searching for something to eat. Camels stalked disdainfully.

I lived alone in an enormous flat over the bank, which was entirely lacking in comfort. As it was in the business part of the town, by night-time all the Europeans had left and it was rather a dreary life. So there was nothing left but to go to one of the clubs.

Karachi prided itself on its cricket club, its pool of alligators and its capacity for consuming cocktails. As nobody in the European community dined before 9.30 there was plenty of opportunity. I saw an English girl drink eight before dinner.

Life there emphasized how entirely aloof the English were from the real life of the people. No native of the country was allowed to put his head inside the Scind Club except as a servant. Segregation was practised on the mail trains and one saw notices placed on the carriages saying, 'Europeans only', but never 'Europeans not admitted'. These discourtesies were adding righteous fuel to the fires of nationalism.

27

I had had trouble with my nose and throat ever since the days I had spent underground in the London office, so I came home to England and had a couple of operations at St Thomas's Hospital and went off to Grindelwald to recuperate. Curling fascinated me, especially the skip's cries of 'Sweep! Sweep!', but I did not get a chance to play until I was over 60. Home again, the question of the date of my return to India came up. I asked for permission to marry. It was refused: I had not had long enough service. I would not go back unmarried and so I resigned and later accepted a post as accountant to a well-known firm of steam-hammer manufacturers in England, B & S Massey Ltd. On a salary of just one-third of what I was getting in India, Miss Barnard and I were married.

Nothing could have been a greater contrast than the life I had been living in India and the life I was to lead during the next two years in Manchester. Fog and dripping skies replaced brilliant sunshine. The scarlet flowers of gold *mohur* trees were replaced by coal-grimed plane trees. Multi-coloured headdresses and embroidered sandals were exchanged for grey shawls and clogs. My wife and I took a house in a garden village and I rode a bicycle to and from the steam-hammer works. We both felt desperately homesick for the south. A little solemn-faced niece, Philippa, used to come and cheer us up.

At my office rapid additions and calculations were no longer necessary. I had to start accountancy all over again. I began by sitting in a hut and watching the doorman 'clocking in' the work people in the mornings. After a few days I sat in a little shed surrounded by machinery in the main shop and learned how the boy gave out job cards. From there I went to the costing office.

Massey's worked on the premium system. Every job had a fixed time of so many quarters of an hour given to it. If a machinist did it in less time he was credited with the time saved and the bonus was added to his weekly wage packet. If a new type of job came along, a mixed committee of management and workers fixed the new standard.

Costing was a specialized task, especially as the firm asked me to get out a provisional balance sheet every month and forecast the profit for six months ahead. As I talked with the men in the works after lunch, or

28

played cricket with them on a vacant lot, I could hardly understand a sentence they said. But I learned to respect and like them. The works were known as 'an open shop' and any man, irrespective of whether he was a trade unionist, was admitted. The directors prided themselves on paying the highest wages in the trade; and during their 60 years of existence they had never had a strike or lockout. There was an extraordinarily happy relationship between masters and men, each respecting the other. I never knew the firm dishonour an obligation to either customer or a workman and if an article had by chance a defect it was exchanged at once. The most spectacular part of the works was the smithy. With the forced-draught furnaces glowing and the hoarse shouts of the smiths trying to make themselves heard above the din and heavy thuds of the hammers, the shop was always a little Dantesque. An expert smith could actually control the drop of a hammer so that he could bring several hundredweights down to crush a mass of red-hot steel or else crack a walnut.

By the end of a year or so, I had fathomed the intricacies of book-keeping and costing and could do everybody's clerical work in the office and works, including the most humble, and, to tell the truth, was beginning to get a bit bored. I realized that, as I had no engineering qualifications or interests, and selling did not appeal to me, nor buying either, there was not much scope ahead and I missed the East and its lighter side of life. I was offered a post by a South American bank in Chile, but as we were expecting a baby I did not accept it.

A few weeks before our son Martin was born I was playing cricket for the village when, out of the corner of my eye, I saw my wife sailing past the ground. Inspired by the sight, I hit out at the next ball and for the first, indeed the only, time in my life hit a six over the top of an elm tree behind the screen. A year later came the threat of war. My wife and I were staying with my mother in Cornwall, teaching our son to paddle, or rather to sit down in minute pools. We talked over the need for men. I sent a wire to the GOC Western Command Chester. 'The following is my experience — six years private London Scottish and trooper Bombay Light Horse. Can I be of any use?' Four days later I was in the train, in my pocket a telegram ordering me to report to the Salford barracks to join up as second lieutenant, 7th Battalion Lancashire Fusiliers. Although I did not know it, I had left Manchester and manufacturing for ever.

3

The Open Desert

The 42nd was the first Territorial Division ready for war. September found my battalion in camp at Turton, Lancashire. We were 1000-strong, organized in eight companies with 28 officers and 52 horses for our transport. I was appointed transport officer and had to have the horses ready for duty from the colonel's charger to the pony and two-wheeled milk float, which had been made into the medical officer's comforts cart. The pony survived Gallipoli, only to be killed later in an accident while crossing one of Cairo's bridges. The transport had been hurriedly got together by inexperienced people and many of the horses, great shires used for hauling cotton lorries across the Manchester granite sets, were unsuitable for military purposes and we started to weed them out.

Reports came that we were to go to Egypt. A call came for volunteers. The Territorials had been enlisted for home service. Many of the sergeants and older men had families and marriage allowances were quite inadequate. They were seriously distressed. Those who did not sign on for foreign service were separated from the rest and an injudicious colonel began allotting them menial jobs. The second-in-command spoke to me about it and asked me to stop with him as he was taking over the details. I had no wish for garrison duty in Egypt and so agreed to stay behind. The battalion was filled up with recruits and the Division sailed.

Five officers and a couple of hundred men were left behind. We were at once given the number of 2nd/7th and began recruiting. Then the rain began. It came relentlessly, hour after hour, day after day. At the end of three weeks the camp was a bog. We lay in water every night.

The heavy horses were so deep in mud that they could be moved only with difficulty. The CO gave nearly everyone three days' leave to go home and get dry. Then the whole Division was moved to billets in Southport. Our equipment was sketchy. An odd assortment of uniforms, khaki and red. Our lethal weapons were Japanese rifles, the bolts of which were always falling out and getting lost, but we got fit exercising on the sand dunes.

Recruits poured in and I was promoted to command a company. After a month or two I was sent for a course with the Guards at Chelsea barracks. I took with me my newly appointed company sergeant-major, an old soldier from the South African war. In the train going down he said to me, 'Sir, when we arrive, say we know nothing.' I acted on this piece of shrewd advice. For the first time since I had left home to earn my living I had no responsibilities whatever. Nothing to do but listen and learn. I enjoyed it to the hilt.

On one occasion on the parade ground, when it was my turn to change from right-hand marker to being commander of a composite battalion, I was letting drive with my biggest voice when the instructing Grenadier regimental sergeant-major beckoned me to him. I stood rigidly to attention. He looked me over for a few seconds, and then, in a voice that would have put a foghorn to shame, said 'You are not singing psalms, SIR.' I wished the earth would swallow me up.

Both Brandrick, my CSM, and I came away with good chits from Major Tryon, the commandant, later postmaster general. But once back I found it difficult to put up with the slovenliness of my men, mostly miners, and I began to give them extra drills on the Southport promenade. My wife heard one of the many women spectators say to a friend, pointing me out with her fingers, ''E's mad, that one.' However, I survived that possibly true criticism and received an appointment to proceed as major on the general staff to join the Egyptian Expeditionary Force, then attacking Gallipoli. One July morning I went up to Manchester and saw my wife with our war baby Anthony, born an hour or two before. In another couple of hours I was in the train for Plymouth.

There, after one false start and all of us being ordered off the good ship *Aragon*, we went aboard the Cunard liner *Franconia* and I received a letter from the War Office appointing me ship's adjutant. There were 2700 troops aboard and 500 unattached officers. But not a gun, and the Mediterranean reported to be teeming with German submarines! A few voyages later this beautiful ship was torpedoed and sunk.

Unescorted, we set off for the Bay of Biscay. There was a lot to be done: to arrange accommodation and constant relays of meals, to appoint orderly officers, arrange for exercise, lectures, fire pickets, boat drill and accommodation in the boats; and in the evenings extend my activities to concert parties.

I was fortunate in finding a Sapper staff sergeant-major who had been trooping before. I let him draft the daily routine orders for my initials and for Colonel Lord Rochdale's subsequent signature. So well did he help me that by the time we got to Gibraltar we had some sort of task for every unattached officer on board. The last 350 officers were formed into six platoons, armed with rifles and instructed to fire at the periscope of any submarine they might see.

I arranged classes of instruction for the officers and felt so sure of myself that I had the temerity to give a lecture in front of three generals and three or more colonels on how to dig trenches under fire, and got away with it, plus congratulations from a couple of the brass hats. Such is the assurance of youth when put to it. As my duties took me up to concert time, the purser kindly arranged for me to be given dinner every night in my cabin and — Oh, spacious days! — champagne was thrown in free and I could invite three guests! Those dinners were very popular.

By the time we reached Alexandria, thanks to my sergeant-major the nominal rolls were complete, the recalcitrant had been inoculated, stoppages of pay recorded, defaulters' crime sheets brought up to date, and barman's bills paid up. Accompanied by my sergeant-major I went up to the third echelon of GHQ to report. I was given an interview by General O'Leary. I spent a couple of days helping to send off drafts and O'Leary was evidently satisfied with the state in which our papers were handed in, for he promptly bagged the warrant officer and me for his own staff. That is why I survived the holocaust of the peninsula.

Records and reinforcements were hard going and we frequently worked all night when casualties were heavy. But I got what would be described in the present age as 'browned off' at being denied an opportunity to take the field against the Turks, especially when one knew from inside information that things were going badly. However, the poetic, discursive soldier Ian Hamilton gave way to Birdwood, the soul of Anzac, and confidence was restored to the decimated forces.

Alexandria was crowded with the wounded and the sick. Our casualties were enormous. No kind of steel shields had been invented for men's protection and they had been mown down on the peninsula by machine-gun fire. Long processions of ships came into harbour bringing reinforcements; they also brought typhoid and dysentery cases, and the wounded evacuated from the battlefields. My old battalion had been filled up three times. Evacuation of the whole peninsula followed at the end of the year.

Gallipoli remains a monument to the everlasting glory of the common man and to the stupidity of entering fresh wars with the mental outlook and weapons of the last.

I lived with a French family and, during my few free hours off duty, spoke French with the children.

Alexandria was a centre for racing and Arab horses were brought in large numbers from Syria and the Persian Gulf. The *gharries* got the rejects and I saw some lovely animals, but as they were fed mainly on green clover, they got too fat and the roads were always in a sloppy condition. Sturdier and less well-bred animals moved the cotton crop in long, narrow four-wheeled carts. Greys predominated.

Pandemonium seemed to reign everywhere. Nothing was done without verbal accompaniment. Yelling and shouting must often have taken as much energy as the physical demands of the job in hand. Cocaine had not yet got a hold on the Egyptians and the labourers were fine, well-built men. They were decent to their animals, except if they lost their tempers over something, and then they stopped at nothing.

The only interest in the war taken by the hordes of Italians, Greeks and Egyptians who made up the population was that it was the cause of great activity in the local cotton market and prices were soaring to unknown heights.

Everyone was gambling. Pelota gave additional opportunity, plus excitement. The game was played by teams of professionals from the Basque country. The men played with incredible dexterity. The courts were full of gesticulating, shouting crowds. There were no new motorcars on which they could lavish their money, so wealthy up-country landowners, thick in the neck and bursting with sweat, would produce bundles of notes from the sleeves of their grey *galabiehs* and, with less thought than they would give to selling a bale of cotton, would wager hundreds on the blue- or red-capped players.

The only silent people in the whole throng were three small men who sat on a bench high up at the back of the court, and formed a board of arbitration. Appeals were frequent. Having got into a huddle and discussed the point, the three men would take off their hats and bow to each other with gravity, and *Monsieur le Président* would pronounce the verdict. Should they give a decision that was unfavourable to the majority of spectators, they were stormed and jeered at.

I was posted to Advanced GHQ, now stationed at Ismailiya on the Suez Canal. There was little doing. The advance into Palestine had not been thought of. A telegram came from the *sirdar* of the Egyptian Army asking for a staff officer. I was asked if I would like to go? I accepted and in a week, a *tarboosh* on my head and bearing the crown and star of a *bimbashi* in the sultan of Egypt's army, I was on my way down to Khartoum. Of war I had seen nothing, but I had seen some strange happenings.

In the early days of the Australian occupation the *tarboosh* or red fez disappeared. This was because the 'Aussies' took a dislike to it; when one of them passed an Egyptian wearing this headgear he would lean across and press it down over the offender's ears.

A number of Australian soldiers had contracted venereal diseases and had been sent home, their bodies shattered. Their comrades, who were very angry about this, set fire to an entire brothel quarter in Cairo. Coming from my office in Alexandria one late afternoon, I saw bedroom furniture flying down from the top balcony of a house nearby, followed by two screaming women, who fell with sickening thuds upon the road.

The Australians had given an example of how brave men could fight and die. Members of the Light Horse were accustomed to living alone in the bush, where every man is master of himself. So they ignored mass discipline. They felt that they had come to fight, not to be treated like schoolchildren. The valour of the 29th Division will adorn military history as long as England lives.

It was May, the hottest month of the year. I left Cairo one evening and next morning transferred at Luxor into a narrow-gauge railway for Aswan and Shallal. The temperature mounted higher and higher in the blazing sunlight. There were no fans and thick sand blew in at the windows. Never before, or since, have I experienced such heat. It must have reached 130°F. There was no ice. My temples throbbed so violently that I thought my head must burst. I lay down on the hard seat too exhausted to pray for death, which I would have welcomed.

The end of this awful day came and, at sunset, I climbed limply out of the train at Shallal and went aboard a Nile river steamer. The ruins of Philae looked like a fairy palace mysteriously set apart by the waters. With iced drinks upon a table and a long chair to lounge in, flesh, mind and spirit were delivered from inferno into paradise.

For 36 hours we chuffed along at a steady seven knots, the stern wheel leaving a square wake behind. The ship was saluted by the whining drone of wooden wheels drawn round and round by blind-folded buffaloes bringing up water from the river in a succession of earthenware pots bound to an endless cord. At the top of the bank the water was emptied into palm-tree troughs, thus bringing life to the barren desert.

Brown and ebony-coloured youths of that strange race, the Berber-eens, who supply Egypt with her domestic servants, waved and shouted as we passed. Long-legged, small-bodied, anxious-eyed fowls and dusty children were intermingled upon dried mud. Dogs kept up an incessant barking until the midday sun drove them to shelter. And the donkeys brayed. However much they were overloaded they still retained enough energy to voice their protests, or indeed their joys, for if they saw a lady of their species the cacophony became exquisite.

The land was divided by irrigation channels into strips of brown earth, which is enriched by deposits of Nile mud left by the annual inundations. This hard-worked soil gives three, even four, crops a year. White-robed red-brown men and black-shrouded women moved about the bright patches of mustard and green — green *berseem* (Egyptian clover) – working the land with their Virgilian iron-toothed wooden ploughs. The pink Libyan hills shone against the sky on the western side of the river and their valleys were filled with blue shadows.

The large boards bearing the names of the stations in Arabic writing made them look as impressive as a prayer. In villages built of mud, with manure stacked on the flat roofs, *sakiyas* (water wheels) groaned

35

in the shade of *jebbek* trees. Burial grounds containing a few saints' tombs with white-washed domes were adjacent to every village and often covered larger areas than the villages themselves. The dusty sterility of the nameless graves gave one a sense of a land too much lived in, where thousands of lives had come into being, withered and perished; and that this had been repeated century after century.

At Wadi Halfa we reached the Sudan frontier and the Egyptian flag flew alongside the Union Jack. The most striking change was the absence of begging. Towns in Egypt are fouled by hundreds of people calling for *baksheesh*, or hawking articles ranging from bogus antiquities and erotic postcards to lottery tickets.

Although of narrow gauge, the Sudan railway train was very comfortable. Once away from the Nile, the land is completely barren and the first six stations have no names, only numbers.

In Khartoum I entered a different century. It is splendidly laid out and beautifully green. As most of the riverside houses are government-owned, the gardens are kept up by an overseeing gardener. It was almost untouched by the war, except that everyone was short of leave. This was a world of officials and officers whose minds, when war was mentioned, automatically went back to the Omdurman campaign of 1896. Newcomers were taken off almost at once to see the battlefield at Kerrari. I was, on my third day.

The reception of a new member at the club was disconcerting. The older members sitting comfortably in their wicker chairs looked up, raised their eyebrows questioningly at each other and returned sadly to their previous activity. They thawed gradually and I realized what an extraordinarily fine lot of men, both civil servants and officers, they were. But the soldiers were disgruntled and disappointed at being kept back from active service in Europe.

I was posted to the intelligence department to learn something about the revolt against the Turks in the Hejaz and also something of the military operations in Darfur. After a few weeks I was sent to Port Sudan to arrange for the despatch of an Egyptian Army mountain battery to Jiddah to join the *sherif* of Mecca's forces. The guns were 20-year-old Krupps with a range of only 3000 yards. They proved of little use because the Turkish guns outranged them. I had of course heard the popular saying that an Egyptian Army officer's promotion depends on the size of his Sam Browne belt. The expansive battery commander's belt foretold his early advancement. His troops were sullen and uninterested. They hated service in the Sudan, but they loathed the idea of fighting Turks in Arabia still more.

Port Sudan had been founded some years before its time by General Wingate, a far-seeing governor general and *sirdar* known to every officer as 'Master'. Nigerian pilgrims did not use it. Arab merchants, although they had all rented shops (which remained empty), continued to do business at Suakin, the old port higher up the creek. Their merchandise was brought up in dhows. As a port, Port Sudan had not yet come to life.

The surrounding hill country was inhabited by Haddendowiehs, Kipling's Fuzzy-Wuzzies, but nothing would induce these wild men to come into the town. Tacked on to my military duties were those of civil administration. Most of the population were Dongalowis, who became such a nuisance with their pilfering and general misbehaviour that, after trying a dozen of them as vagabonds under the penal code, I ordered them ten lashes apiece, which were artistically applied by a police sergeant and two corporals. I was given the nickname of *Abu Gelda*, the father of lashes, and from that time on the problem of the corner boys was settled.

The weather was very hot and also very, very damp. Unless I put my boots in the sun every other day the insides became covered with mildew. Keys were rusty by morning. Newspapers flopped into rag and matches refused to strike. My chest was covered with prickly heat. It was useless to bathe. I was wet again from a fresh burst of sweat before the towel had wiped the water away.

The British community of the port consisted of six people: the governor of the Red Sea Province, myself and a Customs official, the harbour master and two minor officials. Yet such was the social system that this handful of men had to have two clubs, the Red Sea Club for the seniors and the two-roomed Port Sudan Club for the others. However, all met happily at noon to drink cold beer on the verandah of the hotel run by the Railway Administration. Fishing for barracuda was our only pastime.

The Eastern Telegraph Company had an office at Suakin. Its three British employees led the most uninteresting and isolated lives of anyone in the Sudan. Their main work was to retransmit in Morse code the telegrams that passed through their branch. They learned not a word of the local language and knew nothing of the people, nor of the country except for a few yards round their office and sleeping quarters. There were not enough of them for bridge, or for any game, and when not carrying out their monotonous duties they did absolutely nothing. They were normally kept there for three years without a holiday.

Bombay at its worst was pleasant compared to the damp heat of Port Sudan and I was glad when, in October, an order came for me to pack up and proceed to the extreme west of the Sudan to take part in the operations in Darfur against Sultan Ali Dinar.

When Lord Kitchener reconquered the Sudan in 1896, Sultan Ali Dinar was left alone to continue ruling the 170,000 square miles of Darfur Province on condition he paid an annual nominal tribute to the govern-or general of the Sudan.

For years this had been carried out. But when Turkey came into the war, an emissary managed to get across the Sahara and persuade the sultan to raise a revolt against the British. This shaggy ruler sent some spearheads to the governor of Kordofan Province, by way of starting the fight in a gentlemanly manner, and began menacing tribesmen within the Sudan boundaries. We then declared war against him and, early in 1916, a small expeditionary force beat his slave army outside El Fasher, the capital. Arrangements were now being made to finish him off as he had fled to the west.

In Khartoum, I picked up enough boxes of food to last me for a few months. I also got a few lessons in mapping from Boyce of the Surveys Department; and acquired a compass and small board, both of which could be strapped onto one's wrist. At El Obeid, at the end of the rail-way system, I bought half a dozen camels — heavy cumbrous beasts as the best had gone — and started off on a three-week trek. Except for a couple of hours around midnight to rest the camels, we travelled all night through loose sand scantily covered by *heskaneet* grass and thorn bushes. During the day I tried to sleep under such shade as I could find by continually changing the position of my camp bed.

I had passed but two places where there were any wells and had been subsisting on what water my animals could carry in heavy iron *fan-tass*es when, early one morning, I got to the top of a sandy hill and reached Umm Keddada. This was to be my home for the next three years, though I did not know it then. Umm Keddada's chief claim to fame is an excellent water supply. When greetings had been made to all assembled at the well, the animals watered and the men rested, I looked round for somewhere to sleep.

A couple of days later Kelly Pasha and his chief political officer, Harold MacMichael,[1] came in from Khartoum. Kelly was the commanding officer of the expedition and had been down in Khartoum arranging for the winter campaign. But he had not taken Huddlestone Bey, his second in command, into account. Huddlestone had got some fresh information. So he loaded his men onto whatever beasts he could get hold of (only goats were excluded), trekked off 100 miles, attacked at dawn one day, shot Ali Dinar dead, and finished off his troops. The news came through while Kelly and MacMichael were in my grass hut. I have never seen two men so flabbergasted. All their ambitious plans were for naught. Of the shortening of the campaign they thought nothing; personal interests were paramount. Sentences were heard like, 'Not playing the game,' and 'He had no right to start without us.' However, Huddlestone survived this adverse criticism and 20 years later became governor general of the Sudan and head of the Defence Force.

With the campaign over, the troops returned to Khartoum and a quasi-military civilian administration was set up. I was appointed to administer the Eastern District with headquarters at Umm Keddada. The idea was that I should act as assistant to the district commissioner appointed to be in charge of eastern Darfur, but within ten days of his

---

1. Sir Harold MacMichael (1882–1969) was born in Derbyshire, the son of a clergyman. He obtained a first at Cambridge and entered the Sudan Political Service in 1905, remaining there until 1933 in various positions: senior inspector in Khartoum province, political officer on the Darfur expedition and civil secretary. He was a skilled cartographer and a noted historian of the Arabs in Sudan. He spoke fluent Arabic. In 1933 MacMichael was transferred to Tanganyika as governor. He arrived in Palestine as high commissioner and commander in chief in 1938 at the height of the Arab revolt. His implementation of unpopular British government policies such as the land transfer regulations of 1940, made him unpopular with the Jewish community, who distrusted him anyway because of his Arab connections. In 1944 the Stern Gang made an attempt on his life but he escaped unhurt. He left Palestine later that year. During the rest of his life he was involved in government work in Malaya and Malta and for the Joint East African Board.

arrival he received orders to return to Khartoum because he had been appointed governor of another province. I had the luck to be left in charge. I counted myself singularly fortunate. Here was I, in an age of high military endeavour in war but otherwise an age being steadily dulled by the levelling of standards to the mediocre measure of the mass, the first Englishman to live in the last portion of Africa to have been left untouched by European influence. A generation before, Darfur had been visited by Gordon[2] and governed by Slatin.[3] Except for these two officers, and possibly one or two more, no European had ever set foot therein.

The population of the district was unknown, but the boundaries included about 30,000 square miles of mainly sand and thorn bushes. The inhabitants were a negroid people, though they called themselves Arabs — ethnically a blend of Hamitic and Negro. They were nominally Muslims and spoke a pure but simple Arabic. They moved about with unhurried grace. Their tribal marks were slashed across their cheeks when young. They were brave and treated their women well, except, like all Sudanese Arabs, they subjected them in youth to painful Pharaonic circumcision. The external genital organs were cut and removed and the girl's legs tied together for a month while the two lips of the labia majora grew together, excepting for a small hole which was kept open by the insertion of a stick. It was by means of this barbarous custom that a gallant ensured that the bride he purchased was a virgin.

A few months after my arrival the last of the British and Sudanese troops left, stepping proudly over a goat with blood spouting from its cut throat. I was alone with 50 newly recruited police from Kordofan, an Arab officer, a cashier or *shroff*, and a cheerful Sudanese clerk who had just graduated from the Gordon College in Khartoum.

---

2. General Charles Gordon was appointed governor general of Sudan by the Egyptian Khedive Ismail in 1877 and suppressed the slave trade. He resigned in 1879 but returned in 1884 to recommend how to handle a revolt against Egyptian rule led by Mohammed Ahmed Ibn Sayid Abdullah, who declared himself the Mahdi or Muslim messiah in 1880. Gordon was killed on 26 January 1885 when the Mahdists stormed Khartoum.

3. Baron Rudolph Carl von Slatin, Baron of the Austrian Empire, was governor of Darfur under General Gordon and was captured by the Mahdists. He served as inspector-general of Sudan from 1900 to 1914. In the First World War he became head of Aid for Prisoners of War under the Austrian Red Cross.

The Arab district officer was a member of the Bisharin tribe, famous for their riding camels, and he came with the most beautiful animal. She was as dainty as an Arab mare and when really extended could leave us all far behind. I once rode her with a glass of water in my hand to see if it could actually be done without spilling a drop. It could.

The work of starting an organization from scratch was enthralling and however long the day or tedious the hours in the camel saddle, there was always some fresh interest to take away the fatigue. I was well paid and lived on very little, so was able to allot my wife the bulk of my salary, which gave me great relief from anxieties on her behalf. It also seemed to be a job that wanted doing and was worthwhile even in wartime. But the loneliness after the army had moved away was shattering. When I got back to Khartoum after three years I found that I was quite unable to carry on a conversation, especially if there was little to talk about. It seemed so meaningless.

The first job was to get to know the district. Some of my treks took over a month, the longest six weeks, and I never spent more than 15 days at a time in my office. The first march from home was always difficult. Loads slipped, saddles had to be regirthed, or else something was forgotten and had to be fetched. But from then onwards, the trek went like clockwork. Within five minutes of getting to a halting place, my rookie chair[4] was ready and my table set up on a carpet. In another quarter of an hour the meal was ready.

Gradually I got to know every part and before I left I had at least seen every headman. To each I gave a paper of appointment. As few could read, I got a travelling silversmith to cut on a 20 piastre piece, about the size of a five-shilling piece, what he fondly believed to be a replica of the crest on my ring and I used it as a seal by rubbing it on my Indian ink pad. I would give a policeman a verbal order for a sheikh, which he would repeat after me. Then, armed with an impression of the 'Great Seal' upon a piece of paper, he would set off on his journey (possibly of many days) to deliver both message and paper to the headman. The order was invariably carried out.

Although barely one in a thousand had ever seen a white man, the impact less striking than might have been expected. For 18 years a handful of British officials had been spread around the Sudan proper

4. A large cane reclining chair with the virtue of being cool.

and their influence had been enormous. Native customs had been fostered as far as circumstances permitted. For centuries there had been a continuous pilgrim traffic through the province from west to east (somewhat less westwards) as West African pilgrims, impoverished by the journey, would sell or barter their children to Arabs in the vicinity of Mecca and Medina. Death also took its toll. Through these sources, and also through traders in gum arabic and natron (a kind of rock salt), tales of the Ingleeze in Nigeria and Kordofan would spread along the lines of march and into the camps and villages. The people were most friendly and I always slept in the open unarmed.

Only one of my three staff knew any English and I knew very little Arabic. I therefore had to spend many hours each day grinding away at it before I became reasonably competent. For an hour in the evenings, indoors or on trek, six days a week, I would plunge into the intricacies of this difficult tongue — it is written from right to left, there are three versions of each letter (depending on whether it falls at the beginning, middle or end of a word) and all the short vowels are left out. At the beginning, like a Trappist monk, I communicated through copious use of sign language. Then, through sheer necessity, I made considerable progress and, within a year, had passed a couple of examinations. In my viva voce examination I regaled my examiners, two passing British officers, with supplies of cold beer taken from my carefully guarded store, which had been brought up at great cost by camel.

It was surprising how easily the Furowis accepted me and how readily they poured out their woes and, indeed, their joys. Wherever I went I was invariably met by shrill ululations and a village dance. Beginning early in the morning they would go on all day long. Men and women danced together, the women inside the circle, the men for the most part forming the vocal and hand-clapping rhythmical chorus. Although the idea behind each type of dance was sexual and the climax was graphically portrayed, the men would never touch the woman. The only exception was in a dance in which one of them would bend backwards until her head almost touched the ground, at which point a man would rush forward and hold up her head and snap his fingers, or pass his dagger around her head.

The men were dressed in long shirts woven out of local cotton and baggy *kombaz* or trousers. The women wore a *thobe* of cotton stuff wrapped round their waists and another piece of stuff was used as a

42

shawl. They plaited their hair and smeared it with fat. While working both sexes stripped to the waist. The women wore masses of beads round their necks, amber predominating. Little girls wore short kilts made from strips of leather fastened to a belt. Boys ran about much as Nature made them. Everyone wore a leather-bound verse from the Koran.

A portable medicine chest stocked with simple drugs proved a valuable asset. Fortunately trust was placed in my amateurish efforts with quinine and sedlitz powders, and faith undoubtedly helped to make up for my deficiencies. I was called upon to prescribe for many ailments. For the old village headman, who came somewhat sheepishly and said that he had married a young wife and wanted something to enable him to enjoy her more robustly, I gave a mixture of mushroom ketchup, quinine and the contents of my pepper pot, with, as he smilingly reported the next day, the happiest results. I cast out a devil from an old woman who refused to get up and was said to bark like a dog, by lighting a fire of damp straw under her bed; she responded quickly and my fame as a medicine man spread far and wide.

I stumbled by chance upon the only school in the district. Arriving at a village at sunset, I was attracted by a bonfire in the yard of a hut. Riding up and peeping over the wall, I saw an old man teaching about half a dozen lads how to read. The boys squatted upon their heels and shouted out verses from the Koran. When they wanted to write they used little wooden boards and dipped their reed pens into a mixture of gum arabic and soot from the fire. Later I learned that the old man was paid in kind plus a few logs of wood for the fire.

The Furowis live isolated lives, siting their huts as far away as practicable from routes and tracks. Their huts have the appearance of old-fashioned beehives. They build up the conical roofs first from wooden poles and grain-stalks, then lift them up onto three-foot-high stakes stuck into the ground in a circle. A rough hurdle closes the entrance and preserves the decencies.

My own offices were a little more ambitious. After some experimenting on my own, I taught them how to make mud and straw bricks, like the Egyptians of old. A couple of years after I built my house termites destroyed some of the rough poles of the roof and it had to be pulled down. Externally there were no signs, but they had ravaged their way in under the bark and the wood had crumbled into dust. Such is Africa.

43

On tour, day after day, or night after night, one might never meet a soul. Each new turn of the track was like the last. In the hot weather the sun beat down mercilessly upon the sand and a raging metallic heat rose up, seemingly fiercer than the beacon overhead — the same burning, dust-laden wind, the waves of thick sand and arid, stony patches of scrub and thorn bush, enlivened from time to time by troops of gazelle. The impression that nature made was immeasurably deepened by the constant and monotonous repetition.

Sandstorms, *haboobs*, were frequent during June and July before the rains broke. I was caught in one once on tour. A dull saffron smear appeared on the horizon, a rustle in the bushes turned into a whistling wind and the storm was upon us. We couched and knee-haltered our camels, tails to storm, and, drawing clothes over our heads, bent them against the blinding, choking dust and sought refuge alongside the camels' bellies. The sky turned into a great sheet of yellow-brown paper. The wind rose, 30, 40, 50 and more miles an hour, and the sand howled and rushed round us. Visibility was completely extinguished. Sand lashed our faces. Sand was in our eyes, in our ears, in our noses and in our lungs. After hours of misery we raised our heads and looked round. The outlook was unrecognizable. A changed world. High sand dunes had been swept away and new ones formed. I had to find our way by compass bearing.

The few lessons in surveying in Khartoum stood me in good stead. I took a compass and board with me and a kind of bicycle wheel with cyclometer attached, which was run alongside my camel and was used to check on my angles and distances travelled. I plotted my records with a protractor on getting into camp. I recall my pleasure when, having sent my sketches into Khartoum, some months afterwards I received from the Survey Department by camel mail my own records fitted into the general triangulation, and was given credit for them in the corner.

I had no tent, but carried a small waterproof canvas groundsheet for rigging up as a sunshade and that, plus a Persian rug, made my daily camp more luxurious. Water was carried in large iron *fantasses* by the baggage camels and on my own camel I had a small canvas water bottle, which kept the day's supply reasonably cool.

I soon realized that it was essential to maintain certain external forms. Indeed life without them would be impossible. Therefore, however blisteringly hot it might be, whether at home or on tour, I always put on a white shirt and black tie on Sunday nights for dinner and with some ceremony drank a bottle of beer. Three cases containing four dozen each lasted me three years.

Agriculturally, the district is one of the least productive in the world. The main growth, apart from thorn bushes, is a sparse coarse grass called *heskaneet*, which flourishes for a short time during the rains and then rapidly dries up, leaving behind its seed pods covered with spikes, which drift away in the wind and become a continual source of pain to every human being. The spikes find their way into every piece of one's clothing and, once in the skin, take a good deal of getting rid of. Every Furowi goes about with a dagger and a pair of tweezers strapped to his forearm.

Cooking is uncomplicated. The chief meal is *marissa*, fermented grain. The only cereal crop is *dukhn*, a kind of millet of the birdseed variety we usually give to canaries. *Dhurra* (maize), the main crop of the rest of the Sudan, will not grow in the sandy desert, so the people fall back on the smaller but inferior *dukhn*. Cultivation is a quick and satisfying task. Armed with a suitably curved branch of a tree, the good man starts off at the beginning of the rainy season by ambling along. As each left foot advances, he stabs at the ground to make a little hole into which his attendant wife pours a few grains of seed hoarded up from the last season. She covers the seed with her foot and passes on. An enormous area is covered in a day or so. The subsequent weeding is left to madame. The master's only job is to frighten off locusts, if they come, which they do every few years, and to snip off with his knife the heads when the corn is ripe. The wife grinds the corn by kneeling down and rubbing it between stones and the flour, plentifully mixed with sand, is fermented. The result is the main dietary staple for men, women and children. The alcoholic content is high and it is safe to say that the majority of the inhabitants go to bed fuddled.

Trade is carried out by barter.

Acacias grow freely and are regularly tapped for gum, which is taken down to the railhead at El Obeid and there exchanged for coffee, sugar loaves, cloth and amber beads.

Being a naturally indolent people, the Arabs managed to get most of their hard work done for them by Hausa Muslim pilgrims who, leaving Nigeria, would trek across French Equatorial Africa and Darfur on their hadj to Mecca. Since they arrived without money or goods, these pilgrims would work for anyone prepared to hire their services until they had saved up enough money, or food, for the next stage of their journey.

Land disputes were numerous, especially in areas where *tebeldi* (baobab) trees grew. These enormous softwood trees are used in a way that nature at her proudest never anticipated. The major part of the district is waterless, despite a fair annual rainfall. So, since earliest times, the inhabitants have utilized these trees as reservoirs. They cut out their soft hearts and, into the hollows, pour the rainwater that collects at the foot of the trees each rainy season, hauling it up with the aid of leather buckets.

These trees have a fantastic look. Bearing sparse leaves, their great bottle-shaped, bulbous, shiny, purple trunks are of little height compared to their thickness, which averages from 20 to 30 feet in circumference. They are centuries old before they reach maturity, and some may be over 1000 years old.

Where there are no *tebeldi* trees, water melons are planted and, when ripe, the crops are piled up into long mounds, rather as swedes are stored on English farms. Once the melons are eaten, used as water by man, beast and bird, the peasants vacate their villages and drift down south to Bahr al Ghazal Province and other regions near the Nile.

The sultan's rule had been direct and dynamic. He had no police force, but a headman was appointed over each village whose job it was to assess the peasants' crop and hand over a tenth of it to the sultan. Groups of villages were looked after by the leading man of the largest village in the group, who was handed over the sultan's tithe. He, in his turn, took 10 per cent of this total tax, and despatched the rest to El Fasher to feed the sultan's slave army.

As he did not maintain a police force the sultan adopted a quick and somewhat devastating method. If a group of villages refused to pay taxes or kicked up a fuss, he despatched a company of his army who came down, killed the headman and swept the villages clean of everything worth having. He rarely used this force. Memories of its visits were too well known.

Another function of the sultan's representative was to keep his eye open for comely young women to send to El Fasher to enrich the sultan's harem. When Kelly marched into the town after breaking Ali

Dinar's army at Beringiah, a couple of hundred women were found within the palace. Young and old, discarded or newly appointed, they appeared to enjoy life. They kept the sultan's ageing activities going by massaging him from time to time with rancid butter.

There were, of course, no religious courts so matrimonial differences were determined by councils of village elders.

There was little crime. In my time there was only one murder, when one man killed another, journeying with him, to get possession of his camel. I had to arrange for trackers to follow the footprints of the men and camel, and they were so successful that weeks after the incident they found the murdered man's body right away in the scrub. Then the trial began. Assisted by a couple of Arab assessors, I had to be the judge, the council for the prosecution and the advocate for the prisoner's defence. The case having been proven and sentence pronounced, the papers and records were sent by camel to Khartoum and, many months afterwards, came back confirmed by the governor general and council. I then had the unpleasant job of hanging the murderer, who by that time had become a friend of mine. It was a distasteful task and I well remember the severity of my headache.

On tour I appointed or dismissed headmen, assessed crops, levied taxes, settled boundary disputes, had new tracks constructed, carried out animal censuses and listened to complaints.

I got to a remote village one evening after sunset and found tremendous excitement. Everyone appeared to be talking at once. So I sat down and listened to what it was all about.

Two men, Ahmed and Ali, each owned a bull. The animals had had a fight at the well and, in the scramble, Ahmed's beast had pushed Ali's down the well. Before the animal died Ali had been lowered down the well to cut his bull's throat so that the flesh could be drawn up and eaten. By the time I had got hold of all this and had ascertained that normally both were peaceful animals, it was long past my supper time, so I said that I would give judgment in the morning.

After supper of the usual groundnut soup, millet bread and a bit of gazelle, in the light of a candle burning dimly on the table, I was turning over the Bible somewhat idly and in Chapter XXI of Exodus, immediately after the chapter containing the Ten Commandments, I found the solution. Now the Muslims have accepted most of the Jewish prophets as their own and Moses is held in high regard. So next

47

morning, armed with my Bible I went 'into Court' and told them that a similar affair had happened some thousands of years before and had been determined by Musa. I then read: 'And if one man's ox hurt another's, that he die, then they shall sell the live ox and divide the money of it and the dead ox also shall they divide.' I added that I proposed to follow this procedure and I did so to the general satisfaction of the village.

A year later an almost unbelievable coincidence occurred. I got to the same village and again found a great tumult. There had been another bull fight near the well and Ahmed's bull had pushed another man's down the well and it had died. The people sat more eager than before. Again I told them that I would see whether the great Prophet had ever dealt with such a case. In the last verse of the chapter I found the solution: 'or if it be known that the ox hath used to push in time past and his owner hath not kept him in, he shall surely pay ox for ox and the dead shall be his own.' I gave judgment accordingly.

There was rich opportunity for people to enjoy shooting wild animals. On the whole the beasts were tame, for they had little to fear from man, apart from a few trappers who laid snares attached to great logs of wood. Rifles were practically unknown. The men were armed with short spears with wooden shafts and elaborately barbed iron heads. I made a collection of 24 different-headed ones. I was forced to kill a gazelle once every other day in order to live. Herds roamed everywhere. They would run forward, stop, turn round and stare. When one had been shot, others, full of curiosity, would come back, their short tails twitching, and offer themselves as the next victim.

Over the Christmas of 1918 I wanted to give my policemen a feast so an hour or so before sunset I rode out and returned later with seven gazelle. I spent the evening cutting up the joints.

For a change of diet I shot ring doves occasionally — 23 was my best bag, with one shot into a bush. On one occasion I ran into a small flock of crested guinea fowl and a couple found their way into the pot. I came across a herd of ostriches once only. They were black and looked enormous. I chased them for an hour at full gallop but they always had the legs of my horse and kept well ahead.

The prince of all beasts was the giant kudu with his huge curving horns and beautiful body. White oryx came down from the Sahara, but as soon as there was a suspicion of the rains breaking they returned to the north. They get their moisture from creepers and the tops of bushes.

Communications were maintained by camel. The sultan had kept close control and any man proved guilty of thieving a camel from another while on trek was punished by the loss of an arm or leg. There were a good many elderly men going about maimed, but this form of theft had practically died out.

The local camels are of poor quality, heavy and cumbersome. They are very different from the pure breed of the Bisharin Arabs further north. The Furowi are learned about camels and cure mange with juice distilled from watermelon seeds. Camels were watered every seventh day, goats every fourth day and horses were given drink only once a day, even in the hot weather. Grazing was scanty and all animals except camels looked underfed; strong nutritive thorn bushes appeal to camels. A few black and white camels came in from French Equatorial Africa, a unique breed.

In the hot weather the heat was so intense that the morning milk placed in the coolest part of my hut was curdled by sunset. When one put on one's shirt in the morning it felt as though it had come out of a hot oven.

After the armistice had been signed I began to get restless. I had not tasted a green vegetable for three years nor any fruit. I suffered intensely from loneliness. The burning heat made the blood rush through my veins at fever speed. Evening followed evening alone, reading such literature as I could acquire in the light of a couple of candles; I read the Bible right through twice. The miracles baffled me. Exchange of ideas had receded into the background. I was getting bad-tempered from the blazing sun overhead and the glare of the sands beating into my eyes. I yearned for my wife and children. Four years had gone by since I had seen them. General Wingate, the former governor general known as 'Master', had left Khartoum and was now high commissioner in Cairo. He wrote and thanked me for my services and asked if there was anything he could do for me. I felt sure that the British would stay in Palestine, so I asked for an introduction to the chief military administrator of OETA (Occupied Enemy Territory Administration). He replied and told me to get it in Cairo when I came on leave.

I left Umm Keddada ostensibly on leave, but I felt that I should not come back and disposed of my few possessions. Old wooden boxes were in great demand. To the minute granddaughter of the two old women who had, for two years, come daily to my verandah and cleaned the sand and stone from the camels' grain, I bequeathed my precious cow and her calf, which I had bred myself. The lusty youngster was already twice as big as her wilder companions. Feeding is more important than breeding.

My white oryx and kudu heads were wrapped up carefully and, having saluted my staff, I set off along the Mecca pilgrims' route on the three weeks' trek to the railhead. It was hard going. The track was of thick undulating sand. But I had done so much trekking that the journey, with England at the end of it, seemed no hardship.

There were many traces of the military campaign. Supercilious in life, a camel is even more so in death, for he throws his head back until, with lips drawn back, it touches the hump.

My camel, being of a better breed and more lightly laden than the rest of the party, stretched her head out and raced ahead. For mile after mile, the sound of her soft pads was hardly perceptible. The heavens looked like an azure bowl sprinkled with diamonds. Shooting stars streaked across the sky and the rising, deep-red moon turned to a luminous metallic disc. By the end of the journey the moon had become a pencilled silver hoop of light heralding dawn in the eastern sky.

Occasionally native caravans passed and greetings were exchanged: '*Keif halak?*' '*Tiiybin!*' '*El hamd al Allah.*' '*Maa-Salamah.*' 'How are you?' 'Well!' 'Praise be to God.' 'Go in safety.'

We travelled about eight to nine hours, mostly by night and I slept during the heat of the day in such shelter as I could find. All was silent except for the occasional barking of a dog, the sharp cry of a nightjar, or the loud hooting of an owl. Occasionally the camels plunged and strained when the going became uneven and their saddles creaked. As we traversed the undulating sands, I began to shed the feeble struggles of the past three years, which were mirrored against the mightiness of the heavens, so vast, so lovely, so embracing, so strong.

As we were nearing El Obeid railhead and the journey's end, I had a premonition that this would be my last trek. During three years I had spent 18 months on camel back. I was returning to my wife and children. Remoteness and isolation were finished. Readjustments would have to be made.

I called upon the provincial governor. He invited me to tea. As I sat with his wife I suddenly felt unable to converse, so I left her abruptly and sat alone. The next day I sold my camels in the market. They fetched more than I had given for them. I bought my head camel man a clock and gave him the difference plus his balance of pay and a bonus. He was worth it. We said goodbye. There were tears in our eyes.

I caught the train for Khartoum. The capital was looking lovely and restful. The rich green of the gardens facing the river seemed remarkable and the comfort of everyday life was astonishing. But after a few days I began to feel hemmed in and had a strange nostalgia for the harshness of the open desert. I picked up a medallion, a lion awakened by the rising sun, and took the train for the north. There was little to see. A few hours run brought us to Atbara, once famed for a battle fought there but now the main railway workshop. Afterwards for a dozen or so hours we crossed the desert — its midday hue a glistening copper of such intensity that it pained one's eyes.

At Wadi Halfa I boarded a stern-wheeled Nile steamer. Here was bliss indeed. I was grateful for the cool, the quiet and the absence of dust.

Feluccas with great bellying sails passed, gliding along the brown water. Ibis stalked the banks and patient asses and long-eared goats nibbled the naked earth. Camels chewing the cud leisurely gazed in disdain at their unchanging world.

At Shallal a little south of Aswan, the trip came to an end; the Egyptian boundary was reached and I took the narrow gauge train for Luxor, there to change for Cairo.

Cairo was a throbbing metropolis, teeming with officers awaiting transport and demobilization. The air was filled with the plaintive whistles of kites, those big brown birds with a wingspan of up to five feet, that swoop down at incredible speeds to scavenge in the streets. The Egyptians were enjoying unprecedented wealth from the high cotton prices and from exploiting British and Australian soldiers, who spent their money freely.

Having collected General Wingate's introduction, I was glad to get into the train for Palestine and cross the temporary bridge that spanned the Suez Canal. We traversed the desert of Sinai by night and in the early morning I feasted my eyes upon the deep-green leaves and the golden glory of orange groves at Gaza.

4

'Received, One Palestine'

Along-funnelled, shabby engine transplanted from the London and South Western Railway dragging a few dilapidated coaches, nicknamed by the soldiers 'the posh posh' because there were no cattle trucks attached, clanked and sneezed as it carried me across the Judaean hills and came to rest at Battir station a few miles south of Jerusalem. A pipe was lowered from a tank and gallons of water were poured into it. It was early December 1919 and the sun had turned the stark rocky hills to the colour of gold. I climbed down to the ground and, as the Arabs say, 'sniffed the air'. It was sparkling, clear and clean. This was enough. I made an instant resolve to stay in Palestine.

The train moaned its way up to the Holy City and, as we crawled into the station, the words of Blake should have come into my mind:

> I give you the end of a golden string,
> Only wind it into a ball,
> It will lead you in at Heaven's gate,
> Built in Jerusalem's Wall.

Actually nothing of the sort happened. I thought what a singularly unattractive, dirty station it was. I got into a dilapidated victoria drawn by a couple of decrepit-looking Arab ponies for the Mount of Olives. The ponies were so poor and tired that they could hardly break into a trot. The winter rains were late and had not yet started, so it was a lovely autumn day.

There was a brilliant light-blue sky overhead, and dust underfoot and

52

in my nostrils. Tall pagan cypresses rose darkly and phallicly out of bare soil and, at midday, a blue haze, like mist, rose from the gnarled olive trees, which were whitish-grey with dust. Against a crumbling wall, with a few long-eared lean goats nibbling at rubbish, a shepherd boy was lounging, playing his pipes. Dejected donkeys were moving about with their heads drooping close to the ground, constantly blowing up puffs of dust. Humans and beasts were powdered with grey dust and all seemed short of food. But the air was electric, invigorating, compelling.

By the Jaffa Gate we passed the mighty Citadel, the one outstanding monument apart from the Wailing Wall whose foundations were there at the time of Our Lord. A noble remembrance of the Roman domination.

Half an hour later we had traversed the potholes and dust our horses kicked up in clouds, but which the soft pads of the camels hardly stirred as they contemptuously passed us by. We had surmounted Scopus, had had a view of the Dead Sea to the east and were approaching Olivet when, westwards, the Noble Sanctuary, the ancient Temple area, came into sight. I stopped the carriage and looked down. There the Holy City lay, without compare, without parallel. I determined that I would serve her.

In the German Hospice, used as the headquarters of OETA, I had a long talk with Major-General Sir Louis Bols,[1] the chief administrator. He offered me the post then being created of public custodian of enemy property. My resolve was fortified. I accepted the offer.

Within a few days of my appointment, to make sure that I should be working on the right lines, I took a train to Egypt and picked the brains of the public custodian in Cairo. He was a generous-hearted man and gave me the run of his office for a couple of weeks. Bols was pleased with my report and, in military parlance, 'upgraded' me.

I called upon Ronald Storrs,[2] then basking in Pilate's seat. He was

1. Louis Bols entered the army in 1887 and served in the Boer War; as General Edmund Allenby's chief of staff during the First World War, he was involved in the capture of Jerusalem from the Ottoman Turks in 1917. He became chief administrator of the Occupied Territories Administration in 1919.
2. Sir Ronald Storrs (1881–1955) was the son of a clergyman, who took a first in classics at Pembroke College, Cambridge, and entered the Egyptian Civil Service in

sitting at his desk in St Paul's Convent overlooking the Damascus Gate, his massive and noble head outlined by the light of an oil lamp with a green shade. The huge desk had been presented to St Paul's by the Kaiser and was carved with imperial crowns. The building, though built as a convent, had already been redesigned as the future office of a German governor. Storrs was most refreshing and amusing. He gave me much useful advice and introduced me to his civic adviser, C. R. Ashbee,[3] who at once invited me to his house to dinner.

Ashbee and his wife were living in an old Arab house in a valley between the north wall of the city and Mount Scopus. He was a loosely grown, distinguished-looking, imaginative man in his middle fifties. She, a handsome, well-made woman of 40, was obviously at the height of her intellectual powers.

Their dining room with makeshift furniture had an air of distinction, from the tiles let into the sideboard to the old Armenian hammered-copper plates. Among the guests were Dr Eder,[4] he head of the Zionist Commission, and Ragheb Bey Nashashibi,[5] a leading Muslim notable, who later became the progressive mayor of Jerusalem. Conversation traversed a variety of subjects in two or three languages. The contrast between the grass hut in which I had been living and the graciousness of my surroundings here was singular. Ashbee, an old pupil of

1904. In 1909 he became oriental secretary at the British Agency in Cairo. He was posted to Jerusalem in 1917 as military governor and became civil governor of Jerusalem and Judaea at the beginning of the British Mandate over Palestine in 1920. He served as governor of Cyprus from 1926–1932 and then as governor of Northern Rhodesia until he retired due to ill health in 1934. He wrote in his memoirs, *Orientations* (1937), that there could be 'no promotion after Jerusalem'.

3. C. R. Ashbee trained as an architect, designer and town planner and served as civic adviser to the Palestine administration from 1918 to 1922.

4. Montague David Eder (1865–1936), was trained as a physician and psychoanalyst and was one of the first British proponents of the theories of Sigmund Freud. His interest in Jewish affairs was aroused by his cousin, Israel Zangwill, and he joined the Jewish Territorialist Organization. In 1918, at the invitation of Chaim Weizmann, he represented that organization on the Zionist Commission for Palestine, where he stayed for four years. He conducted negotiations with the military and then the civil administration and was a member of the Zionist Executive from 1921 to 1928, first in Jerusalem and later in London.

5. Ragheb Bey Nashashibi represented Jerusalem in the Ottoman Turkish parliament and served as mayor of the city for much of the 1920s.

Bodley's,[6] had created the Guild of Handicraft and the famous Essex House Press (the successor to William Morris's Kelmscott Press) in Whitechapel, and later transferred them to Chipping Campden. After the war had been raging for a couple of years, he came out to Egypt as a lecturer in English at the Khedivial University in Cairo. When Storrs had come to Jerusalem in 1918, on the strength of having heard Ashbee lecture at Charterhouse School 20 years before, he offered him the post of civic adviser.

For two years Storrs and he had revelled in their task. Storrs created the Pro-Jerusalem Society to provide him with funds for the preservation and restoration of the Old City. It needed it. Everywhere there was neglect, dirt and decay. There still remained great tradition in the arts, especially among the stoneworkers. As money began to roll in they cleared the fosse around the city, restored the great walls and gates, removed the clusters of hovels built alongside and cleared the debris of centuries. Splendid and lasting work was achieved. They were now considering a future town plan.

Ashbee had a fertile imagination and his plans for both Old and New Jerusalem were magnificent. Had they been carried out they would have made Britain as worthy of her charge as Italy had been of the Island of Rhodes. Alas, they would have cost more than a year's total revenue for the whole of Palestine.

As I made my way inside the walled city on my first pilgrimage to the Holy Sepulchre and walked down the congested, broad, cobbled steps of David Street, my main impression was one of too much paint crowded upon a small canvas. The steps were hemmed in on either side by vegetable shops aglow with colour. Purple aubergines and red radishes, huge cauliflowers, lemons and golden oranges. Butchers' shops alongside, selling goats' meat and mutton with very naked fat tails, were festooned with intestines and tripe. Flies were rampant.

Laden camels passing up and down caused as much disturbance as a motor lorry passing along an English lane. Stout, bow-legged Kurdish porters, with huge burdens carried on packs fastened across their

6. G. F. Bodley (1827–1907), English architect and friend of the Pre-Raphaelites.

shoulders, brushed past coffee-sellers clashing their brazen saucers. Muslim townswomen enveloped from head to ankles in coarse white winding sheets, with figured muslin or black veils hiding their faces, passed their unveiled Arab countrywomen with tattooed chins and lips wearing dresses of Damascus spun stuffs surmounted with short coloured velvet jackets embroidered with gold thread.

Most of Jerusalem — Arab, Jew and European — appeared to be in the overcrowded thoroughfare. Gesticulating, haranguing, expostulating and bargaining, they went from shop to shop, accompanied by little Arab boys with baskets strapped across their shoulders, turning over, choosing or rejecting the produce.

The city *effendi*, dressed in somewhat ragged European clothes, with a scarlet fez upon his head, stood beside a Russian nun draped in black, her face bound in a black veil and crowned with a high round headdress. An Orthodox Jew with twisted sidelocks under a broad-brimmed black felt hat and dressed in a long coat, trousers finishing between knee and ankle, white socks and black shoes, carried over his shoulder a cream-coloured, black-fringed *tallith*, or prayer shawl. A tall, rough-looking Arab countryman wearing a high cylindrical headdress of undyed camel hair passed me by; I was told that he was a dancing *dervish*, a holy man.

A gamut of smells came up from alleyways and steps, from wood smoke to excrement, from fowls to incense, from baking bread to donkeys, camels and unwashed humanity.

The smooth skin of youth shone in sharp contrast to the weather-beaten, grooved faces of age. Bare legs and feet as hard as leather protruded from tattered clothing.

Bedouin in flowing camel-hair robes and flying *keffiyeh*s bound by ropes of twisted goats' hair passed me by with long, flat-footed, loping strides, proud and scornful, regarding with disdain those who dwelt in cities or turned to the soil for a livelihood. Among them, who consider themselves the most virile of men, it is the women who wear the pants and the men who wear the robes. They were going about their business of finding another load to take back with them, down and up the hills to the deserts far away from the filth that surrounds the town dwellers. Was not their Prophet a herdsman, a dweller under the stars?

A French Sister of Charity with goose-like wings to her white cornet headdress dropped into her large basket vegetables that each shopkeeper gave her as she silently pleaded her convent's needs. A Greek priest wearing a black chimneypot hat, black of eye and of the spade beard curled like that of an Assyrian king, rubbed shoulders with a peasant clothed in baggy trousers and a sheepskin coat with the fleece turned inside. An Englishwoman bargained with an extensive use of sign language, but with an assured air that showed she cherished the opinion that she was already an accomplished Arabist.

A Bethlehem matron swept down the steps wearing a high backwards-sloping headdress covered by a pendant, with a white veil pinned under her chin and falling down her shoulders. Roman Catholic sisters in grey, brown, black or white robes and wearing a variety of headdresses walked beside tonsured and turbanned shoppers. All were equally jostled by the donkeys being pushed and prodded down the steps to the shrill shouts of odoriferous donkey boys — *'Ohya, riglak!* Look out for your feet!' — who, in their turn, were being chivvied by khaki-clothed policemen wearing Russian-looking black lambskin hats.

A bespectacled Jewish lad slunk by, looking furtively at the pot-bellied wineskin bound with a coloured duster around the stomach of a man dressed in *galabieh* and *kombaz.*

Competing with the shopkeepers were many village women squatting upon the steps, their produce, including bowls of sour milk, piled high in round baskets, and with a fowl or two tethered by the leg. They appeared to be having vehement and venomous quarrels with each other, but actually they were discussing amicably some question concerning current prices.

The spice merchants had rows of small brass bowls in which their stocks were piled in high cones. These mounds of dusty-brown, curry-colour and fiery-red sent up warm smells — pepper, cloves, myrrh, cinnamon, a puff of sandalwood and a whiff of jasmine oil.

At the end of the street some Arabs were sitting on stools sipping coffee from handleless cups, or playing *tric-trac* (backgammon) at lightning speed, slapping down their pieces like pistol shots. Others sat peacefully pulling deep at their gurgling, grunting hubble-bubbles, which in full blast sound like bull frogs.

I passed the time of day with a man fanning a charcoal fire surrounded by stones across which lay skewers of meat, *kebab.* He invited me into his shop. There he sprinkled specially prepared flour from a tin canister onto a heated circular iron slab and within seconds presented me with a huge wafer, light as a feather and thin as glass.

There were the harsh metallic clangs of church bells followed by the calls to prayer from Muslim minarets. 'God alone is great: I testify there are no gods but God: and Mohammed is his Prophet. Come to prayer: come to security. God alone is great: there is no god — but God.'

Turning down Christian Street I was assailed by shopkeepers to buy their wares — amber beads, olive-wood boxes, necklaces, cotton shrouds, rosaries, crowns of thorns and all the junk that clusters round shrines and oriental bazaars.

Down some steps I trod to the Holy Sepulchre. I crossed the parvis, stepped over the gravestone of Philip D'Aubigny,[7] the French crusading knight lying at the threshold, which was of special interest to me because my mother's family had intermarried with the Daubeney family, and I entered the half-opened doorway of the basilica. Into that dim complexity of faith and vision, of devotion and tradition, of Orthodoxy and Catholicism, the hallowed shrine of countless millions of pilgrims, I had come. The Stone of Unction lay before me. Calvary was up some steps to my right. A gleam of sunshine on my left led the way to the Rotunda and the Tomb itself. Priests and people in varied dress and of many nationalities encompassed me round about and guides pressed their services upon me. The soft chant of praying voices as well as demands for *backsheesh* were running round the walls and swinging censers added a golden rhythm. I entered the Edicule, the shrine containing the tomb of Christ. As I knelt before the tomb the words of Saint Matthew thundered in my ears: 'He is not here; He is risen.'

There were no carts within the city walls, nor were there streets wide enough to take them.

The duty of the public custodian was to maintain German assets, including cushions and sheets that British officers' wives had collected for their own use from German private houses and convents. I had to register particulars of the fixed properties, including lands at Sarona

7. Philip D'Aubigny went on the Sixth Crusade in 1236. His family came to live in England and the French name became anglicized to Daubeney.

and Wilhelmina near Jaffa, the village of Beit Laham near Haifa, and flourishing suburbs in the three principal towns. I had also to assume the trusteeship of various religious buildings and to arrange for the liquidation of two banks, one German and the other the Turkish Agricultural Bank. The total value of these assets was about £P 2 million.

It was natural that all the most suitable office accommodation had been taken before I arrived and so I had to put up with what I could get. The government advanced me £P 500 as capital and allowed me to take 10 per cent from the money I collected, and from this I financed my office and paid the staff. Many of the German houses were occupied by the military and numerous British married families were in possession of others. These officers, and particularly their wives, resented being called upon to make lists of the German property they were using and I had to put up with a great deal of abuse. But a trustee I had been appointed and a trustee I would be, and I was unsparing in my duties. Eventually, when everybody realized that I was only doing my job, antagonism gave way to a more pleasant way of life. The Swiss consul, a turncoat German Templar, had been in charge of German interests; he strongly objected to my appointment and his own loss of powers. He was very angry when I insisted on knowing where a herd of 30 cattle had disappeared to.

Collecting a staff was rather amusing. I got hold of an intelligent young Jewish woman whom I had met before at the Berlitz School of Languages in Alexandria, teaching French, and I put her in charge of the books that I opened. A somewhat flamboyant Jewish accountant was handed over to me by Major Alan Saunders and the rest were made up of young Arabs. I found a grand old Welshman, Robert Hughes, who had come out 30 years before as a manual worker for the London Mission to the Jews. He had remained in Jerusalem because he had found it the only place he could live without getting asthma. He spoke Welsh as fluently as English and his Arabic was impeccable. I made him a half-time assistant and he was worth his weight in gold. He was a mine of information and had known the old German Templar community intimately. He gave them good characters. Having been to Egypt and seen where they were interned, I too thought they were more sinned against than sinning. Eventually, with the exception of two families, we got them all back. We returned their properties to them intact, plus rentals for any buildings still occupied by the army. And very useful citizens they proved, until they were persuaded over to the doctrine of Hitler and all the young ones joined the Nazi party without much knowledge of what they were doing.

My Arabic was good enough for ordinary needs. Among Jews, German would have been useful but, alas, I knew none. At that time Hebrew was practically unknown except among the most Orthodox. My first task completed, my second was to visit the properties and see something of Palestine.

I set out northwards in an old Model T Ford car. We had no mechanical breakdowns but had to stop frequently on hills to allow the steaming engine to cool down. The journey to Haifa took 12 hours.

How shall I describe what I saw of this Promised land, this Holy Land, this land of the Blessing? It is about the size of Wales, practically treeless in Judaea, with rich olive groves in northern Galilee and with expanses of desert in the south. There the Bedu struggle for a precarious existence among sand dunes, stones and in sterile *wadi*s, dried-up watercourses. Thorn bushes of faint, grey-green foliage were approved of by goats and camels and provided fuel for the ovens.

The central spine of hills, crowned by Jerusalem and standing 2700 feet high, appeared harsh and barren. But the landscape was redeemed by the effect of passing clouds, by the rich colouring of rocks and scanty earth as purples, reds, browns and yellows constantly varied in shade and became splashes of amber or pale patches of amethyst. Deep valleys, bone dry in summer, slashed into the hills and became roaring torrents in the winter rains. Some were carpeted with tiny saffron plants that was so bright that, when viewed from an angle, they appeared to be covered with gold.

Along the seaboard lay the fertile plain of Sharon, of sand and loam soil, narrowing from a width of 20 miles to a few hundred yards in Haifa. Eastward ran the 15-mile-broad rift of the Jordan valley, which falls 1300 feet below sea level at the Dead Sea. The Sea is surrounded by yellow limestone, with salt crystals coating the ground like a brilliant crust of ice. Northwards the plain of Esdraelon cut across two ranges from Haifa to the Jordan valley separating Samaria from Galilee.

The country was a sad sight. An exceptionally backward land, on which the dead hand of the Ottoman Turks had been laid for generations, was now devastated by war. The Jerusalem streets were a series of deeply pitted ruts — in the winter an expanse of mud — which in dry weather produced a thick grey dust that permeated everything, covering clothes, trees and houses as it rose in the air and settled again after every passing cart. Tel Aviv was little more than a cluster of cottages on a sand hill; Jaffa was an entirely undrained town and Haifa a picturesque village.

Not a single town had a public water supply. Though some pumps (formerly used by the military to pump water from the Nile across the Sinai desert) had been installed in Solomon's pools near Bethlehem and were pumping water into Jerusalem, the supply was insufficient. It had to be supplemented by water brought up in tanks by rail from Lydda, which was distributed once in seven days. All householders relied on collecting the rainwater that fell on their roofs into cisterns built under their houses.

There were few animals and they were emaciated and unfit for ploughing. The few sheep did follow the shepherd according to tradition. The trick is done by the shepherd carrying with him a few grains of barley, which he gives exclusively to the biggest ram who, knowing what to expect, always comes to the master when he is called and the others follow. Dogs are used to protect the flock from wild animals and the flock is gathered together by expert stone throwing. I passed few carts for there were no horses to pull them.

Miles and miles of arable land were untilled. Terrace walls in the hills had broken down and were failing to retain the hard-won soil. In no village had there ever been a government school. Few Arabs could read or write. The best cultivated lands belonged to the Germans who had left Germany at the time of the Franco-Prussian war in 1870. Several Jewish colonies established by Baron de Rothschild[8] had flourishing orange groves and vineyards.

In many villages I saw children with enlarged spleens, the result of continued attacks of malarial fever. Malaria was as rampant in the

8. Baron Edmund James de Rothschild (1865–1936) was born in Paris into a banking family and became an art expert and patron of Jewish settlements in Palestine. His involvement began in 1883; as well as providing funds, he visited the settlements regularly and took a keen interest in practical matters of agriculture and industry.

towns as in the villages. The people looked forlorn and hungry. They were badly dressed in old Damascus-woven blue and white striped *galabieh*s. In the village streets, children played on dunghills which were badly needed on the fields, but which obviously had not been moved for years.

Despite this sombre picture, the countryside was a paradise of wild flowers — lilies of the field. Nature was finding her own way in the untilled fields and as the winter advanced into the spring there was a mass of bloom. Yellow, rich-smelling Narcissi, scarlet anemones, deep-blue lupins, red tulips and huge irises, one glorious riot of colour followed later by purple vetch and yellow daisies topped by hollyhocks. The hills had quantities of cyclamen blooming from pockets of sand hidden in the rocks.

There were long-legged partridges and other game birds for sports-men and a few isolated groups of gazelle. But I had killed enough animals in the Sudan, to supply the pot, and for the whole of my time in Palestine I never put a gun to my shoulder. It is the saddest thing to see a gazelle gaily bounding about and springing joyously in the air and then a few minutes later to see it dying on the ground, looking at one with its piteous eyes.

It was only too evident that there was a great deal to be done to get the people on their feet again. Orange groves and vineyards had remained unwatered for season after season. There was a lack of every-thing. Capital, foresight and energy were needed. There were such diverse religions, civilizations, climates and physical characteristics. The Bedu still coped with conditions that prevailed at the time of Abraham; the people in Bethlehem were living as they had during the period of the Crusades; the Arab villages were essentially medieval; and the problems presented in the towns were characteristic of the late eighteenth century.

It was not all flower-gazing. There was a strange feeling of uncer-tainty, unrest and disappointment. The Arabs believed that the promise made to the *sherif* of Mecca four years before for the independence of the Arabs included the Arabs of Palestine. The Jews knew that they had been offered a national home in Palestine. Qualifying clauses made no difference to either party.

Food shortages, fuel shortages, absence of fodder for the few beasts still living, insufficiency of material resources and, for the British temporary officers serving in the military administration, the fear that they might soon be losing their jobs, were serious enough problems, but they were minor compared with the ever-recurring questions of Arab hopes and Jewish aspirations, of Arab rights and Jewish claims. Down the centuries, pious Jews have prayed 'Next year in Jerusalem'. For many modern Jews this was more than a spiritual appeal. It had become a reality, a hope of escape from peril, actual or pending. The keynote to its achievement was Zionism, for Zionism was the Jewish antidote to anti-Semitism.

One can trace anti-Semitism back to the time when Pharaoh hardened his heart and Aaron performed miracles with his rod and the Jews, after eating their Passover supper, crossed the Red Sea into the wilderness and exulted in having 'spoiled' the Egyptians. There is evidence of it in Tangier, for Roman historians described a monument set up there upon which was inscribed, 'We are the Canaanites. We are they that have been driven out of the land of Canaan by the Jewish robber Joshua.' One may find provocation of it in the Bible narrative that tells how Joshua, when he invaded Palestine, 'smote all the land' and 'utterly destroyed all that breathed as the Lord, the God of Israel, commanded'.

It did not, however, become widespread until the Diaspora, when numbers of Jews infiltrated into other countries within easy reach. In Muslim countries they were accepted diffidently, provided there were not too many of them, as 'the people of the book'. In Christian countries they acquired unpopularity on the grounds of religious differences and dislike of their manners and customs. In so-called devout countries they were burnt at the stake; in more tolerant ones they were confined to ghettos and subjected to various vexations and indignities.

Things became a little more pleasant in 1790 when France admitted them to full rights of citizenship, but the improvement in their status was only temporary and partial. In Russia the 'pogrom' became a recognized feature of national life.

In 1882 Leon Pinsker,[9] a Jewish medical man practising in Odessa, wrote: 'The Jews are not a living nation. They are everywhere aliens; therefore they are despised. The only remedy would be the creation of a

9. Leon Pinsker (1821–1891) was born in Poland and studied medicine at the University of Moscow. He published an analysis of the psychological and social roots of anti-Semitism and called for the establishment of a Jewish homeland.

Jewish nationality, of a people living upon its own soil in a home of their own.'

That was the beginning of Zionism. A worldwide Zionist Organization had been set up with Theodor Hertzl, a Viennese journalist, at its head.[10] The idea of a settlement of Jews in Sinai and also in East Africa had been considered, but was quickly abandoned when Hertzl sensed the Russian opposition. There could be no substitute for Palestine. Hertzl died in 1904 and Zionism was carried forward by a committee in Berlin.

Lloyd George[11] claimed that a serious problem concerning armaments was solved in 1915 because of the help given by Dr Weizmann,[12] a Russian chemist and lecturer at Manchester University. Weizmann was introduced to him by C. P. Scott, editor of the *Manchester Guardian*, and, when called upon to find a substitute for wood alcohol used in the manufacture of acetone, an essential element in the manufacture of cordite, went at it full stretch and in a few weeks succeeded in isolating an organism capable of transforming the starch of

10. Theodor Hertzl (1860–1904), a writer who had trained as a lawyer, was the founder of political Zionism. His seminal pamphlet *The Jewish State* (1895) set out the case for Jewish nationhood.

11. David Lloyd George (1863–1945) had a career as a solicitor before entering parliament in 1890. He was appointed president of the Board of Trade in 1905 and Chancellor of the Exchequer in 1908. He was minister of munitions from 1915 to 1916, secretary of state for war in 1916 and prime minister from 1916 to 1922.

12. Chaim Weizmann (1874–1952) was born in Russia and studied at polytechnics in Darmstadt and Charlottenburg and then at the Swiss University of Freiburg. He lectured in chemistry, first at the University of Geneva and from 1904 at the University of Manchester. He developed a strong interest in the Zionist movement during his student years and when his chemical research brought him into government circles as an adviser to the Ministry of Munitions in 1915, he became an energetic and effective proponent of the case for a Jewish state. In 1918 Weizmann led the Zionist Commission, a group of Jews from Britain, France and Italy which went to Palestine after the Balfour Declaration was issued to serve as liaison between the Jewish community and the British military authorities. In 1920 he was elected president of the World Zionist Organization. He resigned from the presidency in 1931 after a period of turbulence in the Zionist movement, but was recalled to the post in 1935. He supported the partitioning of Palestine and in 1947 intervened on behalf of the Zionists to gain US support for partition proposals then being considered by the United Nations. When the State of Israel was proclaimed in 1948, Weizmann became its first president. During his last years he devoted himself not only to this position, but also to academic research and to the establishment of the Hebrew University of Jerusalem and the Weizmann Institute of Science at Rehovot.

cereals, particularly of maize, into a mixture of acetone butyl alcohol. By June 1916 a factory was making acetone from maize, and later, when the shipping shortage forced the restriction of imports, a national collection of horse chestnuts was launched. A number of schoolchildren were given a month's holiday to enable them to collect the nuts, from which acetone was produced in 1918.

The difficulties solved, Lloyd George said to the Doctor: 'You have rendered great service to the State; I should like to ask the Prime Minister, Mr Asquith, to recommend you to His Majesty for some honour.' Weizmann replied: 'There is nothing I want for myself. I would like you to do something for my people.' That, says Lloyd George, was the fount and origin of the Balfour Declaration.

But in saying this, Lloyd George had forgotten that Balfour,[13] when contesting Manchester during the general election of 1906, had had a meeting with Weizmann and had asked him why the Zionists had rejected Joseph Chamberlain's offer of land in East Africa. By way of a reply, Weizmann asked: 'Suppose I were to offer you Paris instead of London. Would you take it?' To Balfour's answer, 'But Dr Weizmann, we have London,' Weizmann said: 'That is true. But we had Jerusalem when London was a marsh.'

After war had broken out the chiefs of the Zionist Executive had moved from Berlin to Copenhagen and declared their neutrality. Weizmann had somewhat arbitrarily assumed the leadership of the organization and three months later Asquith had said in the House of Commons: 'The Ottoman government have rung the death knell of Ottoman dominion in Asia.' Immediately Sir Herbert Samuel,[14] president of the

13. Arthur Balfour was Conservative leader in the House of Commons in 1891–2 and 1895–1902 and prime minister from 1902 to 1905. The Balfour Declaration, favouring a Jewish national home in Palestine, was issued in 1917 when he was foreign secretary, a post he held from 1916 to 1919.

14. Sir Herbert Samuel (1870–1963) was born in Liverpool into a banking family and attended Balliol College, Oxford. He was active in Liberal Party politics at university and won election to parliament in a by-election in Cleveland in 1902. He became under-secretary of state at the Home Office in 1905 and entered the cabinet as chancellor of the Duchy of Lancaster in 1909. He served as postmaster general from 1910 to 1914 and then became home secretary in Asquith's coalition government. He refused to continue when Lloyd George replaced Asquith and in the general election of 1918 he was beaten by a Conservative. In 1920 Samuel went to Palestine as high commissioner. The possibility that the First World War might create a power vacuum in the Middle

Local Government Board, called upon Sir Edward Grey, foreign secretary, and asked him for the restoration of the Jews to Palestine following the collapse of Turkish imperial rule. He followed it up with a memorandum that Great Britain might annexe Palestine and throw in there three or four million Jews from Europe.

At this stage Sir Mark Sykes entered the arena. He and Leopold Amery were assistant secretaries to the War Cabinet. He was a somewhat unconventional Roman Catholic and had been introduced to Zionist principles by Moses Gaster, a Romanian, who was chief rabbi of the London Sephardi community. Gaster was a most learned Oriental scholar and had been principal challenger for the seat that Weizmann had acquired.

There had been prolonged negotiations with Jewish leaders, France and the USA, and a visit to the Pope. And Nahum Sokolow,[15] who was a member of the Zionist Executive and who had come to England, had asked for and obtained a promise that the Zionists should have facilities for communication abroad and not be subjected to censorship. This opened up great advantages and enabled the Zionists to plead all over the world that, in return for services, the British government would satisfy Jewish longings for Palestine. Thus the Diaspora had its eyes upon England.

In 1917 Dr Weizmann and Rothschild called upon Balfour and insisted that the time had come for a final decision. So Balfour asked them to draft a declaration for him to discuss with the Cabinet. Owing mainly to the strong opposition set up by Edwin Montagu,[16] a Jew, who used every opportunity to plead against the British government's

East had sparked his interest in the question of a Jewish state and, by 1915, he was formulating plans for a protectorate, which would give the Jews a national home while taking advantage of the great strategic importance of Palestine to Britain. From 1920 to 1925 he used his term as high commissioner to lay the foundations of a Jewish state. In 1925 Samuel returned to Britain to head a royal commission on the British coal industry and then became Liberal Party chairman. He was elected to parliament for Darwen in 1929 and became home secretary when the national government was formed in 1931. He resigned in 1932 in protest at the government's protectionist policies and remained leader of the opposition until he lost his seat in 1935.

15. Nahum Sokolow (1859–1936) was a pioneer of modern Hebrew journalism and president of the World Zionist Organization.

16. Edwin Montagu (1879–1924) was a British Liberal politician who rose to be secretary of state for India from 1917 to 1922.

Zionist policy, the Cabinet decided to obtain the opinions of eight representative Jews on the draft document and be guided by the results. Among the recipients was Dr Hertz, the chief rabbi. Hertz warmly welcomed the document, especially the reference to safeguarding the civil and religious rights of the existing non-Jewish communities and, on 2 November, the famous letter was despatched to Lord Rothschild. The policy was decided by the Cabinet under Lloyd George, now prime minister, on merit and expediency, but the actual time of the declaration was determined by consideration of war policy. Only Lord Curzon,[17] who was jealous of Balfour, but took longer views than Lloyd George, criticized it severely for the Cabinet (in his own neat deliberate handwriting) and anticipated nearly all the difficulties that would arise. However, he watered down its possibilities and said that 'if the Turks were defeated we must set up some form of European administration (it cannot be Jewish administration),' and added: 'If this is Zionism there is no reason why we should not all be Zionists.'

The text of the declaration, which was embodied in a letter written by Balfour to Lord Rothschild, was published a month before General Allenby[18] took Jerusalem.

His Majesty's Government view with favour the establishment in Palestine of a national home for the Jewish people, and will use their best endeavours to facilitate the achievement of this object, it being clearly understood that nothing shall be done which may prejudice the civil and religious rights of existing non-Jewish communities in Palestine, or the rights and political status enjoyed by Jews in any other country.

It was an adroitly drawn declaration. The question was whether it

17. Lord Curzon had a long political career, which included seven years as viceroy of India, and was especially interested in foreign and colonial policy. He objected to the Balfour Declaration when it was issued in 1917 and succeeded Balfour as foreign secretary in 1919.

18. Field Marshal Edmund Allenby, first Viscount Allenby of Megiddo (1861–1936), served with distinction in the Boer War and during the First World War commanded troops at Mons, Ypres and Arras before taking command of the Egyptian Expeditionary Force in 1917. He captured Jerusalem in December 1917. After the war, Allenby served as special high commissioner for Egypt from 1919 to 1925.

clashed with other declarations made to our Hijaz Arab allies a year before by Sir Henry McMahon, British high commissioner in Egypt, which had not been so carefully drafted and were in much looser form.

There were of course considerable difficulties getting in touch with Arabs from Palestine, but Sykes did not think it necessary or even desirable to discuss with our Arab allies the terms of this letter before it was despatched to the Jews. Nor did anyone except Curzon give a moment's consideration to the inevitable love of the Palestine Arab, Muslim or Christian for his own homeland or appreciate how this form of nationalism would grow. Not one person asked the question: 'How will the present inhabitants tolerate this intrusion?' The term 'national home' was an invention of Max Nordau[19] — 'heimstätte' — as a synonym for 'state'. It was an equivalent all Jews understood. Not for 20 years (until 1920), did he see any reason to disguise the real aim.

For some years an Arab freedom movement had been spreading throughout Syria, and Great Britain had profited by these aims and had opened negotiations with the *sherif* of Mecca, Emir Hussein. Independence was promised to the Arabs subject to certain vaguely expressed reservations: 'Portions of Syria lying to the west of the districts of Damascus, Homs, Hama and Aleppo cannot be said to be purely Arab, and should be excluded from the limits demanded.' No specific mention of Palestine was made. The *sherif*, with considerable personal courage, had declared the Turkish government to be an enemy of Islam and had come in on the side of the Allies. The Bedu Arabs, stimulated and largely directed by T. E. Lawrence,[20] had tied up successfully a couple of Turkish divisions. The promise had also had an effect on the wavering sympathies of other Arab tribes outside the Hejaz.

Although the only Palestine Arabs fighting were the conscripts in the grip of Turkish military service, the local Arabs always considered that

19. Max Nordau (1849–1923) was a doctor and journalist who became one of the founders of Zionism. His books, including *Paradoxes* and *Degeneration*, won him a world reputation.

20. Thomas Edward Lawrence (1888–1935), known as 'Lawrence of Arabia', was a historian and archaeologist who won fame as the organizer of the Arab revolt against the Ottoman Turks in the Hejaz during the First World War. The tribal army he organized captured Damascus from the Turks in 1918. Lawrence both loved and hated his fame and tried to escape it after the war by enrolling under different names in the Royal Air Force and Army Tank Corps. He was killed in a motorcycle crash in 1935.

they were included among those promised freedom. So when, in December 1917, General Allenby's forces were battling before the Holy City, two divergent promises had already been made to two different peoples. In the words of a cynical American, 'Great Britain had sold the same pup twice.'

As a result of brilliant engagements, Allenby forced the Turks to retreat northwards and Jerusalem was surrendered without a shot being fired over or into the city. Some 20 years before, the German Kaiser Wilhelm had come dressed in a flowing white cloak emblazoned with a cross, a gleaming silver helmet on his head. Seated on an Arab horse he had entered the Old City through a breach specially made for him in the walls. But General Allenby came in a more humble spirit. Dismounting from his horse without the walls, he entered through the Jaffa Gate on foot, followed by his staff. His name had mystic meaning for the Arabs — *Al Neby*, the Prophet.

Standing upon the steps of the Citadel he gave the following pledge, which was proclaimed in English, French, Italian, Arabic and Hebrew:

> Furthermore since your city is regarded with affection by the adherents of three of the great religions of mankind and its soil has been consecrated by the prayers and pilgrimages of multitudes of devout people of these three religions for many centuries, therefore do I make known to you that every sacred building, monument, holy spot, shrine, traditional site, endowment, pious bequest or customary place of prayer, of whatsoever form of the three religions, will be maintained and protected according to the existing customs and beliefs of those to whose faiths they are sacred.

Thus General Allenby established maintenance of the status quo in the Holy Places. The occupying power had to administer in accordance with existing laws. Under international military law immovable property could not be disposed of nor could any form of fresh taxation be introduced. Land transactions were therefore prohibited by military order.

But for two years the Arabs had been rather bewildered by the presence of a body of civilian Jews from overseas who had been allowed to enter for the ostensible purpose of assisting the military administration in helping Jews, the representatives of the Zionist Organization. They went about dressed in khaki and wearing Sam Browne belts and called themselves the Zionist Commission. These men, pioneers of the national home, were often more enthusiastic than tactful or prudent. They had raised many questions, they had subsidized Jewish officials and had paid additional salaries to Jews in the civil police force.

Dr Weizmann had declared in a public address in England: 'The Arabs need us with our knowledge and our experience and our money. If they do not have us they will fall into the hands of others; they will fall among sharks.' He had then come out and visited the Emir Faisal,[21] son of the *sherif*, in the Jordan valley and they signed an agreement. This pledged the parties to cordial co-operation between the Arab states and Palestine in acceptance of the Balfour Declaration and the encouragement of the immigration of Jews. The emir added a note of reservation that its execution was dependent on the fulfilment of the claims for Arab independence, which he had submitted to the peace conference, adding: 'If changes are made I cannot be answerable for failing to carry out this agreement.'

Dr Weizmann later raised a delicate question with Ronald Storrs concerning the Wailing Wall, the last remnant of the Jewish Temple area and their most sacred site. He proposed that certain Muslim property in the vicinity, which formed part of a Moroccan pious foundation, should be acquired by the Jews and the owners be given a transfer to other property of equal value. The offer was not pursued further by the administration, but news of its having been made got out and it was bitterly resented by the Arabs.

Despite these dissensions the most sought-after man was an Orthodox Jew named Yehoshua Hankin[22] who was land agent for the Zionist Commission. He wore his hair to the waist and dressed in an old kaftan. He was kept busy receiving options from Arabs for the purchase of their lands once the land registries were opened. Many of those Arabs

21. Emir Faisal became king of Iraq in 1921. His brother Abdullah became king of Transjordan .

22. Yehoshua Hankin (1864–1945) was born in Ukraine and went to Palestine with his father in 1882. He was instrumental in acquiring large tracts of land for Jewish settlement.

most eager to sell were the loudest in their condemnation of the Zionist policy. Tension tightened.

Bols, the chief administrator, was a simple man in whom there was no guile. He was perplexed by the conflicting promises and claims. He informed the British government that the status quo was not being maintained and that the privileges granted to the Zionists had firmly convinced the non-Jewish elements of our partiality. He recommended that the Zionist Commission in Palestine be withdrawn.

Emir Faisal's warning note became menacing when he, whom a congress of Syrian notables had proclaimed King of Syria, was turned out of that country by the French just before Easter. By pure chance I happened to be inside the city walls that Easter Sunday morning. After attending a service at the Church of the Holy Sepulchre, I emerged into dazzling sunshine. Making my way through a crowd of people carrying prayer books and candles I went into a cobbled street.

There was a lot of shouting. Sticks were being brandished. A stone was thrown and hit a Jew. In the twinkling of an eye the street was in a turmoil. Seeing an Arab about to attack another old Jew, I called upon an Arab policeman to help him, but the policeman just faded away and so did the Arab. I tried to stop another Arab who was molesting a Jew, but my reward was to be severely bitten on both hands by the Arab's lady friends. Then I saw a bulky Muslim hurling a piece of rock, so I collared him and took him along the domed lane leading to the Damascus Gate. Next came the ping of a rifle bullet ricocheting off a stone wall and an Arab girl, who had been leaning out of a lattice, slumped down, shot through the temple. As we were nearing the gate, my captive called upon Allah and the Prophet to defend him. Luckily Captain Archie Cresswell came to my assistance and some soldiers of the Duke of Wellington's Regiment ran down through the gate, rattling the bolts of their rifles. They surrounded our man and took him into custody, while I went off to get my hands dressed.

The disturbance spread quickly and continued for some days and resulted in a casualty list of nine killed and over 200 seriously wounded. A committee of enquiry was set up and blame apportioned. A certain Haj Amin el Husseini[23] was sentenced to a long term of imprisonment,

23. Haj Amin el Husseini was leader of the Palestinian Arab nationalist movement . He was *mufti* of Jerusalem and president of the Supreme Muslim Council set up by the

but fled to Transjordan. A Jew named Vladimir Jabotinsky[24] was also awarded a long term by a military court. A few weeks later the Supreme Council at San Remo allotted the Mandate for Syria to France, and the Mandates for Mesopotamia (Iraq) and Palestine to Great Britain.

In July Sir Herbert Samuel assumed office as high commissioner. The first intimation that General Bols received that he was being superseded was a telegram from Sir Herbert saying that he was prepared to take over the general's cook. When the general received the new high commissioner he handed him a sheet of paper to sign. On it was written: 'Received, One Palestine.' With a pretty wit Sir Herbert added: 'E and OE' — Errors and Omissions Excepted — and signed it.

British in 1922. He was an enemy of King Abdullah of Transjordan and thought by many to be behind his assassination in 1951.

24. Vladimir Jabotinsky (1880–1940) was the founder and leader of the Revisionist Party within the Zionist movement.

5

Is Great Britain Honest?

Palestine was on the eve of awakening to a life that had hitherto been denied it. The Ottoman Turks had invariably taken everything and had given the people little chance to use or to develop their natural abilities. Muslim townswomen would benefit much from the change, for they went about so heavily veiled and shrouded that they looked like the dead. When I visited a school for Muslim girls, a bell was rung before I was admitted into a classroom, so that veils might be drawn down over the pupils' faces.

The barley crops were harvested with a sickle and cattle and donkeys trod out the grain from the ear in the fashion prevalent in Abraham's time. The grain was winnowed by being cast up into the air by wooden shovels on a windy day.

It was obvious that if the Jews were to return they must work on the land and be of the land and not drift to the towns. Not only would they assist material production but they would realize that the land is less corrupting than the alleyways and the streets that they had left behind.

The appointment of Sir Herbert Samuel as high commissioner was harshly criticized, but he soon gave proof that he was as determined to carry out the policy laid down by the British government as he was determined that both Arabs and Jews should prosper.

Samuel was a dark-haired, fresh-complexioned, military-looking man with a well-trimmed moustache. He had rather a wooden face with a searching, almost furtive expression. But one never went to him without coming back the gainer. He arrived dressed in the tropical uniform of a civil governor and a white, steel-spiked helmet. His photograph was widely displayed. A small carpet factory had been set up by some

Oriental Jews. What better subject could be portrayed in wool? The high commissioner had to suffer for months knowing that small mats were being turned out with his helmeted head as the centrepiece against a yellow background. Some years later I saw one of these mats in a Muslim hairdresser's window in Damascus. I walked in and asked the owner whose head was portrayed. He looked at me witheringly before replying: 'You don't know? By Allah, that is Mustafa Kemal, the Ataturk.'

Samuel started to form a civilian staff. The majority he chose from the officers who were already engaged in the Occupied Enemy Territory Administration.

He had already invited Brigadier Wyndham Deedes[1] to be chief secretary to the government. Deedes was a remarkable man and the son of a no less remarkable woman who kept house for him. Rosie Deedes was the daughter of a Jewish doctor whose wife had been converted to Christianity, and she was a devoted member of the Church of England. His father had been a soldier and Deedes himself had been an officer in the Rifle Brigade and had long service in the Turkish army. He wrote and spoke Turkish with unusual fluency and served as intelligence officer throughout the war in Gallipoli and the Middle East.

Norman Bentwich[2] was appointed legal secretary or attorney-general. He was a barrister who had come to Egypt some years before as a lecturer in international law at Cairo University. His qualifications for the post were somewhat shaky because some years before he had written a book in favour of Zionism. Though a pleasant, warm-hearted, musical and very intelligent man, he was nevertheless suspected by the

1. Brigadier Wyndham Deedes was educated at Eton and commissioned in the King's Rifle Corps in 1901. After service in the Boer War and in Malta, he spent four years (1910–14) seconded to the Turkish gendarmerie. He worked in intelligence during the First World War and became a brigadier-general in 1918.

2. Norman Bentwich (1883–1971) trained as a lawyer and entered the Egyptian Ministry of Justice in 1912. During the First World War he served with the British Army in Egypt and took part in the conquest of Jerusalem. In 1918 he became legal secretary to the British military administration in Palestine and after the establishment of the Mandate in 1920 he became attorney-general. The fact that he was Jewish made his position increasingly awkward and in 1929 he was recalled to work in the Colonial Office. He retired in 1931 and devoted his life to many different causes, including the Hebrew University of Jerusalem and work before and after the Second World War on behalf of victims of Nazi persecution.

Arabs from the start because he was a Jew. He therefore had a stormy career until he was retired some years later.

A Treasurer was appointed from Malaya.

The man who obviously dominated his colleagues in OETA was Ronald Storrs, who was reappointed governor or district commissioner of Jerusalem. He had great imagination and a flair for the East. He was mentally far ahead of anyone in the administration, although its bare bones bored him. He spoke French, Arabic and Italian well. He had also the gift of picking up a phrase or two of Armenian or Hebrew and producing it at the right moment, with just that effect that gave happiness to those addressed and considerable satisfaction to himself. He was a born showman and had quickly grasped the advertising value of the Holy City to the mutual advantage of city and self. He was a master of the English language.

Colonel George Heron became director of the Department of Health and proved to be a most efficient head of the medical services. William Hudson, the postmaster-general, was a very able man and built up a service which became a model for the Middle East. Major Ley, the director of surveys, carried out a first-rate and lasting job. Humphrey Bowman and Jerome Farrell, an excellent pair, ran the Education Department.

The head of the police service was an astute person. He had been dismissed by the governor general in council from the Indian police for various malpractices, but after his dismissal had managed 'in wartime' to get a job in Iraq and had come to Palestine from there. He proved to be as able and as unscrupulous in Palestine as he had been in India and, after a few years, was found out and allowed to retire.

The rest were fairly mediocre, mostly discards from the fighting services. The bench was supplied mainly from solicitors who happened to be serving in the Middle East. Absence of any knowledge of the local language was apparent. The officers were in the hands of translators, mostly Arab Christians from Jerusalem and the neighbouring villages who had escaped to Egypt and had profited greatly from the war.

When practically every appointment was filled Sir Herbert appointed me to the post of senior assistant chief secretary in charge of administration. Both Deedes, who was 37, and myself, two years younger, had much to learn, but we had faith in one another and the machine that we set up lasted out the Mandate. Our working hours were long. We frequently started before breakfast and did not finish until after dinner at night.

Deedes's and my work was, however, complicated because the political secretary, Ernest Richmond, was an out-and-out champion of the Arab cause and the legal secretary mixed himself up in political matters by ardently espousing the Jewish cause. As, unknown to me, both these officials frequently wrote official letters to the public on the same subject, expressing widely divergent views, my job became at times most exasperating. Both men honestly believed they were of the greatest assistance in the cause of righteousness in Palestine.

Administrative districts had been formed already. Civil law courts were established. From the Turks we had inherited not a single government building. The Turkish pashas of Jerusalem had lived and worked in an old building within the walls, which belonged to a Muslim pious foundation.

The chief secretary's offices were now housed in the German Hospice on the Mount of Olives, which was also used as the high commissioner's residence. The law courts were accommodated in a Russian pilgrim hostel; the Agricultural Department encouraged the growth of corn from a Greek hotel within the city walls; the Customs occupied rooms in a Latin nunnery; the Education Department took over an Orthodox convent on Mount Zion and the Health Department established itself in the old municipal hospital; other departments secured less enviable premises.

It was just as well that as public custodian I had travelled about the country and got to know its geography and something of its possibilities because, during the next four years, I was almost exclusively tied to my office. There was a constant succession of files, telegrams and papers upon my table, a couple of telephones ringing, and an orderly waiting impatiently to announce the head of a department or other visitor. In the evenings I wrote the first edition of the administrative regulations.

Innumerable committees were set up. I had to attend many of their meetings and, once decisions were taken, organize the machinery to implement the findings and then watch over the machine, oil the creaks and keep it running smoothly. Almost every subject raised some question of principle and some seemingly quite innocent hares turned out to be scorpions. Every director wanted to enlarge his department and, incidentally, increase his powers, but expenditure had to be kept within the budget and estimating possible revenue and probable expenditure was no easy task. Papers became for the time being of more importance than people.

English, Arabic and Hebrew were declared to be the three official languages. A general amnesty was given to all political prisoners. Then Sir Herbert published an ordinance prohibiting the display of advertisements outside municipal areas, and thus preserved the countryside and beauty spots from vandalism. Sir Herbert promulgated an immigration ordinance. He limited admissions in the first year to 10,000 Jews and the pioneers began to disembark at Jaffa.

Jaffa was an open roadstead, and ships lying outside were serviced by lighters rowed by Arab boatmen. The emotions of landed immigrants ran riot — the Promised Land was reached at last! The Orthodox dropped upon their knees and kissed the sacred soil, others burst into tears of joy. Long-separated families were restored to each other. Youths broke into song and sang the Jewish national anthem, *Ha-Tikvah* ('The Hope'). Boys and girls shouted and danced. Fanaticism, ecstasy and sorrow charged the atmosphere.

Samuel was a first-rate administrator and set about his work with such diligence that nearly everybody followed suit, and even the mediocre became almost gifted men. Indeed, nearly everyone became somewhat inspired by the thought of working in and for Palestine. An ex-minister and steeped in liberalism, he not only welcomed but sought frank criticism and free expression of opinion from his staff, and never criticized harshly if he thought they were given in good faith. A great many people, therefore, whose opinions were not vital, wrote reams on every possible subject from the interpretation of the Mandate to a fishing monopoly on the Sea of Galilee, from railway rates for oranges to abortion in cows. One of my tasks was to read these effusions.

Samuel could be human as well as frigid. At his office table and in discussion he often repelled those in front of him, but at other times, when it was thought little dignity was wanted, he would assume an almost unnatural attitude of 'hail fellow, well met'. Playing with children he would reveal the real man. My wife and children and I spent many happy hours with him, his wife and family. Official dinner parties were meticulously formal as His Excellency gave five minutes to each guest after the meal. He allowed Ashbee to design and furnish four of the rooms in the German Hospice used as Government House.

Ashbee employed Muslims, Christians, Jews, Englishmen, Germans, Greeks, Armenians, Poles and Russians with no common language. They produced what they could out of local clay and stone, cotton and wool, glass from Hebron and Indian woods left over from the wastage of war. Ashbee described their work as 'an object lesson in the futility of political methods as set beside the cohesive power of the arts and crafts'. Excellent philosophy, but terribly trying to live with, especially in the dining room, where the six-foot-high back to the sideboard was carved by a craftsman whose last job had been to design and build an immense hearse.

A significant measure of control was known as the 'little black book' kept in Sir Herbert's waistcoat. An entry was made for every important subject ranging from a telephone system to an outbreak of measles, but the entry was not erased until he had got what he wanted done.

The country was beset by a strange form of nationalism based not so much on race as on religion, for the criterion of nationality was normally creed. I was to learn later that, throughout the Ottoman Empire, the classification of men had been governed by confessional considerations and that ecclesiastical allegiance and a high appointment in religious office gave a man an impregnable position of power in the world of politics and national affairs. The Muslims accepted with complacency any fellow religionist who belonged to their own sect of Islam, Sunni. The Jews were divided into three groups, the Sephardi, the Ashkenazi and the various strains of extreme Orthodoxy who looked upon the others as purely heretical. The Christians were particularly venomous in their hatred of members of other Christian churches. Even among the Latins or Roman Catholics there were many internal disputes, especially between the patriarch and the *custos*, the head of the Franciscans, who was in charge of Latin interests in the Holy Places. There were several Latin convents whose members would not enter other Catholic convents, even to pay a short visit of courtesy.

The Anglican bishop was not separated from the general feeling. A low-church evangelical missionary from Cairo, he was a wartime appointment and was clearly out of his depth. Ignored by the Latins, he played up to the Eastern Churches and did his best to ingratiate himself with them. This little man appeared in the hot weather dressed in a white, tussore-silk frock coat. His ecclesiastical breeches and gaiters were set off with a purple apron and even the stitching of the button-holes, as well as the buttons on the gaiters, was purple. He had one particular grievance. When the bishopric was founded half a century before by agreement between the King of Prussia and the Archbishop of Canterbury, it was decided that the Church of the Holy Sepulchre and the Orthodox patriarch, a Greek, were respectively Cathedral and Bishop of Jerusalem; so the Anglican representative was styled 'Bishop in Jerusalem'. The absence of the 'of' rankled deeply and, whenever possible, he dropped the 'in' and substituted the greater title. Looking back after 30 years, it sounds almost *opera bouffe*, but of such was the Kingdom of God in the Holy City in the year of grace 1920.

Muza Kazim Pasha,[3] an old deputy to the Turkish parliament, was the leading Muslim, and Ragheb Bey Nashashibi his political rival. Few Muslims could read and write English and, to help him in his political activities, Muza Pasha had persuaded a young Christian Arab woman to act as his secretary. Miss Lulu Jamal was efficient and carried out her task well. The old pasha used to talk to himself in the carriage and was always cursing the Christians under his breath; and so this female member of the 'Brotestant' community used to listen with considerable humour to the fearful oaths against her fellow religionists.

The best-educated Arabs were those who had been educated at the two Anglican schools in Jerusalem, St George's and the Bishop Gobat. They were mostly Orthodox, or else members of the rather despised 'Brotestants', whose clergy went about in the ordinary curate's dress and dog collar with a red *tarboosh* on their heads. They were the most vociferous opponents of the Muslims and were loud in their denuncia-tions of Islamic aggression. Lacking the support of the Vatican, they anticipated the tightening of the screws.

The two chief rabbis, Kuk[4] and Meir, were supposedly co-equals in Jewish religious affairs, but in practice never met in council. For generations the Ashkenazi had been dominated by the Sephardi and

3. Muza Kazim Pasha was Mayor of Jerusalem until he lost the post to Ragheb Bey Nashashibi in 1920 and then became president of the Palestine Arab Executive. He was one of the leading Muslim opponents of British rule.

4. Abraham Isaac Kuk (1865–1935) was born in Latvia, came to Palestine in 1904 and served as rabbi of Jaffa. During the First World War he was rabbi of a London congregation. He was elected Ashkenazi chief rabbi of Palestine in 1921.

now that there were prospects of a rush of Eastern European immigrants, Meir did not like it and feared for his position.

Meir[5] was formerly chief rabbi of the Jews in Salonica, a city of Sephardi Jews speaking Ladino,[6] who had settled there after their expulsion from Spain under Ferdinand and Isabella. He was a picturesque old man who went about clothed in heavy *kombaz*, or Turkish trousers, a long black coat and a black mantle crowned with a black turban. He had made a hobby of collecting minor decorations and on holidays used to turn out with his chest ablaze. He invariably carried an ebony staff to add to his dignity. He always spoke and wrote in French and confined his knowledge of the sacred tongue to the synagogue.

Kuk, the Ashkenazi rabbi, was built of sterner stuff. He looked upon his Sephardi colleague with scant respect. He wore a tall, black silk top hat, always used Hebrew in normal correspondence and was notorious for making the longest and the dullest speeches in a city noted for both.

There were a number of Jewish colonies that had been founded by Baron de Rothschild, which were directed by the Jewish Colonial Association. The JCA had planted orange groves and vineyards at Rishon. Rishon too had excellent wine cellars and the wine, although hardly up to the standard of ordinary French wines, had a wide sale in the Middle East. There were some more Jewish colonies south of the sweet waters of Meirum, Lake Huleh, but these villagers were washed-out and malaria-infested. They spoke Arabic among themselves and were hardly distinguishable from the Arabs who surrounded them, with whom they lived in friendship and many of whom they employed. JCA policy had always been 'live and let live; there is a place for both'.

Van Vriesland,[7] the Dutch treasurer of the Zionists, and Harry Sacher,[8] a former leader writer on the *Manchester Guardian*, were two of the leading social lights until Sacher was lured away from Palestine

---

5. Jacob Meir (1865–1939) was born in Jerusalem, the son of a well-to-do merchant. He was chief rabbi of Salonica from 1908 to 1909 and was elected Sephardi chief rabbi of Palestine in 1921.

6. The language of Jews of Spanish origin.

7. Siegfried Adolf van Vriesland (1886–1939) practised law in Rotterdam and settled in Palestine after the First World War.

8. Harry Sacher (1881–1971) was a British lawyer who settled in Palestine in 1919 and served on the Zionist Executive from 1927 to 1931.

by the Marks & Spencer group to help found a chain of stores and a great fortune.

Miss Annie Landau, the headmistress of the Eveline Rothschild girls' school and a unique hostess in her own right, gave the most wonderful parties. We used to meet in each other's houses to play, sing and recite. There was no other form of amusement — the military cinema had been blown down in the piercing winter winds.

There were other men moving about poking their noses into everything that interested them. And what did not? They belonged to the Zionist Commission. Most of the British officers with whom they had come into contact were fed up with their political views and also their constant demands. Their policy had been aggressive from the start and by the time I arrived I found that there was a general feeling among the soldiers of: 'Better the Arabs we know than hordes of Jews from Eastern Europe.'

Following the promises he made at his inaugural levee, Sir Herbert set up an advisory council composed of ten British officials and ten nominated non-official Palestinian members — four Muslims, three Christians and three Jews. He presided over the council's meetings. Business was slow because of the difficulties involved, not only in translating everything twice, but also because many English legal terms were unknown in Arabic or Hebrew. This body met at monthly intervals for two years in the great hall of the convent, and a good luncheon from Lady Samuel's kitchen added in no small way to the success of the debating chamber.

With infinite patience and wisdom he helped the Zionist Commission along the hard road towards statesmanship and prevented its members from committing excesses, guiding them past pitfalls that have frequently since those days been their undoing.

When the Court of Appeal was established Samuel decided that the wearing of eighteenth-century horsehair wigs would be an anachronism and gave instructions that they were not to be worn by either bench or bar. As most of the members of the bench were demobilized solicitors they were not loth to comply, but five years later, when Sir Herbert had left, three of them resigned from the Law Society and were called to the

Bar. Led by the chief justice, they adopted the trade's legal dress and had the moral advantage of sharing their distinction with ultra-Orthodox Jewish women who, upon marriage, have their tresses cut away and wigs substituted.

Within a few months of my appointment I was made a member of a commission to examine existing sources of municipal revenue. The 22 corporations were a mixed bag, ranging from Jerusalem with an annual expenditure of £P 40,000 to Shefa Amr with £P 600.

My wife and boys came out before the year closed. As our train was nearing Jerusalem there was a huge bump and we were all thrown about the carriage. Martin picked himself up off the floor and said with great pleasure to his brother: 'Tony, this is a real accident.' We went to live in a little chalet with a red roof in the grounds of Government House and had our breakfasts in the garden overlooking the hills of Moab, a daily inspiration. Somewhere near the entrance steps still lies, turning into dust, a favourite dolly that survived the railway accident, but eventually shed so much sawdust that she was given an honourable burial. Some 20 years later our old bedrooms were filled with bottles containing sugar nutrients on which drops of penicillin were growing for use by the army.

In the first year 75 schools were opened in Arab villages and simple elementary education was introduced. Training colleges for teachers were established. A small grant-in-aid was given to 100 Jewish schools set up by the Zionist Organization, which was insistent upon administering its own schools.

The railway system was taken over and the narrow gauge from Lydda to Jaffa was widened. The Post Office was expanded and a public telephone service inaugurated. By the end of 1921 over 1000 telephones had been installed and over half a million telegrams dealt with.

Three organized bands of brigands had been operating under the leaderships of Abu Mudeiris, Abu Sirhad and Nimr. Abu Mudeiris was captured with 20 of his gang. Nimr was shot, and eventually Abu Sirhad was captured. He served a long term, became a reformed character and was employed as a road foreman in the Ramallah area. He became a happily married man with two children and if I were passing in the spring he would bring me wild flowers.

Land came onto the market and the land registries were opened. The district administration was held responsible for ensuring that there was no hardship to cultivators, but otherwise sales and purchases were free.

Menahem Ussishkin,[9] a sturdy Russian Jew who knew Hebrew fluently yet always spoke Russian in his own house, began to acquire land for the Jewish National Fund and bought the rocky hillside near Jerusalem now known as Qiryat Anavim. There he established the first collective village. The settlers spent years clearing away the boulders and building terraces.

Then, despite considerable Jewish criticism, but backed by his colleague Dr Ruppin,[10] Ussishkin purchased from Syrian Christian absentee landlords a large tract of land in the plain of Esdraelon. It was then divided into three areas — the Nahalal, the Affuleh and the Ain Herod. There was some talk of bringing him before a court at the next Zionist Congress for paying so high a price for such a malaria-infested area, but Ussishkin was not only determined but shrewd. He had bought 40 square kilometres of land which, when drained, proved to be the richest in Palestine. He was not impeached but re-elected chairman of the Palestine Zionist Executive.

Ben-Zvi,[11] who had served in the Jewish Battalion, organized the Jewish Labour Federation in which he held the chief office, but subsequently he vacated it for the presidency of the Va'ad Le'ummi, the Jewish National Council. His wife started a farm school for girls in his back garden which developed into a valuable institution.

There were many signs of private enterprise. A silicate brick factory was started in Tel Aviv. In Haifa, the Shemen Soap & Oil Factory was established, a large mill was installed, and plans for a cement factory

9. Abraham Menahem Mendel Ussishkin (1863–1941) was leader of the Russian Zionists in the early years of this century. He became land agent for the Jewish National Fund and chairman of its board of directors. In 1919 he became chairman of the Zionist Commission. Ussishkin opposed the partition of Palestine.

10. Arthur Ruppin (1876–1943) studied law and economics in Berlin and Halle. His *Die Juden der Gegenwart*, published in 1904, brought him a distinguished reputation as a sociologist of the Jewish people. He moved to Palestine in 1907 and became a member of the Zionist Commission, the Zionist Executive and the Jewish Agency Executive.

11. Itzhak Ben-Zvi (1884–1963) became the second president of Israel. He was born in the Ukraine and was active in Jewish self-defence organizations in Russia. He moved to Palestine in 1907. He studied in Istanbul with David Ben-Gurion but was deported by the Turks and went to the United States in 1915. Ben-Zvi was elected to the National Council (Va'ad Le'ummi) when it was formed in 1920 as the effective government of the Jews of Palestine. He served as president of Israel from 1952 until his death in 1963.

were worked upon. Also, a bonded warehouse was about to be erected in Haifa, which had been declared a free port for goods in transit to other countries, but Prohibition in the United States seriously set back our wine industry. This, however, was partially offset by the unprecedented increase in the number of rabbis in New York, to whom Palestinian wine was necessary for ritual purposes.

We did our best to encourage and teach games, for there were only two Palestinian-born players in the football league of 12 teams. I played goal for Olives and for two years we won the championship.

For a brief period efficiency became the order of the day. The story of the Safad table was typical. The district officer wanted one and asked if he could, for 30 shillings, buy an old one he had found in the town. But Colonel Soloman, late of the Royal Army Service Corps, who was in charge of stores, was very regimentally minded and insisted on having made in Jerusalem a standard-pattern office table. True, his tables proved impossible to write upon in comfort, for the strip across the middle dividing the locally cured leather was never flush, but it was an attempt towards uniform battledress.

A table was despatched and invoiced out at £P 3.15s. It was transported from the factory in Jerusalem on a porter's back to the railway station. Thence it went to Haifa, from where it was sent on by narrow gauge to Samakh, south of the Sea of Galilee. From a donkey's back it was put into a boat and sailed to Tabgha at the northern end. From there Jewish settlers took it by cart to Rosh Pinna. Then an Arab took it by camel on the five hours' journey to Safad. Eventually the long-suffering district officer acknowledged receipt of a damaged table-top containing one drawer only and with no legs. He stated that the old table was now sold. What was he to do?

Means of transport were varied, from an old Sunbeam open car with a cape hood for the high commissioner to a victoria brought out at great expense by the senior medical officer in Jerusalem. Miss Hilda Ridler, in charge of Arab women's education, went about her duties garbed in a smart grey riding habit, but the inspector of women's welfare work, much to her chagrin, had to be content with a donkey. The district staffs went everywhere by horseback and acquired valuable knowledge of the lands and people.

The impact of Western methods had come as a shock to Eastern minds, whose former contacts with *frangi*s (foreigners) had consisted of occasional meetings with a few missionaries or being asked to produce horses for tourists to travel upon.

The insistence of the British on cleaning villages, removing dung heaps to the fields, preventing the scanty water supplies from getting fouled, sleeping apart from animals and fowls, attending appointments punctually, or standing up to give evidence in courts were not recognized, or welcomed, as the blessings that officials in their enthusiasm and ignorance believed them to be.

One had only to visit a Bedu tribal court to realize how repugnant to their own ideas ours were. The British judicial procedure of examination, cross-examination and re-examination of one witness at a time and allowing no one to speak or intervene was absolutely foreign to the Arab mind, ignoring his own customs, and remained so to the end. Having to explain everything through translators proved a maddening business. Formerly litigants had got along without many advocates, of whom scarcely any had been left behind by the Turks. Simple legal tests were made and a few ex-clerks were awarded certificates to practise. This created a demand for a law school. So, although there was far more need for mechanics, skilled workmen of all kinds and practising engineers, a law school was opened in November 1921. By 1943 we had a certain number of Palestinian-trained Jewish engineers, but still no Arabs, yet there were nearly 1000 Jewish and Arab advocates.

Confusion of thought and lack of clear interpretation of British government policy made our task difficult. Many of the older Jewish colonists, who had become much like their Arab neighbours, showed little disposition to bustle and change. But most of the newer Jews were exultant in the promise that had been made to them. The Arabs were equally determined to see that their own hopes were fulfilled. The British officials were somewhat bewildered. None had had any experience of the reception of immigrants or of establishing them. There was of course criticism of pro-Arabism or of anti-Semitism, but it was easier for the official on the spot to sympathize with the feelings of those present, who were fearful of an invasion, than with an ideal that concerned itself with people beyond one's ken.

Local Jews, like the Agudat Israel,[12] were by no means adherents of

---

12. Agudat Israel ('Union' or 'Association' of Israel) was founded in 1912 as a movement to preserve Jewish Orthodoxy.

a Zionist policy. These Jews had always led a life apart. They were patient under adversity, were treated with tolerance rather than equality, but still lived on friendly terms with their neighbours. Yiddish was the language of their everyday life and all spoke Arabic. Hebrew, outside the synagogue, was practically unused.

During the first 18 months, 17,000 Jewish immigrants entered — the pioneers of a new era. These young people from Poland had prepared themselves for this moment, by learning Hebrew and farming practice at Zionist camps in Poland, while they waited for the doors of Palestine to be opened. They had left behind them the dirty ghettos of Poland with their indescribable air of medieval squalor. In the Middle Ages the Polish aristocrats had welcomed the Jews, on the grounds not so much of tolerance as of their ability to foster trade and banking and to form the business class between the aristocrats and peasants. But now, with tension growing, the Poles looked upon them as a disruptive element and were glad to let them go.

A new epic had begun. Had not their forefathers built a civilization while Europe was still steppe and jungle? Dirt, overcrowding, bustle, babble of seller and buyer, ignominy and oppression and pungent odour had been left behind. A new world in the Promised Land was about to open where undying pertinacity, industry, ingenuity and endurance would have full scope.

They arrived bursting with enthusiasm. Men and women broke stones for roads or cleared ground for crops. They created a working dress. The men wore a khaki shirt and shorts; the women a half-sailor, half-Russian blouse, Reckitt's blue in colour, and black, full-bottomed bloomers. As emancipation advanced the bloomers changed to attenuated khaki shorts. From tent and shack singing was heard every evening, or a discussion group would get going until fatigue claimed them. Under their hands barren land started to blossom.

Wooden huts became their first homes in the towns. Silicate bricks were the first medium for building in Tel Aviv, but gradually the intricacies of reinforced concrete were mastered. Jews are not as good stonemasons as Arabs, and the cost to them of cutting big blocks of stone with iron hammers was prohibitive.

Arab objections to Jewish immigrants were growing, especially in Jaffa. The 'new' Jews were very different from the 'old' ones, who had lived quiet lives. They aired advanced views, set up labour organizations and proclaimed strikes. Some of the extremists among them, called by their Jewish opponents *mopsi*, the German for 'pugs' (pugilists), were caught distributing leaflets in Tel Aviv in Hebrew, Yiddish and Arabic, exhorting proletarians to unite and extinguish their oppressors.

The day after the distribution, an Orthodox Easter Sunday, a Jewish Labour procession marching down the main street was assailed by Jaffa Arabs. The riot spread and destructive raids followed on five Jewish rural settlements. British destroyers were sent to Jaffa and Haifa. During the riots and subsequent military operations 47 Jews and 48 Arabs were killed and 200 Jews and Arabs were wounded.

Murderous and most brutal attacks, followed by an orgy of pillage, had been made by Arabs upon defenceless people; and in some cases attacks were made by Jews in retaliation, but they had much to avenge. Courts of enquiry were held and blame apportioned. One report gained fame by stating that all the Arab elders in a certain village had committed perjury with dignity and deliberation.

The fundamental cause of the riots and subsequent acts of violence was Arab discontent with immigration and their conception of Zionist policy. Had not the Jewish Foundation Fund advertised that the object of the modern Jewish pioneer was to prepare room and work for the thousands and millions that wait outside? The Arabs feared a steady increase of Jewish immigration, which would ultimately lead to their political and economic subjection.

Many unofficial critics condemned the officials on the spot for having either failed in or overstepped their duty. Immigration was stopped for a time at Jaffa.

One night, when the high commissioner was sitting with Deedes and me debating whether Jaffa should be temporarily closed or not, I had to go outside into the passage for something and I saw Lady Samuel walking up and down, very agitated, saying over and over again: 'They are killing our people. They are killing our people.'

It was an invidious position for Samuel. He was as straight as a die. Much to his annoyance he was said to 'bend over backwards' in his efforts to be fair to the Arabs, but he was known to be a Zionist who had played a part in framing the Balfour Declaration and who had been spoken of by Dr Weitzmann as 'Our Samuel'. It was no wonder that the Arabs mistrusted him. Indeed when Lloyd George had invited him to take up the office, Samuel had pointed out to him clearly the disadvantages and the difficulties.

This was the condition of things after the control of Palestine was transferred from the Foreign Office to the Colonial Office, where Mr Churchill[13] was now secretary of state. At the end of 1920 the prime minister, Lloyd George, who had imbibed some of Curzon's jealousy towards him, was dissatisfied with the jumble of Middle Eastern affairs and listened to the gentle but insinuating voice of T. E. Lawrence that the personality of the minister in charge was of more importance than the office he held. So the prime minister moved responsibility from Curzon at the Foreign Office, and also other controls exercised by the India and War Offices, and gave the colonial secretaryship to Winston Churchill with authority to set up a Middle East Department to deal with the tangled skein. The secretary of state came to Jerusalem after holding his famous Middle East Conference in Cairo.

His visit had aroused enormous interest, and our local paper, *The Palestine Weekly*, made amusing havoc by the insertion of an extra 's'.

> Life in Cairo is very interesting nowadays [wrote the special correspondent], with delegations of international importance. At the Wednesday evening ball at the Semiramis Hotel both Mr and Mrs Churchill were present. Close on midnight Sir Herbert Samuel arrived, and Mrs Churchill at once went upstairs with him and they were seen no more, holding a conference *à deux* which, I understand, lasted well into the small hours.

Mr Churchill placed all this part of the world militarily under the newly constituted Royal Air Force. He also conceived the idea of a British gendarmerie; and a force of 600, including 150 ex-officers, mainly from the Black and Tans in Ireland, was recruited for Palestine. Officers and men eventually became the backbone of the Palestine Police.

13. Sir Winston Churchill (1874–1965) began his career as a soldier, serving in the Boer War and in France in 1916. He entered politics in 1899 and held many offices of state before becoming prime minister from 1940 to 1945, leading Britain during the Second World War. He served as prime minister again from 1951 to 1955.

Brigadier Angus McNeill,[14] the commanding officer, also brought several foxhound couples that had been given to him by masters of famous packs, with which he instituted the Lydda hunt. They hunted both jackals in the vale and some of the descendants of the 300 foxes that Samson had turned tail to tail, put firebrands in their midst, and let go to burn the Philistines' shocks and standing corn.

The gendarmerie also got up race meetings. I bought a black Arab from Damascus, named him Kevimato after myself, my wife Violet and my two children and one year won the two long-distance races, including the New Year Cup.

Churchill came accompanied by Colonel T. E. Lawrence. He first settled Emir Abdullah, who had jumped a claim to Transjordan, to be head there, and then turned to things Palestinian. He did a lot of work in bed and I had several interviews with the future prime minister in his pyjamas, while Mrs Churchill walked about the room in a homely way.

I had to translate to the emir one day for Churchill and found difficulty in giving the correct translation of such phrases as the following: 'Ask the emir if he has seen the new RAF armoured cars: Tell him that he should do so, and add that we have a lot more if necessary for bad boys.'

Lawrence enjoyed king-making and glided in and out of our offices like an elf. Occasionally he expressed himself like an imp. He was extremely sensitive about people yet enjoyed publicity. The settlement of Abdullah he felt was an honourable discharge of a debt long overdue.

After the conference was finished Deedes left to devote himself to social work in the East End of London. He gave me Wells's *Outline of History* and inscribed it: 'In memory of 1920–1923 and with very much gratitude.' He was replaced by Sir Gilbert Clayton,[15] who was political officer to Allenby during the campaign. Clayton was a most loved man. Tiny in stature, he was big in heart and had a happy way with him. In

14. Brigadier Angus McNeill served in the Sudan, the Boer War and the First World War. He raised and commanded the British gendarmerie of Palestine from 1922 to 1926 and served as the chief stockbreeding officer to the government of Palestine from 1926 to 1931.

15. Sir Gilbert Clayton began his military career with service in the Egyptian Army. He was an adviser to the Ministry of the Interior in Egypt from 1919 to 1922 and succeeded Sir Wyndham Deedes as chief secretary to the government of Palestine from 1922 to 1925.

large, clear handwriting he wrote simple but sane minutes on any subject that came before him and when he left for Baghdad as high
commissioner after the Arab revolt in that country, he left a memory
behind him and a position that has never been filled in quite the same
way.

But Palestine's real tragedy once Churchill had given up the colonial
secretaryship was being transferred from Foreign Office guidance to
Colonial Office control. The colonial system of government was then
totalitarianism tempered with benevolence, with a facade of local
executive and legislative councils. A governor was kept in check by the
local press, unless he exercised his veto and closed it down, by the
secretary of state and by questions asked in Parliament.

Although the Mandate instructed Great Britain to administer
Palestine on the basis of an 'A' development, because neither Arab nor
Jew would 'play ball' the regime that was set up was based on the 'C'
system, which was devised for the most backward territories. For this
reason the personality of the man holding the office of high commissioner was to play an extraordinarily important role in the fortunes of
the country.

The transfer from the Foreign Office to the Colonial Office was soon
apparent. The routine was tightened and they expected to be kept
informed on the most trivial matters. The training and outlook of the
two departments of state were so dissimilar. In the one the officers were
linguists accustomed to thinking in three or four languages, who were
continually brushing up their intellects through contact with leading
personalities in Europe, the United States and the Far East. In the
Colonial Office, able officials though they might be, the only Europeans they had to think about were government officials, settlers in the
highlands of Africa and Ceylon, and planters in Malaya. The study of
political aspirations had meant little to them.

Gone without recall was the calm and enlightened experience of the
Foreign Office, accustomed to dealing with the unexpected from the
rise and fall of governments to the murder of a French president.
Ambassadors and ministers stationed in foreign capitals were accustomed to receiving guidance and general instructions only, and the rest
was left to their judgement. Foreign Office officials in Downing Street
or abroad know one another and speak one language. Not so in the
Colonial Service.

To overcome this difficulty, Winston Churchill created within the Colonial Office a Middle East Department and staffed it from without. John Shuckburgh, the head, was brought in from the India Office and T. E. Lawrence, Mark Young and Hathorne Hall from outside. After Lawrence had retired, I came in as a principal secretary on loan from Palestine for a year. Both Young and Hall subsequently became colonial governors. Shuckburgh, the cautious and perfectly trained civil servant, Young the dynamic, Hall the far-seeing and myself the impulsive.

The permanent staff resented the intrusion and by way of giving us a welcome always referred to us as 'the beachcombers'. As soon as they could, when our time was up, we were replaced by their own regular officers. Most of the permanent staff officials had spent their lives in the one dusty office. Indeed in my time, one aged assistant secretary never arrived until noon, left early, and on Saturdays it was too much of an effort for him to come at all.

For decades, the pay of officials working in the colonies was so low that the various services had not attracted a distinguished type of young man; in general it was the failures at the English or Irish Bar who entered the judicial departments. So, presuming it would be unwise to give them much rope, every detail of administration from overseas had to be submitted to the secretary of state for approval. At the Colonial Office the papers were minuted upon by a couple of first-division men whose service varied from one to a dozen years, the answer stamped by a clerk with the facsimile signature of the minister and despatched to the governor concerned. Possibly one in a thousand papers reached the secretary of state's own desk. An ex-civil secretary of the Sudan government, which was guided by the Foreign Office, told me that as civil secretary there he had more powers than ever he had subsequently as a colonial governor. The transfer had also affected the young Palestine civil service. No longer did these officers enjoy the feeling that they were, like officers in the Sudan, members of an entity. Palestine became part of the colonial system and the civil service began to be fed by officers from colonies to whom Palestine was to become an incident in a career. They brought in strange talk of 'tours of duty' and the prospects of 'transfers' at the end of it. The connection was not helped by the frequency of the moves of the secretaries of state. There were nearly a score between 1920 and 1945.

Jimmy Thomas[16] was secretary of state in Downing Street for most of my time. Although he was intellectually lazy and left much of his work to that prince of private secretaries, Eddie Marsh,[17] he displayed a shrewd House of Commons sense. Once he had to reply for the government in a debate on a loan for Palestine. Shuckburgh had prepared a speech setting out the facts and principles. Thomas did not use a word of it. He got up and jollied the House and made them laugh; laughter turned into a roar. He then sat down. After the loan had been agreed to, he came across to us in our boxed-in seats at the right of the Speaker's chair and said: 'I could see the 'ouse didn't want a speech tonight.'

But working in Downing Street on the execution of a policy that is subject to expediency and to fluctuations of interpretation is a soul-destroying task; so, having made arrangements with my friends of Manchester days, Sybil Thorndike[18] and Lewis Casson,[19] for some weeks I left the office at seven o'clock, ate some sandwiches, went to the theatre, donned my motley and appeared with them in the first production (1924) of George Bernard Shaw's *St Joan*, starting as a monk and, owing to illness among the cast, finishing as the Executioner. At the end all the cast autographed a copy of the play and Shaw[20] wrote a large AND underneath their names and signed it.

My misgivings about Palestine became deeper. The more I read the official papers of 1914–20 the sharper grew my doubts. Every standard seemed to have been sacrificed to expediency. I had known little of

---

16. Jimmy Thomas started work at the age of nine as an errand boy and eventually became general secretary of the National Union of Railwaymen from 1918 to 1924 and 1925 to 1931, Labour member of parliament for Derby from 1910 to 1931 and secretary of state for the colonies in 1924, 1931 and 1935/6.

17. Eddie Marsh (1872–1953) served as assistant private secretary to Joseph Chamberlain and Herbert Asquith and as private secretary to Winston Churchill. He was private secretary to Jimmy Thomas in 1924 and from 1929 to 1936.

18. Sybil Thorndike began her acting career with repertory work in Britain and the United States and progressed to leading roles on the London stage and work in theatre management. She made several films but was principally a stage actress.

19. Lewis Casson, actor and producer, was married to Sybil Thorndike and often worked with her. His stage career began in 1900 and continued until 1968, interrupted only by service in the First World War.

20. George Bernard Shaw (1856–1950), playwright famous for works such as *Major Barbara* (1905), *Pygmalion* (1912) and *Heartbreak House* (1917).

international or political matters. But I was certain that the standard of rectitude established by, and expected from, bankers and manufacturers was far higher.

I asked myself the questions: Is Great Britain being really honest to the Arabs? To the Jews? To herself? The questions gnawed at my conscience and refused to be silenced. But I had pledged myself to Palestine. I decided to return.

On my return I found that government activities had increased. Taxation had been assessed more fairly, a Customs code had been promulgated. A cadastral survey had been begun, new roads constructed, village and town water supplies improved and village schools opened at the rate of one a week.

Agricultural progress had been steady but slow. We had made an unfortunate purchase of a considerable number of cast-off army battery mules, which we had sold to the villagers for use as ploughing animals. The mules proved to be worn out and too big to be fed on the meagre rations that could be given to them and they wasted and died. A good many goats had come in from Syria. Goats bred readily and provided the owners with milk and cheese. But in the long term their increase was a mixed blessing, for, like locusts, they eat everything in their path and are a particular danger where one is trying to develop trees.

Sir Frederick Palmer, the eminent consulting engineer, had examined our coasts and Haifa had been decided upon as the site of a deep-water harbour.

A lunatic asylum had been established, for it was considered no longer appropriate for the insane to live chained to the walls of an isolated Orthodox convent near Bethlehem in the hopes that the sanctity of the surroundings would restore their minds.

Pinchas Rutenberg,[21] a Russian Jew of dynamic personality who

21. Pinchas Rutenberg (1879–1942) was born in the Ukraine and studied at the St Petersburg Technological Institute. In 1915 he drew up a comprehensive irrigation plan for Palestine and in 1923 established the Palestine Electric Company, which was later granted a concession to use the waters of the Jordan and Yarmuk rivers to generate electricity.

gained the confidence of Winston Churchill and Samuel, had begun the work of harnessing the waters of the Jordan. He constructed other power stations and a network of pylons was set up across the country.

But the greatest service of all was the advance made in malaria control. The Rockefeller Foundation aided the government department. The help of the villagers was also successfully enlisted and all males were called upon to give ten days' free labour per annum to clean up and clear water courses and swamps in the vicinity of their homes. Wells and cisterns were regularly oiled and mosquitoes prevented from breeding.

Infant mortality was very high. A quarter of all babies born in Bethlehem died before reaching one year. A woman was still 'delivered' sitting upon a stool with a half-mooned wooden seat, 'protected' by a blue bead in her hair, with half a dozen relations around her exhorting her to push. This practice is of ancient origin. The use of 'stools' by Hebrew midwives is mentioned in the book of Exodus, when Pharaoh ordered them to kill Hebrew sons. They excused themselves and saved many sons, among them Moses, whose mother hid him for three months in an ark of bulrushes. Mrs Humphrey Bowman started a welfare centre for training midwives; and, with encouragement and training, the half-mooned stool was abolished, not only by law but also by public opinion. Gradually the work was extended to the country districts. Hadassah[22] and missionary hospitals had also helped.

The hospital of the Order of St John of Jerusalem was doing magnificent work under Dr John Strathearn in reducing blindness, which was particularly prevalent in the area around Gaza.

The Arabs had been given more freedom in religious matters than the Turks had ever allowed them. Haj Amin el Husseini, who had been pardoned for his part in the 1920 riots in the general amnesty, had been appointed *mufti* of Jerusalem. His sole qualifications for the post were the pretensions of his family plus shrewd opportunism. Directly after he heard that his uncle Kamel, the late *mufti*, was ill, he went to Cairo to attend Al Azhar University. After his uncle's death and a short period of religious instruction he returned to Jerusalem sporting a red beard of

22. Hadassah is the Women's Zionist Organization of the USA, which began medical work by sponsoring two nurses to visit Palestine in 1913. It sponsors medical care, training, research and special education.

a few weeks' growth and wearing the white muslin turban of piety wound around his *tarboosh*. It takes seven years of hard study to complete the full course at Al Azhar. However, family 'pull' had then secured him the job. A Supreme Muslim Council had been set up, with the *mufti* of Jerusalem as permanent head. Their revenues, which were a tithe on certain crops, were collected by the government but handed over to them in bulk.

Arab ladies were beginning to peep a little from behind the veil. A beauty parlour had been opened in Jerusalem by an American Jewess, an ex-hospital nurse. Wax figures had been shown in the windows of a draper's shop and had attracted enormous attention from the peasants, who fully expected the figures to speak. Private motorcars began to be used. Agricultural shows had aroused interest. Various devices were tried to catch the judge's eye. At one I was startled to find the fowls' tails apparently steeped in blood; closer inspection revealed that they were dyed with henna. Most of the sheep had yellow topknots. The Arabs were awakening!

When the return to the Promised Land became practical politics, the Jews determined to be as free as possible from government control and demanded the right to maintain their own schools, hospitals, public health administration, rabbinical courts and the succouring of their own poor. A general assembly was established of 300 members elected by Jews of both sexes. A national council, or executive, Va'ad Le'ummi, was chosen by this assembly and constituted in theory the responsible government of the national home. It succeeded in obtaining legal status so that the Jews might impose taxation for their cultural needs and might preserve their own national life. In theory a Jew could 'opt out' of the community, though in practice dissenters merely ignored the demand to pay the taxes. But the permission to levy taxes marked another stage towards the goal that Dr Eder, the acting chairman of the Zionist Executive, had defined when he told the commission dealing with the Jaffa riots: 'The real key to the situation is to give Jews rights and privileges in Palestine which shall enable Jews to make it as Jewish as England is English or as Canada is Canadian. This is the only reasonable or feasible meaning of a Jewish National Home.'

To that doctrine the Palestine government, being entrusted with the protection of Arab as well as Jewish interests, could not subscribe and the high commissioner's considered opinion was impartially set forth in a document, which became a White Paper and was laid before parliament by Winston Churchill. It said the policy was fixed and internationally guaranteed. It did not mean that the purpose in view was to create a wholly Jewish Palestine. It did not contemplate the subordination of the Arab population, language or culture. The Balfour Declaration did not propose that Palestine as a whole should be converted into a Jewish national home but that such a home should be founded in Palestine. 'For the fulfilment of this policy it is necessary that the Jewish community should be able to increase its numbers by immigration. This immigration cannot be so great in volume as to exceed the economic capacity of the country at the time to absorb new arrivals.'

Mr Churchill had sent a copy of the statement before publication to the Zionist Organization, which gave an unqualified assurance in the sense desired. This assurance seemed clear enough, but my doubts were raised shortly afterwards when Dr Weizmann came to Palestine and, in a conversation with the chief secretary and myself, after giving a picture of the international plight of Jewry and — far-seeing man — the ever-growing anti-Semitism in Europe, he said: 'I accept the White Paper because when the time is ripe, I shall make it a blue paper. The Arabs must go elsewhere.'

The policy was uncompromisingly opposed by the Arabs. They had already resigned from the advisory council. Now they declined an invitation to be represented on a legislative council with ten official and twelve elected members — eight Muslims, two Jews and two Christians. The Arabs were insisting that the Jewish national home was depriving them of their natural right to establish an independent government along the lines of those in Mesopotamia (Iraq) and the Hejaz. Emir Abdullah in Transjordan had his own ministers. Egypt had been declared an independent sovereign state. Syria seethed with unrest — a Druze rebellion was to break out there in the summer of 1925.

That was the situation when the first Jew to hold the office of high commissioner, after walking and riding in a farewell tour from Dan to Beersheba, left in June. Armaments had been so reduced that there was not even a gun to fire a salute when Sir Herbert left our shores.

Lady Samuel had upheld the dignity of her position by simplicity and kindness. She was generally known as Auntie Bee. She took great pains to uplift the status of women of all classes and she also assisted infant welfare. She did much to help educate the few English children in Jerusalem, and she got a PNEU-trained English governess out, which was an invaluable asset.

For years after Samuel's departure, Muslims who had been his bitter opponents used to say to me: '*Ah, Samweel, mafish wahid mitl hoo.* Oh, Samuel, there is no one like him.'

In his last report to the secretary of state, Sir Herbert wrote: 'I trust that work, accomplished under conditions sometimes of difficulty, will be considered in the retrospect not unworthy.'

6

Pasha of Jerusalem

F ield Marshal Lord Plumer[1] succeeded Sir Herbert Samuel as high commissioner. His great reputation as a military commander had preceded him. Peace lasted throughout his three years of service. He was helped to some extent by the economic depression, which slowed down Jewish immigration. But when the Arabs made a fuss about a reception for the flags of the two Jewish battalions of the Royal Fusiliers, which were to be laid in the Hurva synagogue, he made it clear from the start that if the demonstration they threatened took place, he would know how to deal with those responsible for its occurrence.

The field marshal decided that the defence of Palestine should be directed from Transjordan, so he disbanded the British gendarmerie, absorbed the British personnel into the police force and built up a new military unit called the Transjordan Frontier Force. He insisted on the cost being borne by the British and not the Palestine taxpayer and, when the secretary of state demurred, said that he would resign if this point was not agreed upon.

1. Field Marshal Lord Plumer (1857–1932) was born in Torquay and educated at Eton. He entered the 65th Foot (1st York and Lancaster Regiment) in 1876 and served in the Sudan campaign against the Mahdists, the Matabele rebellion and the Boer War. In the years leading up to the First World War, he commanded divisions in Ireland and York and during the war he played a prominent role on the Ypres salient and in Italy as commander of the Second Army. He was made a field marshal in 1919. After the war, Plumer served as governor of Malta until 1924 and as high commissioner for Palestine from 1925 to 1928. Plumer was created 1st Viscount of Messines in 1929.

Lord Plumer was a very different type from his predecessor. Rather insignificant in figure, he wore a large walrus moustache. When he descended from his train on arrival, his wife followed him, wearing a light-grey satin dress of the Queen Alexandra period and, perched upon her head, a large hat with high waving plumes. He looked a benevolent grandfather, she a commanding general.

Led by two scarlet-clad *kavasses*, Lord and Lady Plumer moved towards the dais from where he was expected to address the notables and officials assembled. Crash upon the stones went the iron-shod staves of the gorgeously apparelled *kavasses*, striking the harder in honour of the day. Two more blows thundered down the platform and resounded under the roof, a survival of ceremonial reception from Turkish days. Lady Plumer's hat quivered; her features expressed supreme surprise. The baron met the blows stoically, but even his hand went up and clasped his moustache. Two steps forward and another clang shook the roof. Surprise gave way to amazement and amazement to humour and by the time Lady Plumer reached the dais she was twitching with fun and nearly collapsed upon her husband.

The field marshal made the shortest speech yet made in Palestine. After a pleasant reference to Sir Herbert Samuel, he added: 'Lady Plumer and I come among you as strangers. We hope that when I come to leave, we shall leave you as friends. We thank you for your welcome.' The Plumers entered their car and left for Government House, stopping at St George's Cathedral on the way to ask for God's blessing upon their labours. They asked for nothing else; they gave abundantly.

Lord Plumer at once struck the public imagination and until he left had enormous personal influence. Duty to his God and then to his sovereign was in the forefront of his life. He put out no feelers, never advertised himself, but expected his officers and the public to co-operate; they instinctively followed him.

After a flight to Amman (his first trip in a plane) to meet Emir Abdullah of Transjordan, all the tribal sheikhs came up one by one to be presented. The oldest, a rugged old warrior, with a sudden impulse handed him his sword and, as the field marshal touched the hilt, the Bedu chief took his hand and held it to his lips. Every man who followed did the same. This was the first and last time in history that Bedu Muslim sheikhs have paid such a tribute to a Christian official.

Plumer worked in the khaki uniform of a field marshal, his only military display. He and his wife invariably drove about Jerusalem without an escort and she, being an ardent collector of antiques, especially miniatures, spent many hours in the antique shops.

Lord Plumer had none of the pretensions to be '*plus royaliste que le roi*' that beset smaller men. When he gave a dinner party, however official the occasion, he and his wife met and welcomed their guests at their drawing room door instead of having them announced by aides and making a grand circle.

He was as determined as Sir Herbert had been to see that the double implication of the Mandate was fulfilled to the letter and, like his predecessor, he did not brook Colonial Office interference.

On my return from duty at the Colonial Office shortly before the Plumers arrived, I was posted to Haifa as assistant district commissioner of Northern Palestine. I served there for a year and, upon Ronald Storrs's departure to be governor of Cyprus, Plumer appointed me to replace him in Jerusalem. The people gave me the old Turkish title 'Pasha of Jerusalem' and Keith-Roach Pasha I remained until I retired.

Of all my years in Palestine, I enjoyed the ones I worked with Plumer the most. There was nothing petty or self-seeking about him. A keen cricketer, he went to the sports ground every season after Sunday morning service. Some years after he had left he told me that, of all the honours he received, the two he most valued were his election as president of the MCC and the inscribed cricket ball presented to him by the captain of the Jerusalem Sports Club after the last match he attended.

The field marshal arranged for me to have a standing meeting with him every Monday evening at six o'clock. As he and his wife were ardent bridge players for infinitesimal stakes, things so developed that for a couple of years I stayed on for bridge and dinner; but punctually at ten o'clock the stakes were paid over and the evening closed.

Plumer maintained an interest in military matters to the end of his life. I remember sitting on the Hove Lawns with him when the Germans sent over a Zeppelin to show her prowess. The airship flew along the beach at a height of 200 feet. The whole of Brighton was gaping upwards. As the ship flew overhead, the old man gave a fleeting glance, remarked, 'Of no military importance,' and went on with his conversation.

Storrs quite rightly had had his eye more upon restoration of the Old City and ceramics than upon roads and asphalt. Upon my appointment Plumer said: 'I am dissatisfied with the state of the roads. See to it that they are improved.' I asked for three months to study the question of ways and means, including the vexed question of finance. At a subsequent meeting he said, 'I see no improvement. The municipal engineer must be sacked.' I replied, 'His previous experience has been on a railway and erecting tombstones in military cemeteries.' Lord Plumer agreed and, aided by a new engineer from Birmingham Municipality and some extra money allotted to the council, improvements began to be felt.

But municipal improvements were always hard to make because the municipal members, at that time mainly Arab, were always opposed to any increase in rates. These were far too low for the needs of the city. The Arab and Jewish members rarely agreed. If an Arab proposed anything it was always strongly criticized by the Jews and if a Jew suggested something it was soundly sat upon by the Arabs. The Christian Arab members would come and complain to me privately about the manner in which they were suppressed by the Muslims. The Sephardi Jewish member would make similar confidential complaints against the Ashkenazi Jewish members. For generations the Oriental Jews had dominated the Ashkenazi or Eastern European Jews and they much resented the changed conditions that immigration had brought. Their own chief rabbi was hardly on speaking terms with his brother in the faith, the chief rabbi of the Ashkenazi.

A happy way out was developed so that if something essential was wanted, the mayor — whether Arab or Jew — would discuss it privately with all parties, tell me and I would put it forward as my proposal.

Storrs's house had been given up, so my wife and I cast around and found a dilapidated but stately one-storeyed building inside the city walls, which I used for office and house. The walls were a metre thick and every room had a domed ceiling. The rooms were built around an open courtyard where we grew zinnias down below and maidenhair ferns in pots above. The roof was so extensive that when hard-pressed I used to bicycle round it for early morning exercise. We were so centrally situated and our surroundings so picturesque that at our weekly 'at homes' we seldom had less than 100 people in to tea.

101

My wife would not tolerate gossip and we both refused to allow our visitors to talk politics so we often had strange social shake-ups, with people who had not spoken to each other for years finding themselves on either side of the tea tray talking to my wife. Once, I remember, after a particularly savage outbreak of disorder, I saw the grand *mufti* and the Sephardi chief rabbi talking amiably with her. Of all the young assistants who helped us, the figure of Stewart Perowne, later adviser to the Emir of Cyrenaica, stands out. He was indefatigable at parties, thoroughly enjoyed them, and was worthy of the apt description given of him as 'an oiler of social wheels'.

Our own housing problem being solved, my wife and I visited the site chosen for the new Government House. It was a couple of miles outside Jerusalem, south of the Bethlehem road, overlooking the Arab village of Shafaat. The land had been purchased and the Agricultural Department was busily planting trees. It seemed most unsuitable, so we looked for something better.

On the hill of Evil Council looking across the valley, the western walls of the city stood out in all their grandeur. The site was occupied by the town incinerator. The two things against it were its unfortunate name and lack of soil. I felt the latter could be imported so I approached Lord Plumer. He rejected my proposal, saying that all sites had been considered, the other land had been purchased and he could not go back on it.

I refused to give in and I put my case before him a second and a third time. The field marshal became very angry and asked me how I dared to reopen a closed subject. 'Because,' I said, 'I am certain that you are all wrong.' The siting committee was recalled. Plumer opened the discussion. 'I don't want K-R's opinion, I know it. What is yours?'

It was agreed that the hill of Evil Council was a better site. They had visited it on a windy day and been put off by the incinerator smoke. The change was made and the architect, Austen Harrison, secured the finest position possible and proved worthy of it. Shortly afterwards Lillah McCarthy[2] came out with the Masefields.[3] I felt that the name

2. Lillah McCarthy made her first stage appearance in 1895 and her acting career, mainly in London, lasted until the 1930s.

3. John Masefield (1878–1967) was a writer and poet who became Poet Laureate in 1930.

of Evil Council must be exorcised so I took her up one night, sat her down upon a rock and, as the moon rose above the hills of Moab, I asked her to recite again and again Blake's 'Jerusalem'. The very heavens seemed flooded with her glorious voice as she declaimed:

> Bring me my bow of burning gold:
> Bring me my arrows of desire:
> Bring me my spear.
> O clouds unfold!
> Bring me my chariot of fire.

After Rockefeller had offered some millions of dollars to the Egyptian government for the erection of a modern museum, which they rejected because they would not agree to the trusteeship terms he considered a necessary safeguard, our own antiquities director, Professor Garstang, persuaded Rockefeller's representative, Professor Breasted, to give some of the money to Palestine for a new museum.

A committee was set up with Plumer as the chairman, and he made me a member. Austen Harrison came up with an admirable design after visiting most of the museums of Europe to learn what to avoid. The result was not only a first-class workshop, but one of the outstanding buildings in the East. Plumer took the greatest interest in it throughout his term of office.

He was an upholder of tradition and when the English Knights of the Order of St John of Jerusalem came on a pilgrimage, led by the sub-prior, Lord Scarborough, he attended Holy Communion with the pilgrims at the ancient conventual church of the Mar Hanna Order. Later in the day, headed by the sword and standard of the Order and the processional cross, wearing his black mantle with the large eight-pointed white cross, he attended a parade service at St George's Cathedral. This was the first time that the Knights of St John had marched in procession in the Holy City since its capture by Saladin in 1187.

I had the honour of being admitted to the Order at a specially authorized meeting of Chapter General and, with due ceremonial, was exhorted to be true to my sovereign, to my honour and faithful to the Order and 'to remember that the cross you will receive is the sign of man's redemption and its arms symbolise the four cardinal virtues, Prudence, Temperance, Justice and Fortitude. *Pro Fide. Pro Utilitate Hominum.*'

Shortly afterwards, we had a visit from Aimée Semple McPherson of the Four Square Gospel Church. She had bright brown eyes, a large sensuous mouth, and was wearing a wide-sleeved white dress. Having collected 100 Arabs as torchbearers, and given them something on account, she announced that she was going to preach to the world from the Mount of Olives with a living cross of flame behind her. When I sent her word that this innovation would not be allowed, she was most indignant and, to assuage her chagrin, took to the bottle for three days. According to the hotel proprietor, she was seen only when she wished to replenish the stock. She left without saying goodbye.

A couple of years after Plumer's appointment there was a serious drought in southern Palestine. At once appreciating the plight of the cattle owners, he moved the famished herds and the families to the northern district, and kept them there until the rains. He then left with his wife for a holiday in England. Shortly afterwards there was a severe earthquake, and he returned to find that nearly 300 people had been killed and 900 injured. The damage was at Lydda, Ramla and Nablus and at Amman and Salt in Transjordan.

Lord Plumer tackled the problem with confidence. He refused to allow Palestine to make a universal appeal, which so many of the inhabitants wanted, for they had been brought up to trade continuously on the fact that they lived in the Holy Land, but he asked everyone in the country to assist those less fortunate than themselves and to answer the question, 'Who is my neighbour?' He also saw that funds were allotted from government sources for rebuilding. Great stretches of Nablus required rebuilding, but the assistant district commissioner lacked courage. Instead of pulling down a number of houses that had been only slightly damaged, he left them standing, and a unique chance to improve the worst and most overcrowded part of the town was lost. An enterprising Arab mayor seized the chance to improve Ramla and, from that time onwards, the town never looked back.

I had been sitting in my house in the Old City on a stiflingly hot day when there was a heavy rumble followed by a crash, as though a huge lorry had fallen onto the flat roof. The walls began to shake and one, a metre thick, opened up, and I saw daylight through it. I felt a pain in my stomach, like sea sickness. The dome of the Katholicon at the Church of the Holy Sepulchre was badly shaken and eventually had to be taken down. The great dome of the Muslim Noble Sanctuary escaped. The German convent housing the high commissioner was very knocked about and had to be evacuated.

Following the disaster there were many rumours of volcanic manifestations and, in Jerusalem, reports that sulphurous smoke had been seen coming out of the ground. I asked the government analyst to accompany me on a tour of inspection. We found a greyish white smoke issuing with pulsating motion from the drains of many hovels in a tiny street of the Old City. Expectation rose to fever heat when, with an ever-gathering throng, we traced the smoke to the exhaust of an oil engine in a neighbouring workshop connected directly to the sewer.

I heard that the convents of the two enclosed orders, the Carmelites on the Mount of Olives and the Poor Sisters of Clare on the Bethlehem road, had suffered severely. With the approval of the Latin patriarch, accompanied by a Dominican father who was a friend of mine, I visited them.

At the Carmelites, having talked to the mother superior through an iron grille with a black curtain between us, the bolts were drawn back and the double iron gates were opened. Our tiny procession was preceded by a veiled nun bent with age ringing a bell to warn the nuns to shut themselves up in their shattered cells. Some of the rooms had fallen in, but no one had been hurt. So much damage had been done that 15 of the nuns had to be sent to another house in Cairo. Some of them had been inside the convent for over 20 years and ordinarily would never leave while they were alive. Except for a gate sister they had no communication with the outside world. They were amazed by the journey to the station, for they had never seen a motorcar before and the city had grown so much since they had made their first journey up the hill. As they walked haltingly along the railway station platform, they seemed as blind women facing the unknown. An English nun told me that this was only the second time in 25 years that she had spoken English.

The Poor Sisters of Clare, the second Order of Franciscans, a contemplative order, had also been hit grievously. The convent was roughly constructed in Arabic style with vaulted rooms round a courtyard. The roof had fallen in upon the infirmary. When I arrived there I found debris and large stones fallen from the roof lying upon the beds of three nuns suffering from paralysis, but not one of them was injured. The other nuns were forlorn and frightened. Because of the severity of their regime and their restricted diet, they had not the strength to deal with the crisis.

The cells were devoid of comfort. Small iron bedsteads, prie-dieus and washstands were the only furniture. The nuns slept in their habits, lay upon straw mattresses, used rough blankets and, even for the sick, there were no sheets. The stone walls were defaced with numerous little plaques calling upon the inmates to pray for some family or person who had been a benefactor. Contact with the affairs of life was maintained by the prioress through the intermediary of a couple of lay sisters, who lived over the main door and who were denied entry into the choir.

For some weeks I saw a good deal of the nuns in an attempt to make their lives even tolerable and their convent habitable. Utterly divorced from the world for years, they had known no ordinary human joys or human sorrow; they had not known the laughter of a child. Their lives were ordered in the minutest detail by rule. By rigid discipline they lived in remorseless separation from everything that was not God. This hard but golden road, solitude of spirit, was safeguarded by the strictness by which rules of silence were obeyed. There were no subterfuges of sign language, such as are practised by the Cistercians or Trappist monks. Above all, they had found Christ and for His love, they had given up everything and hidden themselves in the secret of His face and in the anonymity of their choir. They had come expecting fasts, sorrows, humiliations and the cross, as well as the trouble, sickness and sufferings that beset human nature. Every night they rose and devoted some hours to prayer and filled the choir behind the altar with their supplications to God. Their lives were ones of purity and holiness and peace. Embraced by silence and enfolded by prayer and sacrifice, their convent was an impregnable fortress of devotion.

Everything was regulated; the way they walked, held their heads and the way they sat in refectory or choir. Bells called to Mass and divine office; bells sounded for strict silence or for spiritual reading; bells summoned the nuns from cloister to choir. No innovations of any kind were permitted. Therefore with childish simplicity they took pleasure in or alarm at the most trivial happenings. Everything that affected them became exaggerated and matters of no importance welled up into problems of grave concern. Some of them talked with me as though their minds had been static for years and they faced the difficulties with the mental attitude of children who had been wakened abruptly from a long sleep. They were touchingly grateful for the smallest thing I was able to do.

Some months after the quake, when life was beginning to become more normal, the prioress invited me to attend the ceremony of a nun making her final profession, and also the reception of a postulant into the Order. I sat in the chapel with the postulant's mother and sister. A priest recited the long office, including the Litany of the Saints, the nuns taking part from their choir behind the altar. Then I was beckoned forward by a lay sister. An iron shutter across the grille was swung open and behind the iron bars I could see the community kneeling in the choir. Veils covered their faces. A crown of thorns, tied with a small white bow, was placed upon the head of the nun about to make her final vows. Placing her hands inside those of the prioress she repeated after her the vows of Poverty, Chastity, Obedience and Enclosure in Perpetuity. The novice was dressed as a bride, in a white satin dress with a crown of flowers upon her head. Two pigtails hung down her shoulders. The prioress slipped the dress from the girl's shoulders and it fell around her feet, and she was left in a white shift. Large shears were handed to the superior and the girl's hair was cut off. The habit and knotted girdle were taken off the altar and handed through the grille by the priest and she was robed and the girdle fastened round her waist. The flowers were replaced by a crown of thorns tied with a black bow. A gold ring was placed upon her finger. The novice repeated her vows after the prioress and then made a tour of the choir and each nun bestowed upon her a kiss of peace.

The young nun then came to the grille to salute her mother. She was radiantly happy and tremendously exalted. The prioress looked up with her cold penetrating eyes, severe and scrutinizing as those of a judge. Her face was as rigid as if cut in marble and her thin lips looked as though they never parted in a smile. After a brief word or two the prioress said '*Assez! Assez!*', the iron doors were swung to, and the girl was cut off from her family and the world for ever.

A week later the prioress died. I was asked to the funeral service. The iron shutter was reopened. Surrounded by the community, the body of this remarkable woman was lying in an open coffin. She was robed in her habit, a crucifix upon her breast, her rosary in her hands. Incredibly old, her noble face wizened like ancient parchment, which even death had not been able to soften, she lay rigid and inscrutable.

7

The District Commissioner

T he day Storrs handed his office over to me, he remarked wittily that I had hitherto been dealing with the affairs of state, now I should have to deal with the state of affairs. He was right. People became of much more importance than papers. For the next 20 years my private affairs sank more and more into the background. With the population increasing at a rate unprecedented anywhere in the world, one's personal joys or tragedies seemed of minor importance. Moreover death was always round the corner.

There is no counterpart of a district commissioner in the constitutional government of Great Britain. The post is somewhat analogous to that of an imaginary official in England who might be supposed to combine in his person the functions of Lord Lieutenant of a county, sheriff, town planner, Home Office official responsible for municipal and local councils, policeman, county councillor, Inland Revenue officer, income tax commissioner, assistant accountant-general, poor law guardian, justice of the peace, coroner and member of parliament. My main duties were to anticipate every want, to provide for all lawful needs and to drive away every evil.

My staff and I had to co-operate with technical and departmental officers to ensure that their work helped to form a harmonious whole. The 60 subjects for which I was responsible ranged from politics to liquor licences and from public security to registration of divorces; from the collection of taxes to maintaining the status quo in the Holy Places; from issuing identity cards to granting agricultural loans; from inspecting factories and prisons to checking government stores and municipal accounts.

Edward and Violet Keith-Roach before their Presentation at Buckingham palace, 1922.

ABOVE. With the 2nd Battalion, 7th Lanashire Fusiliers in 1916. BELOW. Annual spring gathering of Jews, Muslims and Christians near the beginning of the Nablus Road outside Jerusalem, early 1920s.

LEFT. Jews on their way to th
Wailing Wall.

BELOW. King Ali of the Hedja
and the author. c. 1933.

RIGHT. Ready for the Coronation
Parade at Haifa 1937.

BELOW. Edward and Philippa
Keith-Roach on their wedding
day, 4 October 1939 with the
High Commissioner, Sir Harold
MacMichael.

ABOVE. Presentation to the Muslims of the Nebi Musa Banner for the annual pilgrimage to Jericho. BELOW. Edward and Philippa Keith-Roach and Bishop Graham-Brown with (left to right), Alexandre, Patriarch of Antioch, Christopherus, Patriarch of Alexandria and Timotheus, Patriarch of Jerusalem, 1940. This was the first meeting of the Patriarchs for 400 years.

ABOVE. The Armenian ceremony of the washing of the feet with the Patriarch taking the part of Jesus. BELOW LEFT. Greek Orthodox Easter morning procession to the Church of the Holy Sepulchre. BELOW RIGHT. The Latin Patriarch's Easter Sunday procession in the Church of the Holy Sepulchre.

ABOVE. Edward and Philippa Keith-Roach at a village gathering near Quebebe on one of their regular tours. BELOW. Edward Keith-Roach with the Sephardic Chief Rabbi — early 1940s.

I controlled and worked in close collaboration with the police in the detection and prevention of crime and in the preservation of public order. If the public wanted to hold a demonstration, the object of which might vary from a carnival to agitation against government policy, or from an annual tree-planting day to a religious procession, it was the district commissioner, after consultation with the police, who had to give the final decision and bear the responsibility for saying 'Yes' or 'No'.

Assessing and collecting taxes were arduous duties, for I was under a dual obligation to see that the public was not oppressed and the government, as trustees of the people's money, was not defrauded by those who would not pay. Occasionally, household or other goods belonging to our friends had to be seized, or salaries and rents 'attached'. The circumstances were unfavourable when income tax was instituted because we had to attempt to assess and collect, with an untrained staff, a year's new tax in seven months. However, assisted by the advice and knowledge of the commissioner of income tax from India, we managed it. Each assessment involved six different actions from sending the notice to recording the payment.

Even the collection of income tax had its lighter moments. I was reminded that I was in the Holy City by an Arab profit and loss account, where, instead of 'net profit', was written 'And this is what God, may He be glorified and exalted, has vouchsafed to grant us; to Him be praise'; or by the Jew who reversed the headings of his debit and credit columns in order 'not to suggest that the Almighty is first concerned with debit items'. On the other hand, even in Jerusalem a man can ask whether he is entitled to a deduction for 'what the law and convention prevent me from calling a wife'.

As sub-accountants, district commissioners were responsible for large sums of money. Two or three million pounds per annum used to be received and paid out through my offices. Censorship duties brought problems. As head of the board I had to see that no play or cinema film was exhibited unless it had been approved. Licensing cafés and hotels had its own difficulties.

If the Agricultural Department wanted to arrange a demonstration plot of wheat, or provide poison for killing fieldmice, it was I, or my Palestinian district officer, who would obtain the loan of the land, or assistance from the people to wage war on the mice. The district commissioner would help the educational authorities by collecting funds for building and repairing schools, and would assist the medical officer in keeping the villages clean, improving local water supplies and fighting mosquitoes. He might also be called upon to supervise the enumeration of the census, or conduct a locust campaign.

A district officer also had to be something of a civil engineer in order to initiate and build village roads-not easy in a country of either solid rock or deep, rich soil. The most beautiful road in Palestine, which runs from Acre to Safad, was begun by the district officer and the villagers, aided later by a public works foreman and a little dynamite.

Then the ubiquitous motorcar made its appearance and the traffic made it necessary for the government to bring the road up to the standard of a second-class road, until it reached the first-class category. A network of secondary roads was built up in this way throughout the country. Twenty years earlier a village woman would spend the night walking to the town, a basket on her head, to market her produce. Nowadays she could leave her village at dawn in the local bus and, after an hour's run, arrive fresh for the day's bargaining.

Local government took up much time. Control was sometimes irksome to councils, but in exercising control, we did try to maintain their integrity and freedom within prescribed limits and be their friends and guides as well as court of appeal.

As chairman of the District Town Planning Commission, the district commissioner heard appeals from the municipal commissions. Most towns were without public parks and playing fields for want of money given in advance, but the people themselves were largely responsible for much of what was unsatisfactory. Nearly everybody wanted to build a shop on his ground floor, but after the plans were approved and passed, hundreds of contraventions took place each year, and the court procedures were often too long and too tiresome to have offenders prosecuted.

Municipal bodies were helped in varying ways, from criticizing their budgets to arranging receptions. I had induced the Jerusalem Municipal Council to construct a public lavatory for men and women near Zion Square in the centre of the new city to meet what provincial papers described as 'a long felt want'. It had cost some £P 4000 and was fitted up according to Shanks's best specifications. The council, as it neared completion, was justly proud of its latest addition to civic utilities. The new mayor, a Muslim, Mustapha Khalidi,[1] came to see me about the opening. He felt a little diffident about it, yet thought such a mark of progress should not pass unheralded. His Worship caught me when I was in a frivolous mood and, although I had had little experience of similar events, I remembered once having seen in a French comic paper a drawing of a local mayor, assisted by the members of the town council and accompanied by the town brass band and a handful of spectators, performing a like ceremony. All that could be seen of the mayor were His Worship's legs from the feet to the knees and his head and top hat. So, speaking in Arabic, I gravely drew His Worship's attention to the precedent set in France and hinted that that appeared to be the accepted ceremonial. Shocked, and frightened that he might be called to perform a similar rite, His Worship beat a hasty retreat. For once a public building was opened without speeches!

The war naturally brought many extra duties. Finding offices and billets for the military was no small task and brought its own hardships. A woman and two children occupy a basement wanted by the army, who occupy the upstairs room. The woman works all day in an office. She cannot find alternative accommodation. Is she to be turned out? The district commissioner had to decide.

We undertook to distribute flour and organize rationing before this developed into full-time work. In some towns registration had been carried out by the heads of the religious communities and I was pressed to implement the same system in Jerusalem. It sounded simple! But few of the streets had names, let alone numbers. There were many religious communities, and mixed marriages were not unknown. Would the Armenian patriarch agree to accept, as a member of his church, a Bessarabian Jewess married to an Armenian whose origin was Syrian? Would a Jew married to a lady of the Church of the Nazarenes agree to his wife being registered in the Jewish community? Where would a Muslim married to a Jewess, whose children were brought up as Latin Catholics, register his family? In the end I decided that being a spiritually minded bishop, a popular preacher in the mosque, or a devout

1. Mustapha Khalidi was one of six leaders who were arrested by the British and deported to the Seychelles in 1937 after the Arab Higher Committee was declared unlawful.

rabbi did not necessarily make a man a good administrator, or even a tolerable registrar.

As a member of the advisory council I had to examine bills laid before council and to express my opinion upon them. It was my duty to collect, appreciate and convey to the high commissioner every form of public opinion or criticism, whether it was anti-Jew, anti-Arab, pro-Arab, pro-Jew or anti-government — there were never any pro-government.

In the course of a day's work, typical files lying on my table might include a *Report of the Committee Appointed to Enquire into Jewish Ritual Slaughter* (the Holy City has no less than three *shekhita*, or ritual slaughter boards); the sittings of the courts of criminal assizes and my attendance with the chief justice; the *Report of the Custodian of Enemy Properties*; a letter from a gentleman suggesting I allow him to undertake the collection and sale of wastepaper from all houses and, after a suitable commission for himself, present the cash collected to the Red Cross, provided the Red Cross financed the scheme; a letter concerning the question of allowing a young German woman to come out of a detention camp to marry a Swedish subject who was going to Tripoli; a report on distribution in wartime by the Palestine Economic Society; and requests to register an Armenian women's benefit society, to promote a couple of government officers and to deal with repairs in the Church of the Holy Sepulchre.

I would have already dealt with 20 other subjects, for my letter box received 30,000 letters a year. As I started on a fresh pile a note would be handed to me stating that the Coptic bishop was waiting to enter my office to discuss the Coptic pilgrimage from Egypt for Easter. Others would also be waiting.

In the case of a foreigner dying without friends I was responsible for his burial. But, on the other hand, it was my duty to marry all British subjects and my privilege to give the traditional kiss to the bride.

I had a great deal to do with social matters. They ranged from the lady with aspirations, wanting to be invited to an official reception, to impressing upon the head of some religious community that a schismatic member of his congregation must nevertheless be buried in the communal cemetery. I was asked many questions, such as whether an archimandrite takes precedence over an archdeacon, and should both, even if young men, be given the courtesy title of 'The Venerable'.

Personal contact was as essential in Palestine as elsewhere in the East. For years my wife and I were 'at home' every week to receive all sorts and conditions of men and women. At first, among the Arabs, only the Christian ladies attended; but gradually the Muslim ladies ventured forth, having emerged from 'feminine parties only'. Conversation in a dozen languages went on and one had to perform quick mental gymnastics in language, time and place when one switched over from talking French to the Dutch consul on the topic of the Flemish masters to a conversation in Arabic with the Iraqi consul general about the forthcoming date harvest. I would talk in my limited Hebrew about a passage in the Talmud to an Orthodox rabbi as he sipped his tea out of a glass, or chat with a subaltern about a point-to-point held nearby.

For Muslims and Jews a day starts at sunset. For Christians at midnight. There are three days of rest weekly. Each of the three faiths has eight official days of holiday annually when all the banks close. There are four calendars. Therefore for half the year, I never had a complete staff. The only holiday common to all communities was the birthday of His Majesty the King. Except on this day our offices were always open.

The statutory authority of the district commissioner was often ambiguous, yet our practical and personal authority was considerable. Work was arduous, but never dull. I have known occasions when I was made the target of unscrupulous attacks — by the written word, by the spoken word at public meetings, and by bomb and bullet. But on practically every occasion the same people came round to see me privately afterwards and explained that they did not mean it personally. I was often in need of much support. As one village put it, with either sincerity or unconscious humour, on a banner hung up across the road when I was visiting it: 'WELCOME TO OUR PASHA: GOD HELP OUR GOVERNMENT.'

8

The Naked Sword

T he Zionist Organization consisted of 45 autonomous federations, each of which was coextensive with the boundaries of a state. But to meet with the wishes of individuals living within these several boundaries, but subscribing to a definite social, religious or political doctrine, these were allowed to combine into special units apart from the federations. Outside these groups were the Revisionists, created and led by Jabotinsky, who had been arrested for the part he played in the 1920 riots, but who was subsequently pardoned in the general amnesty. Their policy aimed at developing Palestine on both banks of the Jordan with a government of their own.

All these parties had highly organized systems of raising money from self-taxation and from levies upon the rich, called by the Jews *schnorring*. The two main funds are the Jewish Foundation Fund (Keren Hayesod) and the Jewish National Fund (Keren Kayemeth Leisrael), which acquires and holds the land purchased for the Jewish people in perpetuity.

For some years Dr Weizmann had been trying to enlarge the scope of the Zionist Commission; he wished to form a joint Jewish Agency to bring together the socialist groups and US capitalists. He had some success, but the Revisionist Party held aloof. The Labour Party had the largest number of seats, with the Zionists lying second. Communists were excluded and the ultra-Orthodox, the Agudat Israel, excluded itself. This last group looked upon Zionism as a heretical movement, though it liked to share in the benefits it brought. It once went so far as to excommunicate Tel Aviv and to forbid the faithful to set foot therein during the *Purim* festival.

The decision of Turkey to turn her back on Islam, the declaration of a republic and overthrow of the sultan, the abolition of the caliphate and finally the sweeping away of religious endowments, Muslim law and the Arabic script, had passed almost unnoticed in Palestine. Now the *mufti*, taking advantage of a great gathering of Christians on the Mount of Olives of many denominations and countries, presided over by the American Dr Mott, made a violent attack upon the attempts of Christian missionaries to convert Muslims and turn them from their faith.

We had a good deal of trouble with missionary bodies, owing to an Ottoman decree that the religious community a prospective convert was leaving must be allowed an opportunity to dissuade him. The decree was abolished and now all that was required was that a person who changed his faith and wanted the change to have legal effect should register with the district commissioner. This enabled him to gain the benefit of the laws of inheritance of the community he was joining.

Jewish rural settlement was going steadily forward with astounding advantage to the appearance of the countryside. With funds collected in Canada, Ussishkin purchased for the Jewish National Fund the valley of Hefher lying between the Sharon plain and Samaria. Later the Jewish National Fund purchased a large area of swampy land in Haifa Bay, the Emeq Zevulun, and thus a third valley passed into Jewish hands.

Stolid Menahem Ussishkin was more accustomed to everyday clothes than to a 'smoking'. He was invited to dinner at the *Trocadero* by some representative body of London Jews. As his wife and he reached the top of the stairs leading to the dining room, he was confronted by a notice saying 'NO SMOKING'. He returned to his hotel and, having discarded his recently acquired dinner jacket, came back to find his hosts immaculately dressed.

Economically the country was not happy, but some industries, such as cement and soap, were going ahead. Bonds had been bought cheaply by the government and Palestine's share of the Ottoman public debt, with which we were saddled in the peace treaty, was paid off. Local currency based on the pound sterling was introduced and a 5 per cent loan was issued by the Bank of England for £P 4,475,000. But of this sum, £P 1 million was used to pay the British government for capital assets taken over by us, which Winston Churchill, now Chancellor of the Exchequer, had referred to as 'shaking the tree for windfalls'.

Voluntary subscriptions were shrinking, there was a smaller influx of private capital and Palestine could not absorb the numbers seeking admission. Zionist funds had to be diverted from investment in productive capital works to maintenance and welfare services. Lord Plumer was so concerned that he stated that the need for further restriction in immigration was evident as sources of supply were inadequate to meet the economic demands. There was considerable unemployment and some cases of acute distress. In a couple of years 4891 Jews had entered, but 7239 had left permanently, unable to earn a living.

Palestine became the El Dorado of the dragoman and hotel keeper. Some 60,000 tourists came, bringing much wealth. After the day was over the shopkeeper would credit the guide with 10 per cent on every purchase.

We had a visit from Umberto, the crown prince of Italy, ostensibly private but outwardly of the most imperial and ostentatious character.

The consul general let it be known that Umberto had arrived, not only as the Italian crown prince, but also as the Count of Savoy, whose predecessor had raised the siege of Rhodes and in whose memory the Knights of St John wear the eight-pointed white cross, which is included in the arms of the royal family of Italy. He had obviously received instructions from Mussolini to impress himself upon the people and, when he got out of his coach at Jerusalem railway station, he was wearing a light-blue uniform with an exceptionally high collar, two grand cordons crossed over his chest and his breast ablaze with medals. For nearly a week he postured and posed around Jerusalem, but did not endear himself to the mayor when he kept him and his guests waiting for over two hours at a party given in his honour.

The prince visited the Cenacle, the place of the Last Supper, on Maundy Thursday with the *custos*, who gave a peremptory order to the head of the Dajani family, the owners, to remove some carpets so that the crown prince might enter the shrine. This immediately led to a commotion, with the sheikhs shouting and the Italian consul general screaming and the *custos* bawling out that Franciscan rights were being violated. It was an awkward moment and it was some minutes before I could get order and decorum restored.

How different it was to receive a visit from the Princess Royal[1] and

---

1. Princess Mary was the only daughter of King George V and Queen Mary. She married Viscount Lascelles in 1922.

her husband, Lord Harewood, a week or so afterwards. So quiet, so dignified, punctual to the minute, the people took Her Royal Highness to their hearts and gave her a great welcome. An important road was being constructed in the city, so we named it after her — Princess Mary Avenue.

Lord Plumer left, having been unwell for some months. As Mr Amery, the colonial secretary, said, he had given his last ounce of strength to the service of the state.

A few days before Plumer retired, Henry Charles Luke,[2] formerly Harry Charles Joseph Lukach, of Polish-Austrian parentage but of British birth, educated in Vienna, Eton and Oxford, came as chief secretary. He had formerly been assistant to Storrs and had given notable service as a member of three commissions of enquiry and had left on appointment to Sierra Leone. He was a linguist and littérateur and he brought many cultured gifts with him. When Plumer left, Luke was appointed by the colonial secretary to administer the government until the new high commissioner arrived.

World interest in Zionism was sinking. There came an event that was exploited to the full by Colonel Kisch,[3] political secretary of the Jewish Agency.

A storm of protest was raised by the Jews about the action taken by me to preserve the status quo at the Wailing Wall. I was bitterly attacked. The protests were carried all over the world. Lord Plumer would, of course, have clamped down upon the row at once. But there was no Plumer. The agitation lasted for months.

The Western or Wailing Wall is a short portion of the western wall of the Muslim Noble Sanctuary, within the high walls that surround the city. It had formed part of the exterior wall of the ancient Temple area of the Jews. Most of the wall is hidden below the earth or behind medieval Muslim buildings, but this piece, composed of massive undressed blocks of the Herodian period, four rows of Byzantine

2. Henry Charles Luke held a variety of posts in colonial administration before becoming governor of Jerusalem in 1920. He was colonial secretary to Sierra Leone from 1924 to 1928 and returned to Palestine as chief secretary from 1928 to 1930.
3. Colonel Frederick Kisch (1888–1943) was born in India. He joined the Indian Army, was wounded in France and Mesopotamia in the First World War and went to Palestine in 1923, when Chaim Weizmann invited him to be a member of the Zionist Executive. He served as chief engineer of the British Eighth Army in the Second World War and was killed in Tunisia inspecting a German minefield.

blocks, and 13 courses from Saracenic times onwards, is exposed and can be reached by way of a passage through Muslim-owned property.

Upon the rock in the centre of the huge sanctuary, tradition proclaims that Abraham offered Isaac in sacrifice. Some 1000 years ago the Muslims built a shrine, the Dome of the Rock, over this rock. The first Jewish temple, erected by Solomon to the south of this rock, was destroyed by Nebuchadnezzar. The second was built after the return of the Jews from exile and was known as Zerubbalal's Temple. This was replaced by the one built by Herod the Great, which was begun in 20 BC and destroyed by Titus in AD 70. Justinian built a Christian church there, but that too has disappeared. The Muslims built a mosque over the site of the church and named it al-Aqsa, the Farthest, as it was the farthest away from Mecca.

The Jews regard the Wailing Wall as sacred because it formed part of the Temple area, and they believe that the *schekhinah*, or divine spirit, has never departed. The Muslims believe it to be sacred because it forms part of the Noble Sanctuary and because Mohammed tethered his steed, Buraq, in a room in the thickness of the wall when he set forth on his *mihraj*, or celestial journey. The wall is the undoubted property of the Muslims. The pavement opposite it and a cluster of houses facing it, occupied by Moroccan Muslims, are Muslim *waqf* property, that is property dedicated to charitable uses and to the service of God. To this wall, Orthodox Jews turn in thought from all parts of the world, and Orthodox Jerusalem Jews repair to it almost daily, but more particularly on the eve of the Sabbath and holy days, for devotional lamentations. Jews had no legal rights but they claimed ancient customs safeguarded by the status quo.

There had, however, been constant disputes. Controversy had been aggravated in 1918, when Dr Weizmann had suggested to the military governor, Ronald Storrs, that the Zionist Organization should acquire the Moroccan *waqf* houses by exchange of some other property elsewhere to the value of £P 75,000. This would enable the approach to be opened up and secure for the Jews better conditions for free and undisturbed worship.

Under international military law an occupying power cannot allow transfers of land or property. Under Muslim *sharia* law, if all beneficiaries agree, *waqf*s can be exchanged. Nothing came of the proposal. Storrs, after informally sounding the Muslims, reported that it would be unwise to raise the question. But the mischief was done. The Muslims were exasperated and made hostile demonstrations.

Year after year, incident followed incident. The Jews complained that the Moroccan Muslims polluted their pavement and that donkeys carrying burdens disturbed them at their devotions and that boys threw stones. The Muslims complained that the Jews installed tables, seats and benches and tins of water on the pavement.

Matters were not made easier when the Ashkenazi chief rabbi issued a proclamation, after Storrs had ordered Jews to remove some benches, that 'The Holy Sanctum is consecrated to Israel for ever and it should in the end revert to Israel and the Temple be rebuilt with great splendour, as promised by the Prophet Ezekiel.'

That was the explosive state of affairs which had developed and was still developing when I succeeded Storrs. Things came to a head on the Day of Atonement in the autumn of 1928.

The holiest day in the Jewish calendar began at sunset. I went down to see that all was well with the pious Jews, who would be beginning their devotions. I looked down from the Muslim religious courts, above the wall, to see what was happening without disturbing the devout. The courts were full of excited Muslims; I observed that various innovations violating the status quo had been introduced by the Jews at the wall.

The Muslim guardian of the *waqf* complained of these, so I went down to the wall and told Noah Gladstone, the Jewish beadle, what I had seen — notably a dividing screen fastened to the wall and pavement so that women could be divided from the men, as in an Orthodox synagogue, and an Ark much bigger than customary — and gave him instructions to have the screen, at any rate, removed before continuation of devotions on the following morning. He promised to remove them and I accepted his assurance; but I also took the precaution of informing the British police inspector that in the event of Noah failing to carry out his undertaking it would be his business to see that the screen was nonetheless removed.

Noah did not keep his promise. So the police removed the screen. Opposition was shown and one rabbi, who clung onto the screen, was carried bodily, with the screen, outside.

Justice had been done. The status quo had been preserved with as little force as possible. The action of the police, though right and proper, could not be expected to be popular with the Jews and, as I was responsible for it, they attacked me furiously. Led by Colonel Kisch, political secretary of the Zionist Commission, a deputation accompanied by the two chief rabbis was received by the officer administering the government, Mr H. C. Luke, and a bitter personal attack was made upon me by Kisch. Meetings of protest were organized all over the country. The Palestine government felt it necessary to issue a memorandum on the subject.

The Jerusalem Jewish weekly paper published an article entitled 'Holy of Holies Desecrated', expressing the opinion that the removal of the screen (with rabbi) was a blacker spot in the history of mankind than the religious policy of the Inquisition in Spain. It went on to express astonishment that I should trample underfoot the most sacred observations of the Jews merely in order to earn a transitory smile from the Supreme Muslim Council.

The agitation spread. The Zionist official paper, the *New Judaean*, wrote: 'It is revolting to think that anyone holding a responsible position should have the insolence to violate the religious feelings of a community to that extent.' Telegrams were sent to Jews and Jewish organizations all over the world instructing them to denounce His Majesty's Government. At a meeting in New York attended by 10,000 Jews a resolution was passed to the effect that 'Keith-Roach must go'.

The agitation was far more political than pious. The devout Jews who prayed at the wall took little part in it. Rabbi Zonnenfeld, head of the Agudat Israel, came to my weekly 'at home' and told me that he had been that day to the wall to pray for me because of the personal abuse to which I was subjected. The Sephardi chief rabbi came to my house and told me that he had been asked to join the deputation falsely, and added: '*Vous avez très bien fait et tous les ordres que vous avez donnés étaient très justes.*'

The matter was debated in Parliament and a White Paper was issued defending my action. Complaints became worldwide and I received over 400 abusive letters. Many years afterwards, Colonel Kisch gave me a copy of Lord Melchett's moving book *Thy Neighbour* and inscribed it 'To K-R, the best of neighbours'; he admitted that he had organized the world complaint, adding, 'A few telegrams did it.'[4]

---

4. Lord Melchett (1868–1930) served in the First World War and afterwards entered politics and became a writer. *Thy Neighbour* was published in 1936.

To this conflict of ideas Sir John Chancellor[5] arrived in October 1928 as high commissioner. He had an unfortunate start.

As Government House had been evacuated because of the earthquake, we arranged a reception tent at the Jaffa Gate. A violent storm broke out as he arrived. A police escort fell from his horse in front of the carriage. He and his wife were blown about, the tent leaked and water dripped down upon his immaculate uniform and Lady Chancellor caught a severe cold. The butler, who had married Lady Plumer's maid, fell down into a basement coming out of a hairdresser's shop next morning, and, hitting his head on the wall, was killed instantly.

I presented 500 guests and remembered all their names, titles and distinctions except one. By an odd lapse of memory I forgot the name of the American consul and his wife, with whom I had been dining the night before.

Sir John was an imposing man with greying hair and well-defined features. He was strikingly handsome in uniform and gave an impression of a good-looking Shakespearean actor. He was a first-rate administrator.

The Arabs lost no time in asking him to secure a form of government in which the people of the country could participate. The Jews appealed to the League of Nations about the Wailing Wall.

During the following months I repeatedly asked government to define rights at the Wailing Wall 'so that a situation intolerable to both parties might be made clear'. For various reasons no action was taken by the high commissioner.

June 1929 arrived. Chancellor left on leave for England. Luke governed in his stead. I left shortly on leave. A couple of months later, when returning, I talked with two Jewish Labour leaders on the ship. They were very confident that union between Jew and Arab was drawing closer. I said that I doubted this. They failed to appreciate that the

---

5. Sir John Chancellor (1870–1952) was born in Edinburgh and educated at Blair Lodge, Polmont, and the Royal Military Academy in Woolwich. He was commissioned in the Royal Engineers in 1890 and after service in India and a period at Staff College he became assistant military secretary to the Committee of Imperial Defence in 1904 and secretary of the Colonial Defence Committee in 1906. He was governor of Mauritius from 1911 to 1916, governor of Tobago from 1916 to 1921 and first governor of Rhodesia from 1923 to 1928. After his period in Palestine he served on a number of governmental committees and as a director of various companies.

stronger the hold Hebrew had on the Jewish population, the wider grew the gulf between the races.

I found a violent row was in progress about the Wailing Wall.

Luke had given permission for a procession of Jewish young men to march to the wall, where they illegally raised a Zionist flag, sang the Jewish national anthem, and shouted 'The wall is ours.' This enraged the Arabs, who on the following day were allowed to hold a counter-demonstration 2000-strong. The Muslims shouted, 'There is no God but God; the religion of Mohammed came with the sword.' They burnt a table of the beadle's and some devotional books.

Within a few days after I returned it was Friday. Although the *mufti* had no religious training, he was himself a very astute and shrewd man who read a good deal and did his best to educate himself in the intricacies of Islamic law. As *mufti*, he was looked upon as the head of the Muslims rather than as a teacher of the faith. He played his cards well and utilized his position to the best advantage. Despite the theory that in Islam there are no organized clergy, there are in practice religious teachers, *imams*. In the Holy City the right to preach from the *minbar* at the Friday midday prayer was reserved as the hereditary right of a certain Jerusalem family. As the *mufti* was in command of the money that paid for the service, it was but natural that he should decide what the weekly discourse should be about.

The *khatib*, or preacher, dressed in a flowing cloak, advanced with dignity, preceded by a *kavass* striking the ground with a stave. The colour of the robes of the preacher in Jerusalem is green, for the Ashraf or Sherifian Party; in Nablus black, the Abased colour; in other places white, the Omayyad. These three colours with red added form the Arab flag, which means 'We defend them with our blood.'

The four *muezzins* left the minarets, entered the mosque and intoned the call to prayer. The preacher, taking the stave from the *kavass*, mounted the pulpit. It is an old custom at Hebron for the preacher to hold a sword in his hand when preaching. In Jerusalem a famous sword is carried on the Prophet's birthday. It has a handle of wood and a long steel blade. Shoeless, sitting in serried rows, line upon line, the hearers, in whose blood for centuries the spoken rather than the written word has been the means of instruction, can easily and with dramatic force have their feelings worked up to a pitch of religious fanaticism. This Friday the preacher, Saad el Din, carried the naked sword. A violent address followed. After glorifying God and thanking Him, the sheikh touched upon the theme of the Jews and their aggression and he called upon the faithful to defend Islam. He said:

> If we give way an inch to the Jews in regard to their demands at the Wailing Wall, they will ask for the Mosque of Aqsa; if we give them the Mosque of al-Aqsa they will demand the Dome of the Rock; if we give them the Dome of the Rock they will demand the whole of Palestine, and having gained the whole of Palestine they will proceed to turn us Arabs out of our country. I ask you now to take the oath of God the Great to swear by your right hand that you will not hesitate to act when called upon to do so, and that you will, if need be, fight for the Faith and the Holy Places to the death.

The vast majority of the congregation held up their hands in response and swore before Almighty God that they were ready to shed their blood if need be. 'Then go,' said the preacher, 'pounce upon your enemies and kill that you in doing so may obtain Paradise.' Emotion ran so high that many rushed out of the mosque sobbing and declaring that they could not pray. The crowd cried, '*Al bilad biladna wa el Yahoud kilabna*' ('The country is our country and the Jews are our dogs') and, with knives and clubs, rushed towards the Jaffa Gate attacking shops and knocking about any Jews they met, crying aloud, '*Din Mohammed ain bi seif*' ('The religion of Mohammed came with the sword'). Slaughter followed. The riot spread quickly and at Hebron 60 Jews were murdered in a ferocious attack made on the ghetto; there was also wanton destruction. At Safad 45 Jews were killed or wounded and there was a repetition of destruction. At Jaffa the Jews paid back something in an attack on Arabs.

The situation was alarming in the extreme. We had no troops and there were only 175 British officers and men in a total police force of 1500 for all Palestine. Troops were sent from Egypt under the command of Brigadier Dobbie, who was subsequently to become famous for his gallantry at Malta. The few British police were exhausted. Each man had been doing ten men's work for two days when the first of the troops arrived by air. I had gathered everyone I could into a volunteer police force; among those helping us were a number of theological students, led by their tutor Graham-Brown, who some years later became the Anglican bishop in Jerusalem.

Dobbie[6] had the military strength and was imperturbable. He gave a sense of moral force to everyone. Full of Christian faith, he was frequently found on his knees in the office. Refreshed in spirit and in mind and a decision taken, he was resolute. In Jerusalem the water supply had been cut and the lighting system as well. There were no meat or food supplies for some days and, as no scavengers turned up, there was soon an accumulation of filth in the streets. There were similar reports from other places. There were the wildest rumours around and scores of untrue stories circulated about 'the apathy and ineptitude of the administrative officials', but we were doing our utmost with the extraordinary little resource at our command.

Before order was restored 135 Jews were killed and 350 wounded. Arab casualties were 116 killed and 232 wounded, but many of these casualties were caused by rifle fire of the military and police in suppressing the rioters.

The Jews complained bitterly that the Arabs at Hebron had mutilated the bodies, dead or alive, of their victims. Arab opinion resented this and said that Arabs did not behave like that, there had only been 'straightforward killing'. So Chancellor actually appointed a neutral committee of medical men — Strathearn and Orr-Ewing with Stuart of the Medical Department — to go and examine the corpses. On an extraordinarily hot day they arrived masked in Abraham's city and began the task of exhumation. But after a few bodies had been exhumed, the job had to be stopped for the corpses had rotted.

The British government now appointed an international commission under the chairmanship of Mr Jules Lefgren, ex-prime minister of Sweden, to hold an enquiry into the rival claims at the Wailing Wall.

Before the opening session I accompanied the commissioners to the site. I had never seen so many Jewish worshippers before, other than on the Day of Atonement. Prayers and lamentations were delivered with unwonted vigour and there was a continuous cry of fervour and devotion. Inside the *Haram al-Sherif*, the Muslim area, a number of Indian mats had been laid down under the arches leading to the room where Mohammed's steed is believed to have been tethered. The stairs were

---

6. Brigadier William Dobbie was governor of Malta from 1940 to 1942.

covered with carpets and the floor concealed by costly rugs. A well-known character, the ex-town crier, dressed in a green *jibbah*, added a picturesque touch to the sanctity of the place.

At the Moroccan Muslim *zawiya* outside the wall on the Jewish side, everything was extremely clean and no disturbing odours came from the shrine. Several Moroccans were reading the Koran or were disposed in postures of prayer. All had been stage-managed to the best advantage.

The oral evidence took three weeks to hear. I was the last witness and was cross-examined by both Jews and Arabs. The addresses of the Jewish and Arab delegates that followed reached a standard of sincerity and oratory I have never heard equalled in Palestine.

The Jews declared that the wall, from which the divine presence has never departed, even in its ruin, is a haven of religious meditation; and whenever a Jewish heart is stirred, it betakes itself to the sacred spot and finds comfort. The nation has been despoiled of all that was dear, the tombs of its great kings, the holy prophets, the site of its glorious Temple. Only this mute wall remains. We have no design on the *Haram*, which is holy to the Muslims. We only want to continue the age-old tradition to pray to our Maker at the place that is holy to us.

The Muslims replied. The Arabs even in the first days of Islam turned towards the site of the Temple when praying because it was an object of veneration to the Prophet. The status quo is essentially the preservation of privileges and protection from encroachments. The Jews believe they possess by inheritance certain rights in Palestine, that it belongs to them, and that the name should be changed to Eretz Israel, the Land of Israel.

The *buraq*, or pavement in front of the wall, has been a pious foundation for over 600 years and is associated with the *mihraj*, or celestial journey of the Prophet. The site of the Temple of Solomon is now occupied by the third holiest place in Islam. It is by simple tolerance of Muslims that Jews may come and weep at the foot of the wall. And Christians regard the Christian Holy Places as their inalienable heritage.

Who would dare in Europe to expropriate a trust consecrated in perpetuity and adjacent to a Roman Catholic church, in order to erect a Protestant church with a party wall to the Roman Catholic church? Ask the government of Rome to expropriate a Roman Catholic shrine, and immediately afterwards give it to the Jewish community to erect a

synagogue there; or, at the request of Protestants, ask the Vatican to
concede them a piece of land adjacent to St Peter's in order to erect a
temple of worship there! Is there a Pope who would accept all the gold
in the world and acquiesce to such a fantastic suggestion? We stand by
the status quo.

Six months later the report of the commission was published. It
confirmed my interpretation of the status quo in every detail.

January found us engaged in war against a formidable and tenacious
enemy — locusts. Colossal swarms appeared in Palestine, Transjordan
and Sinai. In Sinai, Jarvis Bey called for the Egyptian Army to come
and help. We employed 10,000 Arabs in the fight. Flying locusts have a
certain amount of beauty, silvering the air with the shimmering of their
wings. But crawlers are a dank and loathsome pestilence. I saw the
earth for miles covered by a terrible living sea of insects creeping
relentlessly forward, submerging everything in their insatiable progress.
They missed nothing and they spared nothing. They stopped the trains
because the wheels could not bite onto the rails. Once the crawlers
became hoppers and developed their wings, the insects took to the air
and devoured every green thing, until the time came for the females to
drive the long horn of their ovipositors into the ground and hatch out
two hundredfold of eggs.

We tried ploughs, zinc sheeting, flame throwers and poisoned bait. At
one stage we built up a movable zinc barrier stretching from the Mediterranean Sea across the plain, up the mountains, down the mountains,
below sea level to the Dead Sea. The best weapon proved to be zinc
barriers to stay the march, and bran mixed with sodium arsenic, molas-
ses and water for them to feed upon. We used a couple of hundred tons
of it before we got control. Storks flying northwards to the chimney
pots of Eastern Europe came to our aid in scores of thousands to feast
upon the plague. They were a disgusting sight gorging and evacuating
simultaneously. On the whole they did more harm than good by scatter-
ing the swarms. Having taken a not inconsiderable part in the
campaign, I came to the conclusion that the only good locust is a dead
locust, whether buried, burned or poisoned. No sooner had we coped
with the locusts than we had a plague of fieldmice in Galilee. We

mobilized for battle again, used poisoned bait and smoked them out with gasses over an area of a quarter of a million acres.

An extremely accurate census conducted by Eric Mills showed that the population had increased considerably. There were now 760,000 Muslims, 174,000 Jews and 89,000 Christians.

A rough census had been made eight years before when the population had been estimated at 590,000 Muslims, 83,800 Jews and 73,000 Christians. In ten years 100,000 Jews had come in and 27,000 Jewish immigrants had left. The Jews had established 52 settlements on land purchased by the Jewish National Fund and every acre had been paid for to the Arab owners.

Some 27,000 Muslims, 31,000 Jewish and 14,000 Christian children were receiving education. Unfortunately the cost of trying to maintain public security was so abnormally high that the amount that could be found for health and educational services was only a third of the provision for police services.

Agriculture was making a good deal of headway and communications were improved by 700 kilometres of all-weather roads. Jews were using modern machinery and making full use of their various agricultural experimental stations.

They had imported many hundreds of Friesian cattle and begun scientific dairy farming. Government efforts to improve the local breed of horses were unsuccessful. We had imported stallions from the Crabbet Arab stud in England, but they all contracted 'dourine', a type of syphilis, after serving local mares. They had to be killed or castrated.

Despite the rioting the Arabs had improved in every way. They were better fed and their children were more robust. Some excellent British agricultural officers had helped them with their husbandry and were distributing selected seeds from the government farms. The farmers owned more animals. They still threshed by beasts treading out the corn, but their crops were heavier. Terraces were being rebuilt and fruit trees were being planted. Better attention was being given to olive trees. Orange groves were better planted and cultivated. Yields had increased. A seedless Jaffa was now being grown. But the Arab burden of debt still remained.

The Dead Sea had started to come to life. Novomeysky,[7] a Russian-Jewish engineer, after heated controversy, had been awarded a concession to exploit the salts and extract potash by solar evaporation. As he employed both Arabs and Jews impartially, the works brought a good deal of wealth to those regions.

A commission of enquiry into the cause of the riots had recommended that a statement of policy should be defined by the British government in clear and positive terms. Sir John Hope Simpson, a former vice chairman of the Refugees Settlement Commission in Greece, was invited to investigate and report on land and immigration.

Simpson reported that, under present methods of Arab cultivation, there was no margin of land available for settlement by new immigrants, with the exception of the undeveloped land held by various Jewish agencies, of which there was a large reserve. The position of the Arab cultivator was no better than it had been under the Turkish regime. The Jewish settlers had every advantage that capital, science and organization could give. He recommended an active policy of agricultural development, as a result of which the existing agricultural population's standard of life would improve. Then not less than 20,000 Jewish families of settlers from outside could come in.

The prime minister, Mr Ramsay MacDonald,[8] made a statement in the House of Commons to the effect that it was useless for Jewish leaders to press His Majesty's Government to conform its policy with regard to immigration and land to the aspirations of the most uncompromising section of Zionist opinion and equally useless for Arab leaders to maintain their demand for a constitution that would render it impossible to carry out the double undertaking. The mandatory was responsible for safeguarding the civil and religious rights of all the inhabitants of Palestine. Jewish institutions employed only Jews on works of cultivation. The suspension of immigration under the labour

---

7. Moshe Novomeysky (1873–1961) was born in Siberia and trained as an engineer. He settled in Palestine in 1920 and founded the Palestine Potash Company, which became the most important enterprise of its kind in the Middle East. He was also a founder of the Palestine Economic Society.

8. Ramsay MacDonald began his political career as secretary of the Labour Party in 1900 and became chairman of the Parliamentary Labour Party and leader of the opposition in 1922. He became prime minister in 1924 and served again from 1929 to 1935.

schedule was justified and it would be strictly controlled in future. The government intended to set up a legislative council.

The Jews were stunned. There were cries of 'Shameful betrayal,' and 'England does not want us to build up Palestine.' Leaders of many British parties attacked the prime minister and said that his declaration was a flagrant breach of international conventions. Dr Weizmann and the American, Felix Warburg, resigned from the Jewish Agency.

Mr MacDonald wrote a letter to Dr Weizmann with 'the object of removing misconceptions'. The Arabs considered that this letter went back on the promises given in the House and, with the gift of uncommon quickness of mind, referred to it as the 'black letter'. The old phrase used as a standard of honour, 'the word of an Englishman', was never heard again.

By the end of the year immigration had fallen to 4000 and 600 Jews had left.

Although the damage by fieldmice had been considerable, and the winter and summer crops had been a failure, and grazing was precarious, there were signs that the turn of the tide of depression had come and that the prospects for the incoming high commissioner would be easier economically than they had been for his two immediate predecessors.

Sir John Chancellor left a disappointed man. He had always found the task unwieldy. At a farewell reception given by the mayor of Jerusalem he said: 'I came hoping to increase the country's prosperity and happiness. I am leaving with my ambition unfulfilled. The conditions have been against me.'

9

Dr Jekyll and Mr Hyde

Major-General Arthur Wauchope[1] was the next high commissioner. He moved into the new Government House, which his predecessor had enjoyed for a month. It is a beautiful building and, as one comes up from Jericho, it looks like a sleeping lion guarding the city.

Since Ramsay Macdonald had made his statement in the House of Commons yet another expert, a director of co-operatives in the Punjab, had come to investigate and had expressed his views. The consensus was remarkable. All agreed that immigration should be slowed down. They stated that it was futile to urge upon Arab peasants improved practices involving heavy outlay for equipment. Arab backwardness was due partly to their character and partly to hampering debt. Stability of character is of slow growth, but without it there could be no hope of freedom from debt. A drastic land-transfer ordinance that would in effect prohibit land purchase by Jews was recommended. The Jews

---

1. Major-General Arthur Wauchope (1874–1947) was born in Edinburgh and educated at Repton. In 1893 he was commissioned into the Renfrew militia battalion of the Argyll and Sutherland Highlanders and in 1896 he was gazetted a regular second lieutenant in the Black Watch. In the Boer War he was badly wounded at Magersfontein. In the First World War, by then a major, he commanded his battalion at Loos and then in Mesopotamia. Wauchope was promoted to major-general in 1923 and was briefly a military member of the overseas settlement delegation to Australia and New Zealand. He served as chief of the British section of the military inter-allied Commission of Control in Berlin (1924–27), as general officer commanding the 44th Home Counties Division (1927–29) and in Northern Ireland (1929–31). He was high commissioner for Palestine from 1931 to 1938.

were extremely angry and described it as an attempt to re-establish the medieval institution of *adscriptus glebae* (serfs attached to the soil).

Wauchope ignored these restrictive recommendations. He gave literal and generous interpretation to the policy outlined by Winston Churchill in his White Paper of ten years before. During the next five years he admitted 190,000 Jews, double the number that entered during the previous decade. Colonization leapt ahead and fresh settlements sprang up everywhere.

From the expanding revenues derived from the influx, Wauchope hoped to keep the Arabs happy by assisting their agriculture in every way possible and also by exempting them from rural taxation on some pretext or other, such as drought, poor crops or falls in prices. During the ensuing few years he let them off no less than £P 600,000 in rural taxes and granted £P 150,000 in agricultural loans — repayment was not called for.

It was no use district commissioners expostulating verbally, or by letter, about the exemptions from taxation. All they received were snubs from a brilliant letter-writer, or else they were ignored. The whole structure of government was undermined and, eventually, we were unable to collect any rural taxes worth mentioning.

Arthur Wauchope was a little man with long silvery hair and a habit of holding his head on one side with his mouth open, looking into space. He had a delicate frame and had been severely wounded in two wars. He had an iron and autocratic will and was quite unmoved by murder or loss of life. During the war he had commanded the Black Watch and then a composite brigade. After the war was over he had commanded the British troops in Northern Ireland.

He was most unreasonable to the heads of departments and often very rude. They would come to me with tears in their eyes saying they could not carry on under his treatment. He was amazingly active inspecting peasants' houses or some farming experiment, arguing with and laying down the law to the director of Customs, or port manager, about whether orange boxes should be stacked in the sheds three or four high, advising the general manager on railway freight charges, overriding the director of agriculture about sowing wheat or castrating scrub bulls, casting doubt on the treasurer's figures, or else giving orders direct to a district officer about tax collection.

He was immensely flattered when he was called the friend of the *fellah* (peasant), and also when the secretary of state praised him in parliament for being his own minister of agriculture.

Undoubtedly he had a flair for farming and tree-planting, and enriched Government House garden. He loved making experiments, some of which were most successful, such as cutting down centuries-old olive trees in Galilee and replanting the main stems without roots in Government House garden — 98 per cent lived. He continually over-rode his experts.

Proceedings at legislative council meetings became a farce. Once Harold Crosbie, an experienced and able district commissioner of Jaffa, received a severe reprimand in writing for having asked that his opinion might be recorded in the minutes. He had dared to disagree with Wauchope.

Gradually megalomania possessed him. Signs of this weakness had already shown themselves in France, when he was commanding a battalion in the trenches. He designed and had made in England his own personal war medal, which he 'awarded' to men whom he thought merited distinction, until he was ordered to refrain from assuming the royal prerogative.

But apart from little Arthur's almost brutal behaviour to the officials, whom he worked to the bone — calling for reports on every conceivable subject and, after reading them superficially, casting them aside — in his own house he was a perfect host and gave the humblest official a warm reception. He made all his guests feel really welcome. He enhanced the beauty of Government House. His table was always as well laid-out as if a woman had seen to it and, to add to its glories, he had borrowed some mess silver from his old regiment, the Black Watch. Champagne flowed at every party. He loved and really knew a great deal about music and he encouraged the arts in every way. He gave a hunt ball in Lent and had hounds walking about his ballroom. He authorized a charge of £P 1 a ticket, but he paid the entire cost and had the proceeds given to the Hunt Committee. He showed kindness to those in trouble and devoted the whole of his private income, which was considerable, to Palestine. This little man, with his intolerance and his charm, his bursts of temper, his calculated shrewdness, his inconsistencies, whose many kindnesses were legion, was a living example of Dr Jekyll and Mr Hyde.

I was appointed district commissioner of Northern Palestine just before Sir Arthur Wauchope arrived. The district consisted of Samaria, Galilee and Phoenicia. My headquarters were in Haifa.

My predecessor had come from Africa. A sick and timid man, he had lost his grip and I found collection of taxes upon urban property two years in arrears. I asked who was the principal offender and learned that it was the Christian Arab deputy mayor, who had not paid for some years. He owed over £P 400.

I had a demand note sent, calling upon him to pay within ten days. Nothing happened, except that on the last day he called on me on some pretext and, just as he was leaving, casually mentioned his taxes, coupled with an account of his long and arduous service to the public. I agreed cordially with him about how satisfying public service could be, expressed surprise at any taxes being left unpaid, and asked if our figures were correct. He said they were not disputed, so, as I led him to the door, I asked: 'Then why not pay?'

A reminder was sent, followed by a red note demanding payment within a week, or his movable property would be sold. This brought his bishop along. He had the longest hair I have seen on any man, flowing to his waist. As he sipped his coffee he spoke of the temporality of this life and the difficulties of living according to Christian standards. When I had acquiesced, His Lordship skilfully brought the conversation round to this prominent member of his flock and his long labours for the town and the efforts that he was making to educate his children. As the youngest child was over 20 I said that I hoped this hardship was only transitory and added that, while I was only too happy to talk about His Lordship's spiritual duties, I could not discuss the financial affairs of the deputy mayor with anyone.

I gave a couple of days' grace, then had a seizure order placed on his household furniture. The Arab took to his bed. So I sent the town crier out to advertise the sale on the following day. An hour before the time of the sale his son rushed round to my office and paid in £P 100 on account. I called the sale off. Within a week he had paid up all arrears. I sent for the municipal engineer and ordered the whole amount to be spent on making up the road leading to the deputy mayor's house. I had no more bother. Within a year all arrears, amounting to about £P 40,000, were collected.

As soon as I had got acquainted with the district I began to get a house ready for my wife, for she was then in England. We had had a fair share of trouble. Our elder son, after winning an exhibition at Winchester, had been ill. Our younger son had had severe pneumonia and, after many months of treatment, still had a tube in his back. We had lost our third baby. These domestic upheavals had caused us constant separations and we were eagerly looking forward to being together again.

A telegram arrived from England saying that she had had a stroke. I left by plane. An engine failed before we got to Cyprus and, next day, we crashed into the sea. In another plane we crawled into Taranto harbour and I finished my journey by train. My wife was in a coma and paralysed on one side. After months of treatment, she was able to walk a little, but she was never able to see the home I had prepared for us. So on my return I gave it up and went and lived with the German sisters at the convent of St Charles of Borromeo on Carmel. What I owe to these women can never be repaid.

I failed to appreciate why suffering from perpetual prickly heat in summer should add to the nuns' piety, so, after a few years' residence, aided and abetted by the Revd Prince George of Saxony, who was conducting a retreat, I tried, alas, unsuccessfully, to get the mother house in Germany to sanction the adoption of habits of cream nuns-veiling instead of the five or six obligatory garments of heavy black serge and thick black knitted stockings. We did, however, achieve the acceptance of a few rubber hot-water bottles for winter.

My wife's illness completely changed our lives. For her, six years of enforced inactivity, for me, no longer a brilliant woman by my side who shared every risk and adventure. From now onwards, and for the first time, I had to play for safety.

One hot Sunday afternoon soon after my arrival in Haifa, the air superintendent of Imperial Airways called upon me. He was studying the problem of starting a seaplane service to India. He had turned down Haifa as a base and wanted ideas. I suggested the Sea of Galilee and, much as I sought sleep, I drove him to Tiberias and showed him the possibilities. In two or three weeks' time an alighting place was marked out with buoys and the flying boat came down safely. The pilot then took on board Dr Herbert Torrance of the Scottish Mission Hospital and myself and, with the crew, we had the distinction of being the first mortals to rise from the sacred sea. It was an unforgettable experience to look down over Galilee and see the Jordan river twisting on its tortuous course to the Dead Sea.

The lake was soon given up in favour of the Dead Sea because, while flying boats could safely ride out sudden storms, which are peculiar to the Galilee valley and swoop swiftly over the low-lying sheet of water, one storm caught a connecting land machine that was pegged down to the ground and in a few minutes stripped it. All but the engine was destroyed.

A year or two later Tiberias was hit by a cloudburst. Two inches of rain fell in under half an hour. A sheet of water a metre high came rushing down the surrounding hills, broke through the walls and engulfed the little town. I reached Tiberias within a few hours and found indescribable havoc — 27 people were dead, trapped like rats in sewers. Sewage, furniture, food, corpses, holy books, clothing and bedding were scattered everywhere in sodden masses. The streets were choked with mud and boulders. In some lanes and alleys the water was still over a metre high. Next day about noon, indigo clouds smothered the hills and the same thing happened again, except that as the town was evacuated, there were no dead. The surroundings were crowded with a mass of hungry, wet, moaning and weeping, hysterical people.

It was clear that there was only one thing to be done to safeguard the future; to open up a couple of roads across the town so that prospective torrents could rush through it. Communications were cut. The high commissioner was in Egypt. To write and ask permission from the officer acting for him would have meant delay and possible reference to the Colonial Office. It was a question of now or never while the people were still evacuated and suffering from dread and shock. I told the public works engineer from Haifa to obtain half a ton of gelignite. I showed him roughly where I wanted the roads cut and said: 'Start at once.'

Many of the houses were badly damaged, but as it happened there was a perfectly sound one at the top of the proposed road, which it was essential should be pulled down. It was full of unevacuated people.

They refused to move. The engineer put in the charge, a small one, and then lost heart and nerve and refused to fire it. I was adamant. While the families screamed from the balconies and windows I got a British policeman to fire the charge. The effect was instantaneous. The families rushed out of the house and left.

In three or four days 97 houses were blown up. The havoc was many times worse than the floods. Luckily the stench was awful and kept people away. I was glad of this, especially when I had to blow up a mosque at the end of one of the roads. The stench and filth remained so appalling and the heat so overpowering that I lost all appetite and the only food I could swallow was dry biscuits and, for some unaccountable reason, sardines.

When communications were restored and it was all over, I told the government what I had done and got sufficient money to clear the debris and build the roads. I had to go on leave and H. M. Foot[2] gallantly superintended the next phase. The mass of tumbled-down buildings was dumped into the sea and, for the first time in centuries, Tiberias could boast of a sea walk, which has become its popular promenade and centre for coffee, which is drunk to the creak of an oar or the plash of water against rock. We assessed the value of all the houses that were destroyed and paid compensation. The whole thing cost £P 37,000.

There were many other activities. A government loan had enabled Samuel's plan for a harbour at Haifa to be begun. When the question of putting the work out to tender came up, Mussolini claimed that Italy, as one of the mandating nations, had the right to insist on tenders from Italian firms being accepted. Great Britain countered this assertion by deciding that the work should be done departmentally. A Harbour Department was formed and the consulting engineers Rendal, Palmer and Tritton were appointed to direct the construction. A large area was enclosed by two stone breakwaters, one a couple of kilometres long. Within the two arms, the sand was dredged and many acres of land reclaimed, so that from the value of the fresh land a considerable sum was obtained, which went to pay for the cost of the harbour. I was consulted frequently about labour and rates of pay. It all meant extra work.

2. Hugh Foot, later Lord Caradon, brother of Labour Party leader, Michael Foot, subsequently became a colonial governor.

We had a great day of ceremonies arranged for the opening, but, because of some political wrangle, the whole thing was boycotted by the Arabs and the triumphant little ship, *Lancastrian Prince* of the Prince Line, freshly painted and dressed overall, drew in alongside empty quays. That did not, however, prevent the first two-way broadcast of an exchange between the secretary of state and the high commissioner, in which no mention was made from the quayside of empty chairs or piles of uneaten turkeys, which were later sold at knockdown prices.

As many kings had marched their armies up and down the shores, I named a 25-metre road opened up on the reclaimed area 'Kingsway' and paid tribute to the Crusaders, as well as the engineers, by naming one of the principal gates to the harbour 'Palmer's Gate'. To commemorate the assembly of both battalions of the Seaforth Highlanders, I named a road leading to the barracks and the sea Seaforth Road.

The government granted a building site for a sailors' institute and the British Sailors' Society built an excellent one. The Princess Royal graciously inaugurated the site.

No political events hindered the laying of the pipeline from Kirkuk oilfields by the Iraq Petroleum Company. It was begun at both ends. The physical difficulties were enormous; mile after mile of waterless desert, square miles of land strewn with lava ranging from pieces as small as one's head to thousands of boulders weighing a couple of tons or more apiece. Everything had to be transported and motors were the means used, from small pick-ups to 40-wheeled Marmon Herrington trucks for carrying the pipes.

George Dunkley arranged the supplies and smoothed the political problems and Stuckey, an American from Houston, Texas, was the engineer in charge. Money seemed no object, but Stuckey knew what he wanted and got it: a double line to the Mediterranean. He completed 1200 miles in under four years and, by enabling the line to start earning money 15 months earlier than the estimate, he saved the company well over a million pounds. Stuckey had a delightful and terse wit and once, describing a man to me, said: 'Governor, if that man's brains were made of dynamite and there was an explosion, it wouldn't part his hair.'

I went out to look at the progress. Bumping, banging, jolting, our cars forced their way. Huge boulders and rocks as large as pumpkins or small as cricket balls, littered the ground wherever we tried to go. There were innumerable *wadis*, dried-up watercourses, and low hills. On a low mud flat, which water had so levelled and the sun so thoroughly baked that the going was like travelling on smooth steel, there was suddenly ahead a fissure wide enough to swallow a camel. There were camel skeletons and rusted burnt-out chassis strewn along the way. There were also bad gullies before reaching Rutbah Wells, dug by the Roman Legions.

The Bedu, who for centuries had wandered over the desert virtually alone, or with their wives, children and herds, were actually driving small tractors!

The technique had been built up in the West by trial and error and it was astonishing how quickly the Americans managed to teach the Bedu to use machinery. Englishmen could not have done it.

In sandy areas a caterpillar tractor drew a huge wheel with vanes like an ancient windmill which, going forward an inch at a time, scraped a trench three feet deep and hauled the cut soil up in little buckets on an endless belt and dropped it at the side of the trench. When sand gave way to rock this almost human wheel stopped working, lifted up the scraper and went further forward, leaving the rock to be excavated by men. Compressor-drills driven by portable engines made holes that were fired by gelignite, and the crumbled rock was shovelled away by Bedu who had just learned to use a shovel.

Pipes were brought up a day or two ahead of the excavating parties. Perfect rhythm was maintained. Pipes were set up on trestles in lengths of six or eight and tacked together by three patches. They were then welded together by husky lads from Texas who, in addition to food and lodging, earned salaries larger than many a cabinet minister of a Balkan state. As the welder got going, the pipes were gradually turned by gangs, so as to enable him to do the welding from the top. One welder in a nine-hour day electrically welded 73 pipes and gained the world's record. The joints have to stand a pressure of 750 pounds per square inch and when the line was tested only six leaked.

The pipes were painted and a coating of hot asphalt rubbed on as it was poured out of a can by a Bedu walking backwards along the pipe. A hand roll, to which a gigantic roll of brown paper was attached, was rolled round the pipe by four men until the pipe was enclosed in brown paper. It was then lowered into the ditch and put to bed. It became the longest parcel in the world, 5500 miles of continuous wrapping paper

18 inches wide. Another machine then came along and shovelled in the soil from the side of the trench. It was followed by a body of 'sextons' who completed the job.

The sea line at Haifa was welded separately and carried by dollies or trucks, which were whisked away at the water's edge as the end of the line was drawn into the sea by ropes fastened to an anchored ship. Many of us went down to see the unique sight. It was an unforgettable triumph. As the last job, welding the sea line to the main, was completed, Stuckey's only comment was 'just another sea line'.

With plenty of work available, paid for from loan funds, the Iraq Petroleum Company and other outside sources, the Arabs had never been so well off in their lives. The greater the increase in the numbers of Jews the greater the immediate material prosperity of the Arabs; but this prosperity was ephemeral.

Suddenly an event happened which rent Jewry in pieces.

There had always been tension between the Jewish factions and this was steadily expanding as the Revisionists, the body founded by Jabotinsky to revise the Mandate, increased their numbers. The extremists of the Labour group had been making determined attacks upon the Revisionists and had assailed their meetings with stones and tear gas. A number of Revisionists had been arrested by government, and their public meetings forbidden. A campaign of slander and repression followed and, when this was at its height, Chaim Arlosoroff,[3] a leader of the Labour Party who had succeeded Colonel Kisch as chief political representative of the Jewish Agency, was murdered while walking with his wife along the beach at Tel Aviv.

There was an immediate outcry that this was a political murder and it was ascribed to the Revisionists. A paroxysm of anger and hysteria swept the country.

There was a long delay before the alleged murderer was brought to justice. The preliminary enquiries before the magistrate were allowed to drag on for eight months. Before the assize court the defence argued

---

3. Chaim Arlosoroff (1899–1933) was born in the Ukraine and settled in Palestine in 1918. He was the leader of the Zionist Labour movement.

that there had been an improper frame-up by the police. The court by a majority found that Abraham Stavsky did take part in the premeditated murder and he was sentenced to death.

There was a fresh outburst of passion and rage. It was the first time that a Jew had stood trial for the murder of a fellow Jew in the modern history of Palestine and the Jews were proud of this record. So the Ashkenazi chief rabbi, Kuk, entered the fray and addressed an appeal to world Jewry. The leftists of the Labour Party retaliated by daubing the wall of synagogues and houses with the words in red: 'Pity the nation whose priests protect murderers.'

Stavsky got off at the appeal court on a technical point, though the chief justice stated that, had the case been tried in England, the conviction would have had to stand. Stavsky had entered the prison a blond-haired man; he walked out with his hair as white as snow.

The consequences of this murder had a profound effect on Jewry. The repercussions were felt for years and led to brutal fratricidal strife, which seriously jeopardized Zionist progress. Arlosoroff had stood for everything the Revisionists were against. He had been an ardent socialist, and a student of philosophy and economics. He had undoubtedly had the mind of a statesman and had not been moved by mob criticism. He had been a plain undistinguished-looking man, yet had been very attracted by and attractive to women.

Arlosoroff's death opened the door of opportunity for his assistant, Moshe Shertock,[4] who succeeded him. Born in Odessa, Moshe was brought up among the Arabs of Galilee and spoke Arabic as well as any Arab. By hard work and with gathering stature Moshe developed into Moshe Sharett, foreign secretary of Israel.

Some years after his acquittal, Stavsky organized a gang, which, for handsome remuneration in the Lebanon, brought illegal immigrants into Palestine. During the war he was shot dead in some frontier incident.

4. Moshe Shertock, later known as Moshe Sharett (1894–1965), was born in the Ukraine but spent some of his childhood in Palestine. He studied law in Constantinople and served with the Turkish army during the First World War. He then studied in Britain and was active in the British Zionist movement. He returned to Palestine in 1925 and in 1931 was appointed secretary of the Jewish Agency's political department. He succeeded Arlosoroff as chief political representative of the Jewish Agency and held the post until the establishment of the State of Israel in 1948.

The bulk of Jewish villages were run on communal lines, with the settlers therein, like the early Christians, holding everything in common. Nothing was privately owned — a plant in a pot, the cushion on the divan bed, or even underclothes and toothbrushes. To everyone according to his needs. Even the children in the crêche could only be visited by their parents at stated hours. Women worked as hard as men. This type of settler became entirely different from the townsman and the smallholder. Money and personal progress passed him by. Produce was sold through a countrywide co-operative. But the inability to express individual choice, emotions, tastes and skills in making a home or in change of personal dress or status became intolerable to some people, and that is why every year some members left the settlements to live in the towns and work there, and a few succumbed to taking their own lives. To an Arab such a life was inconceivable. To him family and tribe were the first essentials of human society.

Considerable cultural advance had been made civically. From the many hundreds of gifted musicians being thrown out of European orchestras, Bronislaw Huberman[5] had collected 75 Jews and brought them to Palestine and, despite almost insurmountable difficulties, had' created an orchestra, which now ranks with many in Europe. Toscanini[6] conducted the first series of performances, and returned for a second tour. At the opening concert a horn player turned over two pages of music by mistake and played a wrong bar. Toscanini flung his hand against his head, as though he had been struck, and stopped conducting until the end of the piece. The horn player slunk off the platform in his agony and never returned. The maestro was impressed by the musicians. He told me: 'It is a good orchestra: it will be a better orchestra: it can be a great orchestra.'

This noble band played everywhere: whether it was in a town, settlement, shack or out of doors made no difference. It gave pleasure and spiritual uplift to thousands and was a great unifying force.

---

5. Bronislaw Huberman (1882–1947) was a child prodigy who played the violin in the major cities of Europe from the age of 11. In 1933 he declined an invitation to play in Germany under Furtwängler and in 1936 he founded the Palestine Orchestra, made up of refugee musicians, which later became the Israel Philharmonic Orchestra.

6. Arturo Toscanini was an internationally famous Italian orchestra conductor. He refused to conduct in Germany while Nazi cultural policies were in force.

Hebrew had really become a living language. Drama was catered for by Habima, a co-operative theatre group, and Matate organized a satiric group which, by unmercifully poking fun at everything that the earnest politicians held sacred, added a good deal to the gaiety of Jewish everyday life.

There were now 2082 doctors with licences to practise medicine, but a large proportion had settled in Tel Aviv. With the unanimous approval of heads of all communities, the age of marriage for girls was raised from 14 to 15 years.

Revenues had gone up to £P 5 million and accumulated government surplus was £P 4 million. Our adverse balance of trade was £P 11 million. There was marked industrial development, deposits in the banks were higher and £P 6 million had been invested in new buildings.

By a chain of circumstances and deep Teutonic cunning our shops were flooded with German articles ranging from Bayer's aspirin to pumps for orange groves. Immigrants were allowed to take their capital out of Germany only in the form of German goods.

There were other less satisfactory figures. Murders among Arabs were still frequent; the average was four weekly. Immigrants were flocking in so fast that administrative officers were unable to keep in touch. Our staffs were inadequate. By the time we had made out a case for an increase with the British Treasury, who always had the last word, we were overwhelmed by fresh arrivals.

The Arabs' unabashed habit of stealing from their neighbours' fields gave us constant trouble and was a continuous irritation to the Jewish cultivators. Watchtowers were necessary not only in the vineyards but in every place where crops were growing. We started tracking offenders with police dogs, Doberman pinschers, imported from South Africa. At first we were very successful and traced many offenders, but gradually the Arab peasants became as wise as the dogs and used pepper to prevent traces of their visits; or else after their nocturnal prowlings they would leave for their houses via an asphalted road, however far from their villages they had to go. By this means the scent was lost. There was of, course only one method that could keep this particular crime down: the crude habits of the Americans in the Far West.

Officials were getting tired out. Due to relentless overwork, I developed asthma and for a year was unable to sleep in bed. I had to sit up at night in a chair and be doped with ephedrine.

Dr Jekyll and Mr Hyde

Despite intense building activity there was an acute shortage of accommodation in the major towns and Arabs were being steadily pushed out of houses they had occupied for generations. Large areas of shacks made from old petrol tins and sand sprang up. There was a good deal of talk about government improving accommodation, but nothing tangible was started. The cost of trying to maintain public security was too great! Wauchope, however, was delighted and pushed departments harder than ever.

More demonstration plots for farmers were established. Government stallions, jackasses and bulls were lent to villages free of charge to serve their mares and cows. Some 50,000 hatching eggs were distributed. Beekeeping was increased. Forest plants were issued free of charge to villages and settlements. A million and a half seedlings were raised and given away. Vineyards were extended. Grants to agricultural institutions were freely given and agricultural education pressed forward; £P 30,000 was to be made available for permanent improvement of 93 village water supplies. Building was going on at a furious pace. Even the railways felt the impulse and carried 97,000 tons more cement than the year before. Plans were made for an aerodrome to be built.

Had not the 'economic absorptive capacity of Jews' put into practice proved the solution to the Palestine problem after all? The East was being hurried!

The Jews felt that for the first time the national home was being fostered by the government. But they were still dissatisfied by the 'paucity' of the half-yearly immigration schedule and were pressing for still more of their people to be allowed entry. They realized that the Arab population had also steadily increased following the general prosperity.

The Arabs, with full stomachs, were becoming still more articulate. They grumbled that government policy was encompassing their ultimate economic annihilation and complained. bitterly at the vast numbers of the new arrivals. It became public that, in addition to the published figures, a large number of Jews were coming in illegally and sailing boats from Greek islands were doing a brisk trade. Arab youths started patrolling the coast. Jewish trade unions beset premises where Jews were employing Arabs. Government stopped the manifestations and employed more police.

Unrest was intensified when it became known that an organization for smuggling in Jews had accomplices in the government's Department of Migration. Sir Arthur's public statement that, thanks to the special measures taken to improve frontier control, illegal immigration had been considerably reduced, was not believed. Despite all the omens, Arabs continued to sell their lands to Jews.

There are many ways of earning a living — some choose art or music, others more practical means.

At Haifa there was a worthy old reprobate who used to accompany the local *mufti* when he went to call on an official or other authority. Every religious head — rabbi, bishop, *imam* or *mufti* — has to take with him someone to back up verbally any statement he makes, however outrageous.

Well, the *mufti* died, and his poor old echo, a man of the slenderest education, was left stranded. The old man was almost illiterate, but he had once held a very, very minor post at the court of the *sherif* of Mecca and wore the white muslin of piety wound immaculately round his *tarboosh*. He did his utmost to get himself appointed to the *mufti*iship. He even pressed me to help him acquire both merit and a well-paid job. But I was not to be persuaded and I told him so.

I did not see him for some years, as the new *mufti* brought his own echo with him. One day I met the old man and he begged me to come to his house to tea, and I agreed to do so. With difficulty I prevented him from engaging a band and told him frankly that I would only come if my visit was quite private and *sans cérémonie*.

In some mysterious manner he was doing well. His family house had been enlarged and he now lived on the third floor in two large rooms, with a kitchen and verandah. On my arrival I was shown into one of the rooms, while in the other two naked offspring were sitting on enamel chamber pots attending to the calls of nature. From the kitchen came constant talk and from time to time the curtains moved and almond eyes peeped at me from behind. As I sat on one of the red plush divans I gazed across and, on the wall, I noticed a beautiful *ayat* (illuminated scroll), an admirable example of Arabic calligraphy, in a golden frame, extolling the many virtues of my host. A little cross-examination led him to confess that he had had it written for him when on a visit to Cairo and the script alone had cost £P 5.

There was also a magnificent coloured photograph enlargement of my host, more than life-size, encased in a gaudy frame. He told me that the frame had cost him £P 3 but, alas, the photograph had cost him five. I replied how well these small sums had been invested and awaited the story. Two years previously, before he went to Egypt, he visited an Oriental Jewish photographer to get a photograph for his passport and got two for two shillings. Some months later he learned that in the shop there was a coloured photograph of himself surrounded top, sides and bottom by portraits of a Jewish woman in a very *décolletée* dress. Horrified, he hurried to the shop, found the story to be true and demanded that the photograph be removed from the window. The proprietor argued, saying that it was a good advertisement. His wives visited the shop. Public opinion ranged against him and, in the end, he had to pay five pounds to buy it.

On New Year's Day, the high commissioner announced his decision to extend a generous measure of clemency to those Arabs still serving sentence of imprisonment as a result of the 1929 riots. I drove over to the Crusader fortress at Acre, which was now the central prison, released 14 prisoners and informed others, who had been sentenced to death, that they would be released the following year. Wauchope also remitted the collective fines that had been imposed on certain Arab villages, but which had not yet been collected.

The Zionist Congress at Lucerne unanimously announced that Jewish settlements in Palestine had proved that immigration and settlement could proceed more rapidly — 61,854 had been admitted during the year. The Congress appealed to the government to fulfil its obligation of furthering the national home at a pace demanded by the increasing persecution of Jews by the Nazis. Shortly afterwards, a large quantity of arms and ammunition was discovered in Jaffa port in a consignment of cement from Belgium. It was assumed by Arabs that Jewry was extensively arming itself. There was a vehement press campaign against the government and the Jews.

The *mufti* of Jerusalem was again engaged in beating up the religious issue and speeches in mosques were becoming more violent. Sheikh Izzed Din al-Qassim,[7] a political refugee from Syria, started a terrorist

7. Sheikh Izzed Din al-Qassim led a group of Arab forces in 1935 in the first organized attack on the British since the beginning of the Mandate. His funeral in Haifa led to a strong wave of Arab patriotic feeling.

band, which functioned until he was shot; there were disturbances at his funeral where he was referred to as a martyr. The five Arab party leaders demanded of the high commissioner a democratic government, stoppage of Jewish immigration and prohibition of the sale of further land to Jews.

The high commissioner announced the British government's proposals for a legislative council. It was to be composed of five officials, eleven Muslims, seven Jews, three Christians and two commercial people. The president was to be some impartial person unconnected with Palestine. He would neither debate nor vote.

The Arab leaders said they would deliberate upon the proposals. The Jewish leaders referred to the resolution of the Zionist Congress in Lucerne, when they expressed their grave concern at a step it regarded as contrary to the spirit of the Mandate in the present stage of the development of Palestine, and they resolved to reject the scheme uncompromisingly and to refrain from participation.

A couple of months later, the legislative council proposals were debated in the Houses of Lords and Commons. There was a general opinion among all parties that the proposals were premature. Sir Philip Cunliffe Lister, the colonial secretary, having already seen the Jews, invited the Arabs to England for discussion; they agreed to accept the invitation unanimously.

But these fluctuations in policy concerning what the high commissioner had described to both Arabs and Jews as 'the pledge given by His Majesty's Government' created further tension, which was fostered in both the Arab and the Jewish press. With the brutal murder by some Arabs of two Jews travelling in Samaria in April, the storm broke.

10

Retrospect

It is well to pause and consider what had happened during the 20 years since Balfour, on behalf of His Majesty's Government, made the promise to Rothschild. How had the country progressed? Nationalism had become a pest and its flags were flaunted everywhere. Racialism displayed itself in its crudest forms. Arabs relied upon mob violence. The Jews were cleverer and more subtle.

Despite the growing antagonism and Arab hatred of Jews, much progress had been made. Arab living conditions had entirely altered. They were better fed and, except in Haifa, better housed and better clothed. Despite the sales of Arab land, better use was being made of that which remained. Schools flourished in every Jewish settlement and in some hundreds of Arab villages. Communications had been opened up, not only within Palestine but also with its neighbours. Water now flowed in places where it had not been known to flow before. In some places ancient sources had been improved. In one Samaria village scheme, I decided we should investigate a stream that just trickled down a hill. Inside an ancient conduit, we found the roots of a tree that had penetrated for 50 yards and it was completely blocked up. We removed the roots, cleaned up the passage and there was an almost immediate response. The flow of water was sufficient for the whole village and in the evenings the elders were able to sit and reflect to the tinkle of plashing water with its gentle monotonous reiteration.

In suitable land on the plains many Arab landowners now owned orange groves. The stony slopes of mountains, which for hundreds of years had been barren, were now being terraced by Jews and becoming forests or orchards, and trees were laden with fruit. Farm stock was heavier and bigger. Little strings of blue beads, which formerly served on the necks of mules and donkeys, now 'protected' the steering wheels of cars and lorries bringing produce to market. The earth was bringing forth her increase.

By the introduction of drastic regulations and by the oiling of all water sources, in which both Jews and Arabs co-operated with government, malaria had been stamped out, except in the Lake Huleh marshes and along the twisting banks of the Jordan.

Arabs are pleasant people to live among and their long loose garments cover a multitude of sins. They inherit good manners and, although when roused they go absolutely mad with passion and will commit murderous assaults with indifference, once the mood has passed, they will regret that Allah had taken away their senses. In their fight against Jews, they sincerely felt that they were waging a holy war and that their reward in heaven would be great. The fact that many of them had sold land to Jews through brokers left them entirely indifferent. The justice of their cause was unimpeached.

If I visited a village, however poor and slatternly, I was received by adults and children with perfect manners. Yet if I scattered a few sweets for the children, in the twinkling of an eye they were fighting and clawing each other like wild beasts.

Jewish children were free and casual. There was little discipline in the schools; they argued with their teachers and flatly refused to accept any statement with which they did not agree. They showed scant respect for their elders and disregarded anyone else. Jewish settlements were generally dirty and there were more flies about than in Arab villages.

Jewish youth, girls and boys dressed in khaki shorts, started going around in large numbers singing songs and generally absorbing the road. They looked and appeared to behave like Hitler Youth on holiday. This behaviour was very irritating to the Arabs, who regarded such conduct with opprobrium. I often felt that if only we could explain to each party in the presence of the other what their different customs and habits were, it would be a good thing. But they remained quite intransigent and refused to meet.

The price of Arab wives had gone up and some young men were going off to Cyprus in search of Greek ones. Educated young Arabs were ceasing to return to their villages to try to improve farming methods, even after they had passed through the agricultural school. Their parents' ways were too strong to be countered with a diploma, so a fresh class of townsmen were appearing who had little sympathy with the life of the major part of the population.

Distinct changes were appearing everywhere. Arabs are fine stone-masons and, given time, produce excellent vaulted buildings. They had not mastered the intricacies of inside staircases, but several Arab architects were returning after a European training and outside steps to upper rooms were disappearing along with mud houses. Jews had started off with silicate bricks but, as the cement works in Haifa developed and this material became more plentiful, they learned with experience and mastered reinforced concrete. Of course, with architects from nearly every country in Europe, their new buildings embraced every type, and local authorities had great difficulty controlling building activities. In Haifa alone, 2000 contraventions were recorded in one year.

Owners got round any regulations. Once a building had been passed and approved for occupation, inside walls were quickly demolished and new ones inserted; and a place approved as a three-family house was soon converted into one holding double that number of families. But public opinion approved of a law I succeeded in introducing, allotting a certain percentage of open space in building estates as playing fields. But all Jews had an urge to own shops, for which larger rents could be obtained, and garages were frequently found converted overnight for this purpose.

Formerly there had been a good deal of personal contact between everybody. Now social cleavage had wormed its way in and was never bridged. The Jerusalem Sports Club, which was opened for and used by all classes and races, had become a purely British meeting place, with no Jewish members and only one Arab. The American-built YMCA was the one place where Jew met Arab, but it was barred by local families of any position and the Latin patriarch issued an order that he would excommunicate any Roman Catholic found within its walls. But Jews and Arabs could work together. For some years I had a Karrieme Jewess cook, a Muslim butler and a Christian houseboy. Rutenberg's electricity organization and Novomeysky's potash industry employed both races impartially.

The Jews, turning their words to the political needs of the moment, are nowadays adamant that it was Hitlerism that drove them to insist on entry into the Promised Land. But actually the numbers from Germany were very small compared with those from Eastern Europe. The members of the executive of the Jewish Agency and the Jewish National Fund were mainly Russians, and it was they who directed policy and saw that it was carried out. It was they who created and built up a nation speaking Hebrew. It was these people, who had left everything for Palestine, who were the real pioneers and inspirers of the national home.

Only Samaria kept aloof from sales of land to Jews. It has always been a stronghold of Islam and kept to itself. No blandishments won Muslims in what was jocularly known as the Triangle of Error.

An important factor was the attitude of English women towards Palestinians. It is extraordinary how soon an English woman abroad forgets her status in life and assumes an unnatural one. I know many people who have spent their working lives in Palestine, have lived in it and of it, but who have never had what they term a 'local' inside their own homes.

I never met a Jew in an Arab house nor an Arab in a Jewish one, except on those occasions when the Jewish Agency, for the purpose of propaganda, collected some Arabs, dressed them up in new garments as a gift, and photographed them with their Jewish neighbours. Yet Arabs continued to sell their land to Jews.

Most British officials thought that the Arabs had had a raw deal, but did not realize that the Arabs' future lay largely in the Arabs' own hands. They sympathized with the peasant who was quite content to sit under the shadow of his single tree and watch the Jews plant scores of new ones on land that had formerly belonged to Arabs.

I often thought that there would be less ill will if the Jews would develop the virtues of tolerance and humility and shout, push and encroach less, and also look less upon everything that they had gained as their due. They played into the hands of their detractors by the gracelessness they displayed and by their incessant egotistical clamour.

Lady Hester Stanhope[1] had described the Jews in Jerusalem, 100 years before, as 'a nation of old-clothes dealers, without imagination,

---

1. Lady Hester Stanhope was a British traveller who left England for the Levant in 1810. She made a pilgrimage to Jerusalem, crossed the desert and camped with Bedu in the ruins of Palmyra in 1813. She settled on Mount Lebanon in 1814.

without courage, without any of the qualities necessary to a great nation'. And she decided to transfer 'her empire' to Palmyra. But the modern Jews, the immigrants, were different. They were bursting with energy, full of imagination and prepared to turn their hand to anything; they were prepared to live hard, to face any difficulties and achieve their goal. In short they showed guts.

But almost every European Christian who came to the country soon got tired of Jewish aggressive advertisement and saw only the Arab's virtues under his picturesque robes. That he thieved from Jewish village gardens, stole the fruit and poultry as a matter of course, was brushed aside as a simple Arab failing or way of life. Did not every Arab have a watchtower in his vineyard as security against his own brethren?

We tried to teach the boys scouting, but without much success. When not engaged in acquiring an inordinate number of badges, Arab boys used to line the streets at political funerals, or were used for other political purposes. The Jews would have nothing to do with Lord Baden-Powell[2] and set up their own mixed troops.

Soccer was now the great game in Palestine but neither party met the other in competitions.

But, although living conditions and environment were easier, we had not changed the Arab character. It remained much the same. The only real change we had made to Arab life was to get their women to accept the abolition of the use of wooden stools in childbirth. For short spells they would show intense physical activity, but their efforts would burn out for lack of endurance and routine. Deprived of constitutional outlets, they turned to revolution. The Jews looked upon the government as an obstacle to the achievement of their national home. Every screw must be tightened to allow them to select and get their fellow men into the country by whatever means. A national army, even an underground one, must be assembled. Restraint must give way to action. Dr Eder had been right when he gave evidence before the Riot Commission in 1929: 'There could be only one Home in Palestine and that a Jewish one.'

---

2. Robert Baden-Powell (1857–1941), first Baron Baden-Powell, hero of the siege of Mafeking, who founded the Boy Scouts and Girl Guides movement in 1908.

11

The Christian Holy Places

The claims and rights of the various churches in the Christian Holy Places were a never-ending problem, particularly upon the great festivals, and especially in those rare years when the Western and Eastern calendars coincided. The arrangements that had to be made for the diverse services and the space that might be occupied by the various congregations worshipping were most complicated.

The Turks, when they retreated, left no records behind them. The different churches had many records, but they only gave particulars of decisions that had favoured their own church, as the rulings had depended upon which side at the moment enjoyed the greater influence. Therefore, my predecessor and I had a great deal of difficulty compiling an official record of rights and claims, and also determining exactly what the status quo was.

The Church of the Holy Sepulchre, called the Church of the Resurrection by the Eastern churches, embraces many shrines. The Stone of Unction is opposite the great entrance and Calvary is up some stone stairs to the right. Huge pillars support the great dome of the Rotunda, erected over the Edicule containing the tomb of Christ. The Katholicon is east of the Rotunda. Other commemorative shrines are built round the main building.

Two Muslim families, descendants of those to whom Caliph Omar committed the keys, occupied a *diwan* near the entrance and still retained their ancient privileges of opening and closing the entrance doors. They were paid by the three patriarchates in rotation. These rights went back to AD 637 when the Caliph Omar, riding on his camel from Mecca to Jerusalem, imposed terms on the inhabitants. In the conditions of their surrender he said: 'I grant the people of Jerusalem security for their lives, their possessions, their children, their churches and their crosses. Neither shall they be exposed to violence in following their religion.'

The Orthodox, Latin and Armenian patriarchates had possessory rights. The Syrian Orthodox and the Coptic Church of Egypt had some lesser rights, while the Abyssinians could erect a tent annually on the roof and process around the dome of St Helena's chapel. A Muslim pious foundation had access to another part of the roof.

Services were given in many languages. The Copts used the language of the Pharaohs, the Abyssinians G'ez, an ancient Semitic tongue, and the Armenians their old Indo-European speech. The Greek used in the Orthodox services was that of the Gospel, while the Syrian Orthodox or Jacobites used Aramaic, the language of Christ, and the Roman Catholics prayed in Latin.

Every priest on duty considered it is his sacred task to guard the interests of his own church and I was called upon continually to give rulings in settlement of disputes.

One day I was called hurriedly and found inside the Edicule a Franciscan friar with blood pouring down his face from scratches and a Greek priest lying across the tomb of Christ, holding his stomach and moaning that he had been hit by the Franciscan. I had a long talk with the parties separately. The brawl had arisen because the Greek had thought that the Franciscan had prevented an old Russian Orthodox woman from kissing an icon at the head of the tomb. Actually the friar had merely asked her to wait while he got out a candle, but the old woman, who spoke no tongue known to either of them, had protested and the Greek had sprung to her aid. The differences of opinion were settled satisfactorily and a day or two later I saw both clerics talking amicably together. The Franciscan had put the case tersely to me: 'We are all soldiers here to defend the rights of our fathers.'

The Syrian Orthodox, sometimes called Jacobites, had rights to a little chapel off the Rotunda and the Copts held fast to a tiny altar attached to the Edicule. Once the Syrian patriarch, whose throne was established at Mardin in Iraq, paid us a visit, and, perplexed because he was not awarded the same honours as were the heritage of Palestine's three patriarchs, he worked up the enthusiasm of his local clergy and started off on a full-dress procession of his own in the church. I arrived in time to find his way barred by a phalanx of Armenians, breathing what amounted to: 'Only over our dead bodies may you pass.' As the swarthy prelate was unversed in status quos and was covered in sweat from anger and also from the weight of his vestments, it took some persuasion to reconcile him to the inevitable. But he had his revenge. Inside the Syrian chapel was an ancient painting claimed by the Armenians to belong to them. Little by little, pieces disappeared off the right-hand corner where there was some Armenian writing. Constant were the appeals to me. Finally I had the painting glazed and covered with wire netting.

The Anglican Church became involved through the late Cosmo Gordon Lang,[1] Archbishop of Canterbury.

In 1931 it was announced that he had been ill and was paying a purely private visit to Palestine during his convalescence. When it became known that he was setting forth from Monte Carlo in Pierpont Morgan's luxury yacht, *Corsair*, there was much adverse comment.

For many years a section of the Anglican Church had been seeking to obtain from one of the older churches confirmation that Anglican orders were valid and that their priests enjoyed the blessing of Apostolic Succession. The Roman Church had turned a deaf ear. After a good deal of lobbying, the ecumenical Orthodox patriarch of Constantinople had informed Archbishop Randall Davidson that he recognized the 'charisma' of the priesthood derived from the Apostolic Succession. Anglican orders therefore had the same validity as those of the Roman, Old Catholic and Armenian Churches. This declaration had been affirmed by the Orthodox patriarch of Jerusalem.

No one had been more assiduous than Archbishop Lang for reunion of all Christian Churches. Indeed many Anglicans held the view that this service was his only ecclesiastical contribution of lasting importance.

1. Cosmo Gordon Lang was Archbishop of York from 1909 to 1928, after which he succeeded Randall Davidson as Archbishop of Canterbury.

Bishop MacInnes,[2] the Anglican bishop in Jerusalem, was anxious to get a closer relationship with the Orthodox for more personal reasons. He was a low churchman and whether or not the validity of his own orders were recognized by the Latins made no great appeal, but, as he ad been consistently snubbed by the Latin patriarch, he had turned for solace to the Orthodox.

As the archbishop's visit had been announced as being private, when I went to accompany him on a visit to the Holy Sepulchre, I was astonished to find Bishop MacInnes wearing his doctor of divinity gown and the Anglican clergy he could muster in their cassocks and university hoods. Lang arrived wearing a light purple silk cassock, cape and skullcap. As we walked down the cobbled steps of David Street, except that his cassock lacked the brilliance of scarlet, he looked for all the world like a Roman cardinal.

At the portal many dignitaries of the Eastern Churches were gathered in their best robes, while a solitary Franciscan friar stood by, ungreeting and ungreeted, a sentinel on duty to see that no Latin right was violated. Lang was still a sick man. But from the moment we entered the great doorway, the primate, whom Sir William Orpen[3] had found difficult to paint — 'I see seven archbishops. Which am I to paint?' — threw his lassitude aside and became the actor and, aided by his glorious voice, carried out his inspection of the shrines in the grand manner. Certainly on this occasion he suffered none of the inhibitions of his undergraduate days when he tried to convince a fellow lodger 'infected with "High Churchism" of the irreconcilability of the Divine appointment of Episcopal Orders'.

The archbishop was placed in a gilded chair in the Katholicon and I could see that some sort of ceremonial greeting was about to be held. I had but a moment to think. It was clear that the archbishop was expected to take some part, so I said quietly to His Grace that he must not speak in reply as it would be contrary to the status quo. It was a

2. Bishop MacInnes served a curacy in London and then went to Cairo, where he became secretary of the Church Missionary Society in Egypt and northern Sudan. He became honorary canon of St George's Collegiate Church, Jerusalem, in 1909 and was bishop in Jerusalem from 1914 to 1931.

3. Sir William Orpen was a painter who served as official war artist from 1917 to 1919 and painted the peace conference in 1919. He was also a successful portrait painter.

tense moment. Lang was undoubtedly annoyed and at one moment seemed to be prepared to brush my remarks aside, so I repeated them as an instruction and it was obeyed. After a welcome had been sung by the robed choir and His Grace had been addressed by Archbishop Timotheos as 'the successor to the throne of Augustine', he bowed and was then taken inside the iconostasis where he knelt before the altar. Returning through the royal doors, in place of a blessing, which I heard later was to have been given, he made a dramatic gesture of resignation and left.

To the archbishop, my action had seemed a piece of pedantry and he was visibly annoyed. Bishop MacInnes and his fellow priests were discomfited. By keeping their intentions secret, MacInnes had over-played his hand. But to all who knew, my ruling was correct. No official comment upon the incident was ever made to me. Neither did the Orthodox patriarchate question the decision. They were too wise.

Patriarch Damianos gave the archbishop one of his mother-of-pearl patriarchal staffs, which Lang took to be recognition of his own almost patriarchal status. It has been stated that the archbishop's fleeting visit left a lasting impression. Actually it cut very little ice.

Down the centuries countless pilgrims had come to pray at the Holy Places. Kings had come in sackcloth and thrown dust upon their heads. The less fortunate had crossed continents on foot and sailed in the holds of sailing ships. Others, like the holy family, who returned across Sinai, have come astride an ass. But Cosmo Lang, the primate of all England, had chosen the primrose path in the most luxurious yacht afloat. That and the port of embarkation killed the visit.

Five Churches had rights at the Church of the Nativity at Bethlehem, but the Orthodox enjoyed almost exclusive use of the 1600-year-old church. Its dignity was considerably enhanced by Sir Ronald Storrs, who, during the military occupation, with the consent of all parties, had a disfiguring wall hiding the transepts and main altar from the nave taken down.

The little altar in the grotto under the main building, over the place of birth, was used in turn by Orthodox and Latin. One year, I was asked to go urgently to the grotto. There I found a mass of blood on the floor, hangings pulled down, vestments strewn about and two dishevelled priests, a Greek monk and a Franciscan friar, breathing heavily and looking much the worse for wear. Each held tenaciously to a brass candlestick that had been snatched off the altar and used as a weapon. Each accused the other of overstepping his legitimate time for holding Mass. Two courses were open: either to have the men prosecuted for brawling before an ordinary magistrate's court or to deal with the matter myself.

Both patriarchs agreed that it was undesirable for a priest to appear in a local court; indeed, I think they would have refused to deliver them up for trial. After hearing the evidence, I asked the Latin patriarch to order the Franciscan to return to Italy and the Greek patriarch to confine his priest to three years at the convent of Mar Saba, a desolate spot in the hills overlooking the Jordan valley.

But out of evil came good, for I took the opportunity to have the grotto thoroughly washed, the first time within living memory. Two charwomen spent much soap and a profitable day.

12

Religious Services

I attended many types of religious services; from the grandeur of a Christmas Mass at Bethlehem with the Latin patriarch pontificating, to the simplicity of an English service at Christ Church, from the austere services in the Church of Scotland, to the singing and the laughter, the pushing and the fervour of the Orthodox Holy Fire ceremony in the Rotunda of the Holy Sepulchre, with twirling banners, sword dancers and the shouts of triumph as the patriarch appeared from the tomb, his arms aglow with torches, the lights carried from candle to candle until the whole church was ablaze with fire.

I have seen a Muslim *zikr*, when the faithful squat and gyrate slowly in a circle, clap hands and repeat for hour after hour, '*La 'ilaha illa 'llah*' ('There is no God but God'), gradually moving faster until the eyes blaze and the breath comes in gasps, producing a state of ecstasy wherein the mind is withdrawn from earthly things.

The Maundy Thursday ceremony of the washing of the feet, conducted by the Armenian patriarch in his cathedral, assisted by a dozen bishops and vartabeds vested from neck to feet in flowered capes of exquisite needlework, and accompanied by the harmonious droning of the choir of young men and maidens, was grandiose ceremonial.

I went annually to a similar ceremony held by the Syrian Orthodox bishop in the tiny church of St Mark, when, after the bishop has washed the feet of the 12 Armenian priests (representing the 12 disciples), they in turn washed his feet and then, placing His Lordship on a throne, lifted him shoulder-high to read the Gospel.

I have taken part in the *Seder*, or Passover service, held at the houses of the chief rabbis, eaten the bitter herbs and drunk wine from the traditional three cups and heard the children ask the questions, Why do ye this? Why is this night different from all other nights? I have attended service on the Day of Atonement in the Great Synagogue alongside the weeping worshippers fasting until the sunset.

I have heard the Russian nuns chanting the office unaccompanied in their convent on the Mount of Olives and eaten bread with them afterwards. I have listened to the Franciscans sing Mass as only Italians can at Emmaus with His Paternity the *custos* celebrating, vested in the gorgeous scarlet and gold vestments presented to the convent by the people of Naples, and sat at luncheon with 100 of them afterwards in their refectory.

I attended annually the three Christmas liturgies celebrated by the Latin, Orthodox and Armenian patriarchs at Bethlehem, clad in their gorgeous vestments of brocade, gold and silver when in the light of guttering candles they knelt in prayer in the grotto of the Nativity.

I have been invited to Benediction at the Chapel of the Reparatrice Sisters who, clad in their light cerulean mantles and cream cashmere robes, kneel in constant vigil before the exposed body of the Lord in perpetual adoration.

I have been to a Mass held at dawn on Mount Thabor; and a few nights later have made a pilgrimage with Jews on the feast of *Lag Ba'Omer* to Hillel's[1] tomb at Meiron and stayed on for the bonfire at night.

I have attended the annual service of Holy Communion held on St John's day for the Knights of the Order of St John of Jerusalem, robed in their black mantles and eight-pointed white crosses, which is celebrated in the ancient church dedicated to the saint in the Old City, 30 feet below the present ground level.

Many times I have visited the Karrieme community, originally from the Crimea, who reject the Talmud and are now reduced to a handful of women and one man, and heard the man, their only rabbi, read the Pentateuch in modulated sing-song Hebrew in their little underground synagogue.

I have climbed the almost endless steps banked with trailing red bougainvillaea, rustling palms, hibiscus aflame with flower and rows of

---

1. Hillel the Elder was a great Jewish sage who lived around the end of the first century BCE.

canna lilies like vivid flames on green candlesticks, and prayed with the Baha'is at the tomb of the Bab on the summit of Carmel.

I have attended High Mass in the Cistercian or Trappist monastery in the Judaean foothills and stayed on to a silent meal with them afterwards, the silence broken only by the solemn reading by a monk of a holy book of meditation. On St Stephen's day, after the conclusion of Mass, I have lunched with the Dominican fathers in their convent just outside the Damascus Gate.

Three services are, however, unique.

At Easter time the Turks were formerly seriously perturbed at the large influx of Christian pilgrims into Jerusalem so a century or so ago an imaginative governor had a miraculous message that the tomb of the prophet Moses had been found in the Jordan valley and that it was necessary for good Muslims to come annually to Jerusalem at Easter time and, after the ceremonial reception of banners, go down in procession and pray at the tomb.

The Turkish governors had always taken a prominent part in the ceremonial and, in order to maintain the privileges conferred by the status quo, the district commissioner had carried on the old tradition. Thus, in the third-holiest place in Islam, a Christian official took an official part in Muslim prayer and ceremonial.

I was met at the principal entrance to the *Haram*, the 'Gate of the Chain', by the *mufti*, the Supreme Muslim Council and the sheikhs of the mosque, surrounded by thousands of worshippers. The proceedings began with prayers, at the conclusion of which we marched in procession to the Muslim law courts. Green, gold, red and silver village banners, embroidered with texts from the Koran in brilliant colours, fluttered in the breeze. Each was followed by its own particular contingent of young and old, arms locked, bodies swaying in a joyous dance. One by one the banners were taken out of their bags, fastened to the great shafts and handed to me to deliver to the bearers. As I handed to each bearer his banner I bade him 'to receive it and to bear it with honour and in peace'. Then, having concluded our prayers to the one God, the great standard of the Prophet, of green silk embroidered with gold lettering, was ceremoniously presented, held aloft and carried into the mosque for the final prayers before being taken down to the tomb.

The slopes of the eastern hills were dotted with tents, houses of hair, kneeling camels and picketed horses. Within the tents sat elders awaiting the respectful visits of friends and enemies. In silence the tea and coffee started their passage from hand to mouth.

Here, in the hot valley, thousands of the faithful devoted their time to resting, talking or showing off on horseback, while their children sucked sweets and drank sherbet, or rode in primitive swing boats, while my party was handsomely entertained by the Muslim authorities at a sumptuous banquet, where we ate a little of the many tons of rice that were cooked in the great Nebi Musa copper cauldron and given gratis to the pilgrims.

One ceremony had traces of pagan worship, Egyptian dynastic ritual, Judaism at the time of King David, Coptic evolution, sixteenth-century Portuguese Catholicism and Turkish ceremonial.

On the Saturday before Easter the Abyssinian abbot and his priests erected an embroidered tent upon the roof of the Holy Sepulchre and bewailed the crucifixion. After the abbot had read the words 'He is risen' from the Gospel held ceremoniously before him, the priests and people, each bearing a lighted taper, set forth from the tent to search for the body of Christ.

Kavasses, attired like Turkish janizaries in light-blue baggy trousers and Albanian jackets elaborately embroidered with silver thrown across their shoulder, led the procession. Girded with scimitars cased in silver scabbards, they struck the flagstones with silver-headed staves with iron bases ceremoniously as they moved. The cross-bearers came behind them, followed by the melancholy-eyed priests, black as ebony, clothed in vestments of green and gold, of yellow and of plum colour, with mantles of silk, velvet and brocade. Each priest wore a crudely fashioned silver crown of barbaric proportions, studded with roughly cut coloured stones.

As the procession got warmed up, the priests, stimulated by the thrumming of the great silver-tipped, barrel-shaped drums and by the shaking of brazen sistra,[2] indistinguishable from those used formerly in the Temple of Isis, danced with a swaying side-stepping shuffle in front of the abbot, as King David danced before the Ark of the Lord, as they circumambulated the dome of St Helena's chapel.

---

2. A sistrum (plural sistra) is a musical instrument, a set of loose metal rods in an oval metal frame and a handle to shake it with. It was originally peculiar to Egypt, where it was used in the worship of Isis.

The splendour of the abbot, crowned with a golden crown and clothed in a golden vestment surmounted by a scarlet mantle and sheltered under a gold embroidered and tasselled umbrella of state held aloft by a huge man, was breathtaking. Other umbrellas of green and of gold were borne behind, and thurifers censed the worshippers with spirals of sweet-smelling incense and grease from guttering candles.

What matter if the bearers of the two golden crosses were the two handsome Abyssinian Muslim waiters at the American YMCA! The monks were few, and so were the Abyssinian Christians, and did not our Lord command men to help one another?

Unaccepted by the rest of Jewry, an antipathy dating from the division of the Hebrew kingdom, the Samaritans, now reduced to 150, remained the only distinct survivals of ancient Israel. They had kept their sunset sacrifice of Passover on Mount Gerizim unbrokenly for over 3000 years.

Invited by their high priest and accompanied by the Muslim mayor, I set out from Nablus on a horse amidst a throng of people. After stumbling and sweating for an hour or more we reached the plateau on top of the hill. The Samaritan women were confined to their tents, but the black-robed girls and boys in coats of many colours were much in evidence.

Seven lambs with curling horns, of the first year, without blemish, their heads and tails touched up with saffron dye, stood by a trench munching green leaves. They were tended by men and priests robed in spotless white.

As the sun dropped lower the venerable high priest, a brilliant scarlet turban on his head, came forth and led the devotions. He prostrated himself in Muslim fashion with his forehead touching the ground. With arms aloft he chanted the story of the Passover from the twelfth chapter of Exodus. The sun disappeared as he reached the verse, 'the whole congregation of Israel shall kill it.' With a sweep of his arms he gave the signal. Seven knives flashed, seven scarlet founts gushed, seven quivering bodies were stilled and a triumphant shout filled the square.

A bunch of wild thyme was dipped into the blood and the doorways of the women's tents were struck. The kidneys and the fat above the liver were offered to Jehovah and consumed with fire. The priests' portions were set aside, the tendons, symbolic of the hollow in Jacob's thigh, were drawn out and the carcasses were roasted in the trench; long after midnight the symbolical meal would be eaten. In the morning any that remained would be burnt with fire.

The dignified high priest committed me to the divine will. I bowed my head before beginning the arduous journey down to the valley.

13

Funeral Rites

In the East there is little time between death and burial, for the heat with its powers of decomposition races the mourners for possession of the body. The limit is generally 24 hours, but in the case of an Armenian patriarch I have known an extra couple of days' grace. His Beatitude, dressed in his scarlet vestments, lay upon a table covered with a cloth of gold, which hid a couple of zinc washing tubs loaded with ice, replenished as need arose. Incense smouldering away in brazen vessels at head and feet soothed our olfactory organs and endeavoured to make us forget that nature wins in the end.

Diversities extended to those last rites, many of which went back to remote antiquity, and where we ourselves will one day be the central figure. All communities agree that rotting flesh is sacred, having been the temple of the soul, and to earth it must return, but at its own pace. Short cuts, such as exposure to the sun as in Parsee practice, or burning pyres like those the Hindus adopt, or ordinary cremation, were vetoed in the Holy Land.

An Orthodox patriarch was buried sitting in a chair, his rich vestments and episcopal ring being whipped off at the last moment. Orthodox Jews were carried in a litter, covered by their *tallith*s (prayer shawls), and laid to rest in swaddling bands of white cotton; wealthy Muslims were carried upon a new mattress and covered with a quilt of fine needlework, while the poor were put into a communal coffin and taken out and dumped at the graveside; Syrian Orthodox or Jacobite Christians were borne in an open coffin, the head of the defunct being encircled with a wreath of flowers, with one placed in the mouth for good fortune's sake.

But irrespective of their faith everyone enjoyed the resplendent glories of a good funeral; its pageantry, the crowds, the excitement, the pushing, the shouting, the keening, the mourning and the laughter.

The greatest welcome ever given to a dead body was the reception for King Faisal of Iraq, who died in Switzerland and was brought back in a cruiser of His Majesty King George's Mediterranean Fleet.

I had spent days making arrangements for the arrival in Haifa. At all times of the day and night, especially at night, telegrams kept arriving — from the Admiralty, the Foreign Office, the colonial secretary, the army and Air Force, the young king of Iraq, Emir Abdullah of Transjordan, and nearly every consul in Jerusalem. Advice was abundant.

I accompanied the ex-king Ali, brother of Faisal, aboard. Inside the Customs enclosure were dignity, decorum, gold lace and plumed head-dresses, guards of honour of sailors and kilted Highlanders, bugles blowing and bagpipes wailing; but once outside the fence, crowds, who had come into Palestine in their tens of thousands, promptly and very properly took charge. Police and soldiers were swept aside as every faithful heart did his utmost to touch the coffin or give a hand at bearing the body. My Irish superintendent of police enjoyed himself enormously sitting astride the ornate Swiss coffin, lashing out good humouredly with a riding whip to prevent more than a dozen persons at a time jumping upon the decorated pick-up that bore it. After all, could Ould Ireland herself have put up a better show? In the scrimmage, his assistant lost all his medals and they were never recovered.

We had started at dawn. I had been told that the aeroplane in which the body was to be flown to Baghdad must be airborne by 7.30. As the swollen mass of heaving, shouting, gesticulating people surged down the roads and across the open space of the aerodrome, the reception committee, Supreme Muslim Council, bishops and notables, government and military officers, as well as the carpeted dais, disappeared in the midst of the roaring mass of humanity. By some miracle I got both coffin and aged King Ali into the plane and, at 7.29, the machine took to the air. Sweating in every pore I struggled through the mob back to my office to write the inevitable report for Downing Street.

At first, would-be orators were enraged at their lost opportunity to make speeches and wrote angry letters to the government and local press. But it was no good! Public opinion was against them. The crowd had won. After all, it was their man they had honoured. Congratulatory letters poured in. The postmaster general must have made scores of pounds from the telegrams. Even the Colonial Office unbent to offer its thanks.

King Ghazi,[1] Faisal's son, joined in the general felicitations and, some months afterwards, I received a communication from St James's Palace that His Majesty King George had been graciously pleased to allow me to receive and wear the Order of the Rafidain, which had been awarded to me by the king of Iraq for the personal services I had I rendered to the throne. King Ali came especially to Haifa to place the insignia round my neck with his very delicate hands. But the British sent me a bill for ten shillings to pay for having my name placed on the roll permitting me to wear it.

Jewish mourners still rent their garments — generally with prudence along a seam — and sat upon the floor for the requisite number of days, while friends sat with them at intervals to help them to bear up. Directly after death, Jews were washed, shrouded and placed upon the floor. They were buried without coffins so that there might be nothing between them and the hallowed ground. There was a good deal of mercenary exploitation by the owners of burial grounds. A funeral was generally an occasion for numerous secular speeches after the *Kaddish* had been intoned. Coming back from such an occasion I commented on the practice to a Jewish friend and he replied blandly, 'I wouldn't call a funeral a religious ceremony, but a secular one tainted with religion.'

Arab women took up more comfortable positions upon cushions on the floor of the house and, in their emotion, tore their hair or beat their heads against the wall, fortified by numerous cups of coffee. Arab men were stoical and, sitting apart, resigned themselves to the will of Allah.

Muslim funerals were gradually losing their simplicity and the practice, borrowed from the Christians, of carrying great hoops of green leaves and withered flowers, to which were attached streamers of black ribbon embossed in gold lettering advertising their donors, was creeping in. It was the custom for everyone to help bear the deceased to the

---

1. Ghazi succeeded Faisal as King of Iraq in 1933.

mosque and to the grave. Across the expanse of the *Haram al-Sherif*, the Noble Sanctuary, the body swayed as the bearers continually changed and a five-foot man took the burden from a taller. Occasionally an old man desiring to touch the coffin for 'the honour and the blessing' had the whole burden of that side suddenly thrust upon his frail shoulders with disastrous results. But as decorum was the last thing anyone was thinking about, least of all the man in whose honour we were attending, we set our black silk 'cylinders' more firmly upon our heads and trod along at one mile per hour until we took leave at the door, where the awaiting sheikhs, with arms held out, recited as quickly as possible in staccato tones, as though each would outstrip the other, appropriate sentences from the Holy Book.

There was no gloating over funeral furniture as in Europe and America. Coffins, when used, were of a simple type and were bought off the pegs they were hanging upon in the shops. They were generally made of two long pieces of wood forming the sides and joined together by bits of old boxes for bottoms and tops. Tops and sides were covered with cotton cloth of garish pink or silver blue.

I got a surprise the first time I saw a Syrian Orthodox procession coming along a cobbled road in the old city. Choir boys wearing black and red *galabiehs* carried candle lamps on the top of poles and in the centre was a cross bearer. Two young men preceded the corpse, carrying the coffin lid bolt upright. The front was covered with pink and tinsel but as the lid passed I read on the inside: 'Bottled in Liverpool. Keep in a cool place. Stow away from boilers.'

The funeral of Dr Musa's wife was a complicated affair. Dr Musa was a pious Jew from Persia who, when he was not translating petitions outside the Department of Immigration offices, devoted himself almost exclusively to the mystic message of the Wailing Wall. On a brief visit to England he had married a Cockney woman from the East End. Every day he rode a shaggy pony down to the wall and his wife walked behind, ready to take over the pony when he got there.

Dr Musa's fancy in dress was never to cast a clout. Upon several waistcoats he invariably wore two overcoats. His swarthy complexion was hidden by a bushy beard and his eyes were protected by a forest of

167

eyebrows. He wore a black Persian pillbox hat. The doctor often dropped in to see me. One day he announced that God had spoken to him on a visit to Damascus and informed him that the Messiah had come incarnate and He was revealed. I asked the old man how he could recognize Him. Getting up from his chair he bowed to me formally and said: 'Sir, you are in the presence of the Messiah.' I bowed with equal gravity and, after giving me his blessing, he left.

His wife fell ill and one hot day in July she died. Two days later he came to see me, talked about his divine message and then mentioned casually that he was having difficulty about her burial. Would I give him a letter to the Ashkenazi chief rabbi. I did so. His Eminence replied in Hebrew that, 'As Dr Musa is a Persian he should apply to the Sephardi chief rabbi.' I wrote a letter to this rabbi, who styles himself 'the First in Zion', and awaited a reply. With it came a deputation of neighbours from the quarter where Mrs Musa lay.

Chief Rabbi Meir answered in French: 'Not only was I district commissioner, I was his personal friend and well known for my piety, but unfortunately he was not sure that the deceased was a Jewess. He must have proof.' The neighbours were more vociferous and callous. They said that Mrs Musa's body was making life unbearable and demanded her removal.

Questioned, the doctor admitted she was a Christian but believed in the divine message of the Wailing Wall. He did not know to what church she belonged. As the Abyssinians were the lost tribe of Israel, he would like her buried in their cemetery.

I pacified the delegation and sent the medical officer up. I wrote to the Abyssinian abbot and asked him if he would bury the dead woman. Next morning came the reply, written in picturesque Amharic, together with what the Abyssinian translator fondly believed to be a French translation. 'His Reverence's duty towards the government was profound and any order of mine would be obeyed, but the key of the Abyssinian graveyard was kept by the Armenians and, in accordance with ancient custom, none but Abyssinians might be buried there.' There were more protests from the neighbours. The medical officer could not move the body to the mortuary; it was too near the hospital.

The Anglican bishop came to my aid and agreed that the archdeacon should bury Mrs Musa, provided the doctor would sign a statement that his wife had been a Christian. Dr Musa refused to allow his wife to be

buried in a coffin, but I insisted, so off he went with a Greek Catholic
district officer to buy one. They were away some time, but returned
flushed with pride because I was paying for the coffin and they had
succeeded in getting a shop to reduce the price from £P 3.5s to
£P 2.15s. 'Would I please come to the door and see it?' I sent them off.
In an hour they were back. No one would carry the coffin or the body.
It was all too irregular. I put off the archdeacon for an hour and sent off
another district officer with orders to rope in at the Jaffa Gate half a
dozen professional Orfalli Kurdish porters, pay them enormous
largesse, and get the lady buried.

At five o'clock the streets suddenly cleared as all that was mortal of
Mrs Musa was carried to her final resting place followed by Dr Musa
and three district officers, a Jew, a Greek Melchite and a Protestant,
each looking a little ill. There was a slight controversy when Dr Musa
wanted to make a speech at the grave but the squall was weathered.

Next day, clad in a third overcoat, Dr Musa came to thank me. While
we sipped our coffee, his in a glass, he told me why he objected to
coffins, but we agreed that the one Mrs Musa had had was a bargain.

A wealthy Syrian who had returned after living in the United States for
many years lost his daughter, who died in New York. He had done
much for the development of Haifa and had acquired a lot of property.
The daughter was unmarried, so he decided to give her the finest
funeral in Haifa that money could buy.

Six Arab horses were covered with white palls braided with yellow
cord and attached to a special hearse. A couple of bands followed, and
a Melchite choir was imported from Tyre. The route round the town
had been selected with care so as to embrace as much of the father's
house property as possible. Upon the roofs people had been posted to
throw down flowers. Traffic was stopped.

A boat set off from the quay and brought back an enormous black
crate. Opened by a shouting, gesticulating body of Arab porters, it
revealed a thing of wondrous beauty in oxidized silver. When I saw it I
realized why Chicago caskets cost so much!

When the procession had trailed round the streets I joined it outside
the temporary cupola. A deft swing and half the top of the coffin

opened and the long-haired bishop and I were invited to look through the glass. Taking off his inverted top hat the aged prelate picked up his skirts, climbed up on a stone and peered in. He gave a gasp and fell backwards.

The girl was dressed as a bride in white and gold raiment. Her right hand was clasping a cross and a bunch of lilies was in her left. Her dark features seemed slightly self-conscious as, acting on the principle that 'gentlemen prefer blondes', the crematorium beauty specialist had done his utmost with powder and paint, and rouge sits so feverishly on dark skins. I stepped down almost as shaken as the bishop.

When Mr Menahem Ussishkin, the notable Zionist leader and president of the Jewish National Fund, died aged 78, and in harness up to the day of his death, he left a paper saying that there were not to be any customary speeches or eulogies. So much was this grand old man respected that even in death he was obeyed. Delegates came from every Jewish National Fund settlement and covered his grave with a unique pall, little bags of earth from all their villages. He lies alongside his old friend Pinsker in the Cave of Nicanor on the Mount of Olives.

The Syrian Orthodox metropolitan of Jerusalem shared the distinction of seated burial with the Greek patriarch. When my friend Bishop Philoxinos passed away in hospital, priests who had been anticipating His Grace's end were hurriedly called to vest the dead man and sit him upon a chair. He was carried down the narrow tortuous cobbled steps to the tiny Church of St Mark in the heart of the old city, which, according to Syrian tradition, is built upon the site of the Last Supper, and he was placed before the altar.

Philoxinos had been one of the strongest priests I ever met, and a notable figure with his height and flowing beard. He had done good work and had built a church at Bethlehem. He had loved being made a bishop late in life and never quite got over his surprise and joy; with a sheepish and happy look he would fondle his jewelled pectoral cross, much as a child handles a toy.

As I saw him, shrunken in death, robed in golden vestments, a heavily embroidered gold cap (the Syrian monks' cowl) upon his head and an ivory crosier in his hand, seated upon the episcopal chair in which, for five successive years I had seen him elevated shoulder-high, proudly reading the Gospel after washing the feet of the 12, I recalled an incident of 20 years before, for what he may have lacked in saintliness he made up in virility.

In the scrimmage round the Holy Sepulchre after the Holy Fire had been distributed, while guarding his bishop, he saw a young Coptic priest trying to prevent His Grace's traditional chair being carried to its rightful place in the procession. Priest Yacub, as he then was, stepped back a pace and, with one blow on the chin, knocked the offending Copt completely out, so that the man had to be carried away over the heads of the crowds to be revived. The procession went triumphantly on!

After an elaborate mass attended by the community and a short service, later attended by officials and consuls, Philoxinos had his hand fervently kissed by his followers; he was then stripped of his outer raiment, carried down and deposited in the vault under the chancel. The decaying body of another old friend, Bishop Elias, who had died a few years back, grimly awaited him on the stone throne. This body was unceremoniously brushed into a corner and Philoxinos replaced him. There we left him, in the light of one guttering candle, sitting bolt upright — awfully alone.

Among the hills bordering the valley of the Jordan nestles Mar Saba, a fortress-like convent used formerly as a penitentiary for refractory Orthodox monks. Visiting it one day to attend a service in commemoration of the patron saint, I learned that a monk had died, so I stayed on for the funeral.

A heavy stone had been raised up in the courtyard floor and a strange, unsavoury smell permeated the whole establishment. After a short service we walked down a sloping pathway into the vault. There, sewn up in black cotton cloth, lying upon stone slabs, were the bodies of monks ranging from one who had died a week before, to another who had been placed there a month before, to the remains of those who had been dead for years. Elsewhere there were skulls, row upon row.

Why the whole community was not dead of some disease puzzled me, but the manner of disposal may account for its poor physical condition. Only the abbot looked flourishing, but he, like myself, was only a visitor and of titular rank.

The wife of a distinguished British Jew died in the Holy City as the result of an accident. The husband, who had been himself injured, was forced to agree that she should lie in Palestine, but he insisted that she be buried in a coffin. He was beaten by tradition in the end. To the consternation of the British nursing sisters who had prepared the body for the grave, a couple of professional washers thrust their way into the mortuary at night, stripped the corpse, rewashed it and wrapped it up in their own shroud. Male watchers then proceeded to tear one side out of the coffin so that the remains could touch mother earth. Their end accomplished, they sat down in the midst of the sodden floor and smoked cigarettes until the dawn.

A dear, very fat American lady, who had given long service, especially in the cause of temperance in Palestine, died and I was invited to her funeral at the Church of the Assemblies of God. She was one of the oldest residents in the Holy City and I felt I would rather go in person than send a representative. So one hot July day I donned my black coat and set out for the bare little church. Many flies were buzzing about the crowded building. I was led to a front pew and, after saying my prayers, opened my eyes and found myself gazing into the face of the deceased, who was somewhat gaily decked in her best party frock. I sat out the long service and sang nearly a dozen verses of a hymn, 'He is Coming Now', in alternate Arabic and English verses. Meanwhile mourners came up and, breaking forth into dramatic sobs, affectionately patted the lady's cheeks. The service ended, the minister in charge, a Palestinian educated at a small Western American university, called in stentorian tones: 'Now all those who desire to view the remains of our sister step up this way and file past the coffin. Step this way and see the remains. The remains this way.' However, I managed to step the other way and escape further ordeal.

Funeral Rites

In the early days of the civil government an elderly American tourist died and his widow decided that she would like to take his remains back to the United States. Her wishes were blocked because at that time corpses could not be taken from Palestine. She was advised by the hotel to go and see the Muslim mayor, who was a man of great resource. She found the mayor worried, pacing up and down his room. The municipal purse was empty and there was a shortage of money to pay the scavengers. £P 70 were lacking.

Always civil, Ragheb Bey Nashashibi listened to her plea and, as her story unfolded, enlightenment and vision shone in his eye. He suggested cremation and that the matter be left in his hands. And the fee? 'Seventy pounds,' he said firmly. The bargain was clinched. The widow left. Rapid orders for the municipal refuse destructor to be cleaned were given. The body was spirited away and next day the tactful mayor called in person at the hotel, followed by his uniformed *kavass* carrying a small olive-wood box, normally associated with cigarettes, bound with purple ribbon. With a decorous bow, the mayor presented the box of ashes and pocketed the dollar bills. He stopped long enough to convey the corporation's condolences, for, as he says when telling the story, the cigarette box and purple ribbon were worth the money, as he made more than their price on the exchange of the dollars at the bank, and many local homes were made happy beside the breast of Mrs Silas B.

However, when they came to hear of it, the public health authorities were shocked and the director of medical services stopped further incursion into the business of a mortician by His Worship.

Our village buses were like carriers' carts of old and took everything. When the bus was full inside, 'jump on the roof' was the custom. Near Lajjun, on the Haifa-Jerusalem road, a young peasant signalled the bus and asked to be given a lift. He paid the fare but there was room for him on top only. Mounting the roof, he found a shiny coffin being taken to Jerusalem and got inside for shelter from the rain. Some distance further on, two other villagers halted the bus and the large-hearted driver, for a consideration, agreed to take them on top. Clambering up, they muffled themselves in their *abaya*s and the vehicle rolled on.

173

As the bus was going slowly up a hill, the lid of the coffin began to rise before their horrified eyes. A hand came forth groping to feel if it were still raining. The two villagers edged away, howling: 'The dead has come to life! *Allahu Akbar!* God the greatest! Save us!' Without waiting for the bus to stop, they took flying leaps to the roadside. Fortunately only slightly bruised, they picked up their skirts and fled into the hills.

14

The Giant Turtle

I availed myself of every opportunity that was offered to go on local
leave. It gave me a chance to see something of our neighbours. The
brief escape from work and officialdom kept my sense of proportion alive and I saw all the interesting things and places surrounding
Palestine.

My wife and I paid an early visit to Petra, crossing the Jordan by the
Allenby Bridge, which was erected by Canadian lumberjacks in 1917
under such murderous fire that every rivet is said to have cost a life.

As we dropped down to the river we entered a succession of dead
hills carved by the winds into improbable shapes — a cone, a cube, a
queer isolated pinnacle, a ridge looking like a battlemented castle, the
whole mass impregnated with salt.

An old motorcar carried us in seven hours from Amman, the
Ammonite capital of Rabbath-Ammon, which the Greeks had renamed
Philadelphia and which had just been made the capital of Transjordan,
to the head of the Wadi Musa.

Low peaks confronted us, coloured claret, mauve, pink and gold.
They barred the way to what for hundreds of years had been a closely
guarded secret. Behind them for centuries the Nabateans had made their
capital. Neither Bedu in the East nor Jew from the West had ever dared
to explore; a few who had set out to solve the mystery had never
returned.

Except for Persian, Macedonian and Roman military expeditions,
these mountain men had maintained their dominion for centuries and
taken toll on the commerce of scents, silks and spices passing between
the Indian Ocean and the Mediterranean Sea.

175

Mounted upon scraggy horses, we dropped down a steep path. We reached a gash in the mountain side, Es Sik. For half an hour our horses stumbled along beside a stream that ran down it. Traces of an old aqueduct still remained. Cherry-coloured flowers from oleanders brushed our faces. The light got dimmer, the walls higher, the air stiller, the sense of unreality keener as we descended. The winding track narrowed so that we could touch both dark red walls. At a slight turn the sunken way enlarged and, facing us, in brilliant sunlight, was a temple carved from the living rock. It was here that Nabateans had prayed for protection when going on expeditions, or had given thanks on their return. What must the temple have been in the days of its glory with its statues, its sphinxes, its columns and sculptured capitals in perfect condition?

We turned southwards and the gorge closed in, and then abruptly opened out to a flat of about a mile long and two thirds across to the mountains rising on either side. Here had been the city, and here remain the carved tombs of vivid colours and varied architecture. We passed an open-air theatre with 30 tiers of sandstone seats that would accommodate a couple of thousand spectators.

We were quickly made aware that the Nabateans had departed as various members of the present inhabitants showed themselves — thin, debased and emaciated. They were not looked upon by the Bedu tribesmen as Arabs and were called the '*Badul*', literally the 'Changelings' because they were believed to have been Jews who, some years after Islam was founded, changed their faith *en masse*.

They scattered their fleas, quarrelled among themselves for scraps of food from the kitchen and later, led by a cadaverous dame with a sword in her hand, danced at night to the flickering light of a bonfire. The old woman worked them up to a perfect frenzy by cursing them, calling them cowards, bewitching them until they had exhausted their energy and all they could do was to fall upon the roasted sheep and rice I had prepared for them. My wife and I departed to a tomb and slept.

Some 15 years later I left Zarqa, near Amman, in an aeroplane, flew as far as Ma'an, then mounted the escarpment and crossed over Es Sik and looked down upon the mystery city tucked away between the hills. We then banked steeply, heading for the south, passed over El Quweira and, coming down to 50 feet above ground, flew along the length of Wadi Rum, the limit of the Nabatean kingdom. On either side of us was red rock going straight upwards for 1000 feet. We went too quickly to pick out features, but it was incomparable, like a jewelled avenue in Valhalla. I had the impression that our small open machine was standing still and a fence of jewels in the rough was rushing past us.

Banking again we headed westwards and arrived over the Gulf of Aqaba, intensely blue; we then went up to the northern end, where traces of the castle with its triple gate, similar to the one built by Solomon at Megiddo, could be seen.

We soared over the spine of hills passing Petra again, then descended to the Wadi Araba, with the needle registering our drop below sea level as we reached the southern shores of the Dead Sea. The potash evaporation pans gleamed white like snow.

We went the length of the salt sea as far as the mouth of the Jordan, then rose from 1000 feet below sea level to 4000 above and, crossing the Judaean hills, dropped down onto the aerodrome at Ramallah near Jerusalem.

Rather breathless I descended from the machine and grasped the pilot's hand. We had traversed together some of the wonders of the world.

One winter's morning in glorious crisp weather, invigorating every fibre of one's being, my wife and I left Jerusalem station to stay in Her Sultanic Highness Princess Kadria's yacht moored on the Nile.

Our train dipped down to Battir, the station where I had got out and sniffed the air on my first journey up. For some miles alongside the railway there were a series of terraced and irrigated garden plots, which supplied the city with vegetables from a unique spring of water.

Small boys held up crimson anemones and purple cyclamen plucked from crevices in the hills. The train rocked down to Lydda station over 2000 feet below and then we settled down for the journey through the orange groves to Gaza, El Arish and across the Sinai desert. The orange groves were hung with golden balls glistening in the sunlight. At every station Arab children crowded the line offering a dozen oranges for a piastre (2½d).

At El Arish scores of children, looking more like Egyptians than Arabs, lined the route and called for *baksheesh*. They dashed to a window and picked up a coin or a cigarette as seagulls pick up a piece of bread thrown to them in Oban harbour, keeping one half eye on the train and the other one and a half on the Egyptian policeman who carried a stout wooden *nabout* and called upon Allah to shatter the homes of these dogs who did not hear his voice.

As the train left El Arish for the four hours' journey across Sinai the sand got heavier and cultivation ceased. A wind with the taste of a furnace rose up. The sky darkened and, in an hour or two, with a roar, a sandstorm born in Transjordan was upon us. We were closed into a detached world with what the Royal Air Force describe as 'visibility nil'. The storm had not the majesty of a Sudan *haboob*, but the wind shrieked and was terrific. The train was brought to a standstill; no driver's eye could cope. We crawled into Kantara some hours late accompanied by a crescendo of biting wind. Customs formalities were carried out in sepulchral gloom, as was the journey across the Suez Canal.

Abbas I, son of the great Ibrahim Pasha, viceroy of Egypt who died in 1848, reigned but a short time, but he reigned long enough to purchase for his own use the finest paddle-wheeled yacht that art, skill, workmanship and money could buy. Tod & MacGregor of Glasgow built the ship and delivered it in 1852. The Princess Kadria had acquired the yacht by inheritance and had very graciously invited us to stay there. Swinging past the crescent formed by the British embassy in Cairo, we pulled up at the top of gaily lighted steps leading down to the Nile. We were greeted by the captain. It was over 40 years since he had first taken service with Sultan Hussein, the princess's father. Born and bred by the riverside, to the Nile he belonged. The butler, robed in a dark blue *jibbah* trimmed with scarlet, opened a doorway at the forward end and the clock had gone back a century. Passing through a mahogany-lined dining room we entered the saloon, similarly panelled. The walls were decorated with a series of pictures painted on porcelain in oils, lustre and gold paint. A portrait of Mohammed Ali[1] looked

---

1. Mohammed Ali (1769–1849) was an Albanian officer in the Ottoman army who ruled Egypt from 1805 and founded a dynasty which lasted until King Farouk was overthrown by an army revolution in 1952.

down upon us. Exquisite furniture, brocades and carpets harmonized with the surroundings.

But if the upper rooms were magnificent, the two rooms below could be likened to the *Arabian Nights* themselves. The walls were broad panels of rosewood surmounted by a gold frieze that ran right round. But our 26-square-foot bedroom was the most beautiful of all. Upon the walls and door panels exquisite flower scenes had been painted in oils upon the rosewood and each picture had been enclosed in a frame of carved wood covered with gold leaf. Persian carpets were upon the floor and a heavy blue and gold silk tapestry covered our bed. Period chairs covered with gold leaf were before the dressing table. There were large armchairs to rest in. The ceiling was white panelled wood lined with gold and mahogany.

Added to this splendour was a charming note of welcome from Her Highness, plus the warmth of an electric stove and shielded lights. The service and cooking were excellent.

We looked out from the cabin windows. The waxing moon was about to set. It made a silver ripple across the Nile like a streak of phosphorus. We went to sleep as the river lapped the sides of the yacht that had known her rise and fall for 90 years.

I went with Dr Orr-Ewing and his wife to Palmyra. The journey from Damascus was somewhat dramatic because Orr-Ewing was a happy-go-lucky soul and had not seen to his tyres before we set out. After several punctures and 50 miles from anywhere we had run through the lot of spares.

With hundreds of camel drivers we had exchanged the courtesies of the desert. 'Where do you come from? Where are you going? Go in peace.' Proceeding cautiously on our last four inner tubes we passed between two towers built on a low escarpment of hills and beyond lay the walled city. The main avenue was so long that from the distance the mighty colonnade looked like a Canadian ring-fence. The lofty columns arising out of an ochre-coloured bed were surrounded by hills upon which not a living blade was seen. It was hard to realize that these stark remains were all that was left of what was once a great city teeming with people.

Originally Tadmur had been a small Arab settlement, but it was transformed into a place of first importance, especially when the Nabateans, reduced by the Emperor Trajan, vanished from Petra and secretly diverted the desert trade with the East to Tadmur or Palmyra. In the third century of our era Palmyra had become an outpost of the Roman Empire and Zenobia became reigning queen. Her husband, Odenathus, had by his own energies raised himself to become the leader of the people, the government and the army. He was assassinated by his nephew at a public function. But vanity and ambition overreached themselves. The queen had conquered Egypt and her legions had poured into Asia Minor; throwing off all pretence at allegiance, she had coins minted without placing the head of Emperor Aurelian thereon.

For ten years Rome had suffered these indignities. Then the emperor struck, and when the inhabitants of the conquered city revolted against the Roman garrison he placed there, the city was destroyed. Zenobia was granted her life by the emperor and taken to Rome, a solitary but great figure in Aurelian's triumphal march.

In the eleventh century Palmyra was struck by an earthquake, but recovered something of its trade and, a century later, there were 2000 Jews living among its inhabitants.

Today the tiny population is entirely Muslim. The main avenue of limestone columns 55 feet high once formed the supports for the statues of successful merchants who had succeeded in convoying caravans from the Persian Gulf. But the majority of the busts have long since been destroyed or sold by the Bedu. The Temple of the Sun is of huge proportions, enclosed by four outer walls of which one remains. The present population live in a collection of flat-roofed, sun-baked brick hovels within the ruined walls.

I saw young Bedu gallants, with long plaited hair and the faraway look in their eyes one associates with sailors or desert dwellers, walking with natural dignity in their picturesque rags, armed to the teeth, within the walls of what to their ancestors must have been the most stupendous monument in the world.

As I left at sunset the crudeness of the day softened, the sinking sun leaving an afterglow of amber that touched the tips of the lofty columns. On the rustle of the evening breeze came the murmur of sonorous Bedu voices and the rhythm of drums from within the temple. One could almost hear the voices of those who, kneeling down at

180

sunset, offered up their prayers and supplications to the sun god.

Cairo seemed a teeming metropolis after Jerusalem, but once away from the mosques, the museum and the green grass of the Gezira Sporting Club, the zoo was far and away the most delightful place to go to. A beautiful garden of 50 acres on the west bank of the Nile, it was the only place in Egypt where soliciting for *baksheesh* was absolutely forbidden. How the director achieved this is a modern mystery. At holiday times the people flocked in from palace and slum and in a hushed mood shared their groundnuts with the inmates.

As the keepers did not have to work any of the animals in order to make a living out of their labours, they were kind to them. The beasts looked contented and happy. The climate suited them. The hippopotamus, a royal beast, mighty of muscle, spent most of the day under water. Yet if the keeper called to him or hit upon the water, the great animal ambled up from the tank and opened his prodigious mouth. The seals performed tricks and the lions put up their heads to be scratched. Huge giraffes had hides like spotted velour.

The oldest inhabitant was a giant turtle. His exact age was uncertain, but he had been there ever since the gardens were opened many years ago, and he was very aged then. Usually the Egyptians did not take much notice of him, as he rarely walked about his pen with the others but spent his time sleeping in a corner.

One day when I was alone I saw a number of Egyptian women standing round the pen and I heard a succession of extraordinary grunts coming from it. The women were beside themselves with laughter. There were screams of delight. They yelled and slapped their sides in ecstasy. Mothers held up their children to have a better look. Little girls peeped between their skirts. I have never seen Egyptian women so animated and eager.

I walked up and found that the aged reptile, attracted by a female of the species, had decided that he was not as old as he thought he was and was taking the opportunity, in calm and deliberation, of mating with his love, whom he mounted in the traditional manner. His labours and grunts of satisfaction were too much for the women, whose daily lives were so near those of animals. For the next quarter of an hour he was

181

the most popular exhibit in the gardens. I am bound to confess that the whole proceedings were so comical that at the finish no one was laughing more heartily than myself. The incident was rather like watching the tree that blossoms once in 30 years.

15

The Storm

I n April 1936 two Jews who were travelling between Tulkarm and Nablus were first robbed and then shot dead by Arabs. The following night two Arabs were murdered in a hut near Petah Tiqvah. In a few days 16 Jews and 5 Arabs were killed and 100 from both communities were wounded.

A general strike was called for in Nablus by Arabs and it spread rapidly. The various leaders put aside their family and party quarrels and formed the Arab Higher Committee under the presidency of Haj Amin el Husseini, the *mufti*. Emergency regulations were promulgated by the government and district commissioners were given wide powers, including authority to detain persons without trial for one year.

Incendiarism of Jewish property spread all over Palestine. There were four cruisers and two destroyers at Haifa; British officers and seamen came to our aid and ratings acted as engine drivers on the railways. Naval officers took charge of lorries converted into armoured cars protected with steel plates and mattresses. The first of six, with a two-pound pom-pom in the head, was painted Mediterranean grey and named 'Pip', and this name stuck to the flotilla of six which operated all over Palestine. Not to be outdone by the sailors, the Royal Artillery set about mounting a three-pounder, originally intended for the local defence of Haifa, onto a lorry and this vehicle was referred to officially as 'Squeak'. The trinity was completed by the army naming its searchlight lorry, improvized to work with them, 'Wilfred'.[1] One of the trains, manned from the cruiser *Sussex*, was known as the 'Jordan

1. Characters from a popular cartoon strip.

Queen' as it ran on the Haifa-Samakh line and was frequently in action. On his last patrol a midshipman flew a long white surgical bandage from his armed truck by way of a paying-off pennant.

I dined in the gunroom with the young officers a night or two before their ship left. Five young men were seriously worried because, on their return to Malta, they had to sit their promotion examinations and, as they had spent the last weeks in operations, they had had no time for special work at their books. Next day I went and saw the captain and, with his permission, I wrote to the president of the forthcoming board and asked that their good work under active service conditions might be taken into account to balance the possible lack of theory. Some weeks later the captain wrote to me that all five had been given first classes.

General Wauchope urged the Arab Higher Committee to restrain Arabs from violence. He advised them to send their delegates to London. The Higher Committee refused until immigration was stopped. Cunliffe Lister, the colonial secretary, expressed in the House of Commons his complete confidence in Wauchope and stated that there was no question of stopping immigration and that the invitation for an Arab deputation was still open. Then, 12 days later he announced that the government was sending a Royal Commission to Palestine to investigate and make recommendations for the removal of grievances. The same day the high commissioner published a labour schedule for 4500 Jewish immigrants to enter.

Immediately the storm broke out again, more seriously. Arab bands began to form and volunteers from Syria and Iraq appeared among them. Thousands of forest and citrus trees were destroyed, and trains were wrecked. Mr Ormsby-Gore[2] succeeded Cunliffe Lister as secretary of state and he too expressed confidence in Wauchope, and added that the government would not be moved by violence.

Two events now took place that seriously undermined discipline in the local administration. Wauchope allowed, as a safety valve, both first- and second-division government Arab officers to submit memoranda to the government, stating that insufficient regard was being paid to Arab grievances and recommending the stoppage of Jewish immigration. Then, in order to obtain better control over the port, where sniping had been continuous, Wauchope authorized the blowing up of

---

2. William George Arthur Ormsby-Gore (1885–1964).

250 houses to make a wide road in Jaffa; the government stupidly camouflaged the reason for the action by stating that it was part of a town-planning improvement scheme. The act was severely criticized by the chief justice, McDonnell, in an action brought before the High Court by an Arab householder. His Lordship said: 'The petitioner has done a public service in exposing a singularly disingenuous lack of moral courage. It would have been more creditable, instead of endeavouring to throw dust in people's eyes by professing to be inspired with aesthetic or other quasi-philanthropic motives, if those responsible had said frankly that it was primarily for defensive purposes.' This criticism by the High Court electrified the Arabs, who promptly had the judgment printed and distributed as a pamphlet.

Wauchope felt that whatever one thought about the *mufti* of Jerusalem he was a force to be reckoned with. So he tried to be sympathetic and make him his friend. To this end, despite the vigorous protests of Morris Bailey, my deputy, acting for me while I was in England on sick leave, he had allowed Haj Amin to make a tour of Northern Palestine, ostensibly to calm Muslim opinion. He had given instructions that police were not to be present at these meetings. Full advantage of this trust was taken by the Muslim leader.

For some months I had been very ill, the result of continuous overwork. I suffered grievous pain from acute iritis. Thanks to the wondrous skill of Dr John Strathearn and Sisters Roulstone and Sadlier I am not blind.

For weeks and weeks I could not sleep, so I went off to Austria to try and get better. In the village of Kitzbühel I met an old acquaintance from the League of Nations. We had a great evening. We laughed and talked, ate enormous Wiener schnitzels and drank libations of white wine. I went back to my *schloss* and slept the clock round and from that moment steadily improved in health.

I was away from work for many months. On my return I found that the strike had not ended and violence continued. A number of police were murdered. My most senior Muslim officer was wounded in the jaw and a few days after his return to duty was shot dead.

The Iraq Petroleum Company pipeline was damaged a score of times by firing at the pipe and lighting the oil as it spurted out. To repair it a special technique was developed by the repair parties. The fire would be put out with sand, then an Arab worker would rush forward and sit on the hole. Holding a block of wood between his legs he worked it into the hole and drove it in to block the flow. The place would then be welded over and, just before the weld was completed, the piece of wood would be driven home, and, in a few days, it would appear with the oil at the next pumping station.

The British Cabinet cancelled the army manoeuvres and sent two divisions to Palestine under Lieutenant-General J. G. Dill,[3] former director of military operations. My colleagues and I had warned the Arabs about the drastic military action that would be taken against them, and urged them to call off the strike. I met Dill in Haifa, but there was delay in deciding what form military law should take, and he had to wait before it was determined under what power he was to operate. While matters were being delayed, seven weeks passed.

The three Arab kings and Emir Abdullah of Transjordan[4] were called into conference by the Arab Higher Committee and, in October, Their Majesties sent identical letters to the committee, asking it to resort to quietness to avoid bloodshed, relying upon the good intentions of the British government. The response was immediate. The strike was called off. 'God is on our side,' said the manifesto.

Kauwakji,[5] the Iraqi, as commander-in-chief of the Arab armed forces, signed a special order of the day ordering them to keep their arms safe and praising their courage.

Dill also issued an order of the day stating that the calling off of the strike was in great measure due to the resolute action of the three services. Wauchope did not agree with the terms of this proclamation and ordered that it be not published in Palestine, but of course it could not be suppressed and came over the BBC.

---

3. Lieutenant-General J. G. Dill served in the Boer War and the First World War and then worked mainly in training and in military operations and intelligence.

4. Emir Abdullah was the second son of *Sherif* Hussein of Mecca. He was established as King of Transjordan in 1921 and assassinated in Jerusalem in 1951.

5. Fawzi el-Kauwakji was the most important leader of the Arab forces during the Arab revolt which began in 1936. He was a Syrian who had fought with distinction in the Turkish army during the First World War and afterwards became an intelligence officer with the French army in Syria. He took part in a Syrian rebellion against the French in 1925 and later became military adviser to the king of Saudi Arabia. Kauwakji was an experienced and skilled commander and, when the British succeeded in driving him out of Palestine into Transjordan, the Arab revolt began to disintegrate through lack of effective leadership.

Within a month British units began to leave. Some 21 British soldiers, 16 police, and nearly 300 civilians had been killed and 100 soldiers, 100 policemen and 1100 civilians wounded. Photographs of Kauwakji inspecting his troops began to appear and it was obvious that many armed bands were sitting tight in the hills. So the military, who mistrusted the ability of civilians and the police to keep secrets, made a plan to block the exits, surround the bands from Syria and Iraq, and disarm them.

The high commissioner was faced with a problem. It was desirable to get the Royal Commission out. The foreign bands were anxious to leave. So the military operations were cancelled and I was ordered to send word to Kauwakji. He was allowed to leave by crossing the Jordan into Emir Abdullah's domain; there he stayed until Abdullah induced him to go back to Iraq.

Major-General Archie Wavell[6] replaced Dill. I saw a good deal of him and his family when I went back to Jerusalem. They loved wandering about the Old City and learning about its little-known corners. Before that, he had stayed with me in Haifa while he was writing his book on Allenby. One evening he was talking to me about soldiers and said that a successful general must be steeped in his textbooks, but once he starts to give battle he must throw them all behind him and conduct operations out of his original thoughts. How well he was to prove this later!

Economically the country was having a bad time. Crops were lower than average and their transport was difficult. Citrus exports had dropped. Building and other industries had suffered a setback. Government revenues from imports had begun to fall. The six-monthly schedule of immigrants had been cut to 1800.

New Year's Day 1937 was the dawn of expectation for Jew and Arab, and also for the British official. We had passed through a harassing year. The British police had been sorely tried. There were few British administrative officers. Some of their Arab colleagues were found to be disloyal: one of my Arab district officers had been in active

6. Major-General Archie Wavell's early military career included service in the Russian army from 1911 to 1912. During the First World War he served first in France and then in Palestine, where he became Allenby's chief of staff. In 1937 he was given the Middle East Command. He defeated the Italians in North Africa, but failed against Rommel. In 1941 he was transferred to India where he became viceroy in 1943.

touch with Kauwakji while the rebel leader was operating in his sub-district.

We had had to get to know and co-operate with new army command-ers, and get them to accept our opinion about whom they could trust. They were most sceptical and their motto was 'sack the lot'. There were bickerings between military intelligence officers and police. The army was inclined to criticize the high commissioner and asked continually for 'a free hand'. The police asked permission to 'use Turkish methods'. It was my and other district commissioners' duty to maintain the prestige of the high commissioner and carry out his policy.

The Royal Commission had arrived in November and been received with considerable ceremony, but no Arabs had attended the reception.

Lord Peel, the chairman, had been chairman of the London County Council and secretary of state for India, as well as holding various other political appointments; Sir Horace Rumbold had been British ambassa-dor at Constantinople, Madrid and Berlin; and Professor Reginald Coupland, the sixth member, was professor of colonial history at Oxford. At the opening session the chairman emphasized that a Royal Commission was an entirely independent body, uncontrolled by His Majesty's Government in the present or in the past.

The commission had made a deep impression. It listened, heard, and cross-examined. The dignity, the courtesy, the searching questions, the promptitude and the accuracy of the transcript of questions and answers had won respect and everyone who met its members was loud in their praises. The Arabs had at first refused to give evidence, but did so later.

I had a long day with the commission in Haifa. I said that even in England difficulties had been caused by immigration and that, owing to the trouble created by immigrants, an agitation had been set afoot against alien Jewish settlers, and that the Ashkenazi authorities in London had appealed to the Home Secretary in 1771 to adopt a policy of restriction of Jews from Poland.

Some 70 years later a circular had been printed in Jerusalem by rabbinical authority making charges against members of the Anglican Church resident in Jerusalem. It complained that Jews had been compelled to give of their substance to build a hospital and that, by paying higher rents, the missionaries had taken several houses in which Jews lived and had driven them out. The circular ended on this note: 'The Congregation of the Lord is oppressed and cast down ... they cry and none delivereth.' In 1907 the entry of a million and a quarter immigrants into the United States of America had caused a revulsion of feeling and this led to restrictions being imposed. After the Great War, 6000 Italians entering Australia had caused serious disturbances. But to draw a parallel with 60,000 let into Palestine in one year, it would be necessary to put the entire population of Australia into Tasmania and to send to the island 360,000 immigrants in the same period.

I urged that economic absorptive capacity should not be the sole factor. It ignored all psychological considerations, housing accommodation available for present inhabitants and the adaptation of newcomers to local conditions. It also swamped the administrative services. I recommended that a 'political high level' for immigrants be introduced. The adoption of this measure was as much in the interests of Jews as it was of Arabs.

The commission left with everyone's goodwill.

Unfortunately the terrorist campaign did not stop there. In Jerusalem 19 Jews were wounded in a bomb outrage and, within a few hours, four bombs were thrown into Arab cafés. Attacks by Arabs were made on Arab mayors in Haifa and Bethlehem. There was also intense intimidation with violence upon Arabs by Arabs.

The chief justice, McDonnell, who had adversely criticized the high commissioner, had departed and the attorney general, Harry Trusted, was appointed to replace him. The immigration schedule had been again drastically curtailed, but the Arabs were discontented, even with this, and decided to boycott the king's coronation celebrations. However, despite the boycott, political strife was stayed for the commemoration of the coronation of King George VI on 12 May and we had a great day of rejoicing in Haifa. I took the salute at a parade of the Essex Regiment. All the British children in the district were collected and, after a feast of buns and cake, I gave each one a mug that I had designed and had thrown by a local potter: on one side the town arms were emblazoned and on the other a suitable inscription. I held a large garden party in the convent grounds on Carmel and presented a number of coronation medals to those who were doing useful if inconspicuous work for Britain in Palestine: doctors, missionaries, social workers and teachers, as well as officials and other British notables.

In July, the report of the Royal Commission was published. It was recognized at once as a great state paper. It is the most exhaustive and fairest document ever written about Palestine, a model that every person in public life should read.

The commission agreed that a 'political high level' should be introduced for immigration, but it considered that all schemes put forward were only palliatives and that partition (and if necessary the removal of population) was the only solution. 'While neither race can justly rule all Palestine we see no reason why each race should not rule part of it. Partition seems to offer at least a chance of ultimate peace. We see none in any other plan.'

It recommended that should disorders break out again, requiring the intervention of the military, there should be no hesitation in enforcing martial law under military control.

The British government agreed with the arguments and conclusions but all parties in Palestine expressed their dissent vehemently. I wrote to the high commissioner:

> Jews, Christians and Muslims are like three bewildered, discon-
> solate children at a party. 'We don't want jam; we don't want
> honey; we don't want cake. We want jelly.' Alas, there is no
> jelly. The horn of Haj Amin is exalted and the one who waits
> outside the gates, Emir Abdullah, is denounced. The Jews state
> that Eretz Israel without Zion is become as sounding brass.

The suggestion that there might be an exchange of land and population revived the spirit of revolt among the Arabs and, from that moment, the revolution really started. Murder and arson were again rife. My able young Australian assistant, Andrews, was murdered as he was attending evening service at Nazareth. I saw him lying upon his back on an army blanket, a smile upon his lips, his dead British police comrade by his side. I thought of his wife and three children. His only crime, love for and devotion to Palestine.

Wauchope was in England, so Battershill, the chief secretary, who was administering the government, took action. On our insistence, the Arab Higher Committee and all national committees were declared unlawful, and Haj Amin el Husseini was deprived of his office of president of the Supreme Muslim Council. A few weeks later, disguised in woman's clothes, he fled by sailing boat to Beirut. Military courts were set up and the carrying of arms was punishable by death. Andrews's death shook Palestine and there was a lull for some days. Then the airport at Lydda was attacked, and trains were mined and many people killed.

The secretary of state sent out still another commission. This time it consisted of a couple of former Indian policemen, one of whom was Sir Charles Tegart of the Calcutta police. Tegart was an amusing as well as a brave man. When his car was ambushed near Nablus and a colleague was shot dead by his side, he did not get rattled. He got the British government to provide a couple of million pounds for the construction of 50 strongly fortified police barracks all over the country. He also had a barbed-wire fence erected from the Mediterranean to Lake Huleh. It proved useless. The Arabs dragged it apart with camels.

Tegart's other innovation was not good. He started what he called 'Arab investigation centres', at which 'selected' police officers were to be trained in the gentle art of 'third degree', for use on Arabs until they 'spilled the beans', as it is termed in criminal circles. When I heard that such a centre had been established in a Jewish suburb of Jerusalem, I warned Wauchope that I would not tolerate it. It was closed soon after Wauchope retired.

Wauchope's tenure of office did not survive the Royal Commission for long. He followed it to England and, shortly after, Ormsby-Gore announced that owing to illness he had resigned. He returned and spent the next three months as mentally and physically active as ever.

His final departure was distressing because he did not want to leave the garden of Government House, which he had planted with olive trees, and with flowers and seeds gathered from all over Palestine. It remains a lovely memorial of the best side of his dual character.

The British government announced that it was sending a fact-finding commission to make recommendations on the tentative plan for partition and its practical possibilities, but it had not accepted the proposal for the compulsory transfer in the last resort of Arabs from the Jewish to the Arab area.

During the previous six years Northern Palestine had developed so much that it was now decided to divide the district into three separate ones. Each was to be administered by a district commissioner, and I was asked to go back to Jerusalem where security was very bad. I went back. My old offices within the city walls had been evacuated because Jews, rightly, were afraid to enter the Old City. William McGeagh, my deputy, and Robert Greig and Jerry Cornes gave me the most loyal service and help, and so also did Jamal Beq Tuqan and Jacob Kisselov.

Constant attacks were made on traffic passing along the highways. Mr John Llewelyn Starkey, a British archaeologist excavating at Lachish and employing hundreds of Arabs, was murdered near Hebron in 1938 by armed Arabs and half his head was cut away. I had warned him of the danger. He had replied, 'I can trust the Arab.' We got police dogs to the scene, and Tegart and I ran behind them across country from dawn to noon, a distance of 20 kilometres. From time to time the dogs stopped and pointed to a piece of torn clothing or a dropped cartridge. Eventually the dogs stopped at a dry wall in an Arab village and we dug into it and found a revolver. But, despite all our efforts, we never found the perpetrators of this ghastly crime.

To attempt to describe 5700 recorded major cases of crime committed during 1938 would require a book to itself. To leave out all details would be to ignore historical facts. There were 430 cases of assassination when 77 British, 255 Jews and 500 Arabs were killed. Many hundreds were wounded and between 2000 and 3000 members of Arab bands were killed and wounded in encounters with the military.

On three occasions I missed death from bombs by a few inches, and Arabs were caught with revolvers in my garden a couple of times. Things got so serious that after a time bomb went off under my sitting-room window, just as I was walking upstairs to bed, the general insisted on a double military guard being posted there at nights, and three British policemen accompanying me wherever I went during the day. These police were very good fellows, but as days lengthened into weeks I began to hate never being alone by day and hearing the tramp, tramp, tramp of sentries during the nights. When I wanted to go out and see things for myself, I often gave my protectors the slip, which was wrong of me, but human.

Scores of my acquaintances met their death by bullet or bomb, and one never knew from day to day who would be the next victim. Nearly every day someone would come to see me with tales of atrocities or sorrows that would wring the heart, but one had to keep a stiff upper lip to maintain morale. Police and military were attacked 1000 times and

Jewish settlements over 600. The telephone lines were sabotaged on 700 occasions and the railway and roads on 340. The Iraq Petroleum Company pipeline was damaged at an average rate of twice a week, and Captain Orde Wingate[7] was given the job of guarding it. He enlisted a number of Jews and, with a mixed group of commandos, shot everyone who approached after dark.

Lieutenant-General R. Haining replaced Major-General Wavell and reinforcements arrived. Major-Generals R. O'Connor and B. Montgomery[8] commanded divisions in the Jerusalem and northern districts respectively. Three more different temperaments would have been impossible to find.

General Haining was a barrister as well as a professional soldier, but the lawyer always predominated. He was an excellent administrator, but suffered from an inability to control his temper, 'getting hot under the collar', as he expressed it. His strategy was unimaginative; he was a good disciplinarian but even he could not subdue Montgomery.

O'Connor, the divisional commander with whom I had most to deal, was a quiet little man who was a soldier's general rather than a staff officer. On the North-West Frontier of India he had learned Indian dialects and loved the rough life. He was a religious man, very happily married, and in his sense of duty used to remind me of Plumer. His war career was nipped in the bud by his falling into Italian hands in North Africa.

I first met Montgomery in 1924 when I was lecturing at the Staff College. We met again in 1929 when he came to Palestine with his battalion of the Warwickshires, which he had just been appointed to command. It was a somewhat inefficient battalion because it was unhappy. Montgomery, fresh from staff duties, never left his officers alone; he was always nagging at them like a prep-school master. To

7. Major-General Orde Wingate (1903–44) later achieved fame in the Second World War for developing tactics of fighting deep behind Japanese lines in the jungles of Burma. He was killed in a plane crash over India.

8. Field Marshal Bernard Montgomery (1887–1976), first Viscount Montgomery of Alamein, entered the army in 1908 and served in the First World War. He achieved great fame by winning the battle of El Alamein in 1942, which marked the turning of the tide against Germany in the Second World War.

dine in mess was an ordeal because, even in the ante-room, he kept ticking them off one after the other. This officer's tie wanted straightening, that one was having too many drinks, and the third was leaning up against a plant pot. Even then he selected a couple of young subalterns to trail after him all day like embryo aides.

There were only two battalions in the country then and the senior battalion commander acted as OC British Troops in Palestine. For a brief fortnight before he took his battalion away to Alexandria, Montgomery acted as OC Troops. He made full use of it by sending a memorandum to the War Office, pouring ridicule upon the defence scheme that was then current and had been drawn up by Sir John Chancellor, the high commissioner, in consultation with the military authorities. Montgomery left Chancellor a copy before he set off for Egypt. Chancellor, who had formerly been assistant secretary to the Committee of Imperial Defence, was livid with rage. I had lent Montgomery my house, as my wife was in England, and when I saw him off at Jerusalem station, he was quite exhilarated by the stir he had created.

Montgomery had then spent four years at the Staff College at Quetta as a senior instructor and followed on with some years as a brigadier at Portsmouth. He now returned to Palestine as a major-general, with a very shiny hat and a very young lad as his aide-de-camp. He had always been a hard worker and, even when commanding his battalion, had spent many hours a day at my house, studying the higher strategy of war. When he had left for India, he had sent me a long and charming letter thanking me for what I had been able to do for him, and finished up by saying that he looked upon me as one of his few friends. We were therefore no strangers when he arrived back the second time.

The army's job in Palestine was a difficult one. All parties had the ear of the House of Commons by some channel or other. None of the three generals at the top liked each other. Conferences were unpleasant. Most of them made use of newspaper correspondents.

Following the running amok and committal of atrocities by British troops against the village of Bassa in Northern Palestine, Bishop Graham-Brown, who in the previous war had been adjutant of his battalion, went up to investigate for himself the truth of the Arabs' condemnation of the troops' action. He had a long interview with Montgomery and came back absolutely bewildered. To every question, he said, Monty had but one reply: 'I shall shoot them.' 'The man is blood mad,' the bishop moaned across my office table. Very soon Montgomery had the civil administration by the ears and eventually, instead of co-operating in the fullest sense, he and the district commissioner approached each other through their own subordinate, the superintendent of police.

Despite the fruitless expenditure of much ammunition, by the time the world war was in the headlines, two divisions of troops had not succeeded in capturing or killing a single one of the real leaders of the Arab revolt.

Some weeks before war was to break out, Montgomery was very ill but he recovered in time to get off to England before the cataclysm swept across the world. From that time onwards he became world-famous.

With the arrival in March 1938 of Palestine's fifth high commissioner, Sir Harold MacMichael, came a complete change at Government House. Gone were the old masters from the dining room; the arched cubbyholes in the walls no longer held choice pieces of china or glass, but were filled with heads of African deities, carved by Tanganyikans in black woods, giving the long domed room the appearance of a mausoleum. In the drawing room maps replaced landscapes. The bookshelves no longer housed the poets, but cheap editions of crime novels. Gone were the spacious days when the goblet rang and the music of the harpsichord and violin was heard, and visitors flocked to and fro.

'Macmic' had been the outstanding civil servant in the Sudan and had passed on to be governor of Tanganyika. A classical scholar with a vein of shrewdness and cynicism, he had never allowed his heart to rule his mind. Three years of lonely service in Kordofan had established unchangeable habits. He cut himself off almost entirely from personal contacts. His hobbies were maps, reading detective stories, collecting semi-precious stones and cutting down trees.

All agricultural and horticultural stations were attacked by Arab bands, including a hill experimental fruit station that had been paid for out of Sir Arthur Wauchope's own pocket to help Arabs. The agricultural school for Arab boys at Tulkarm had to be closed, for the entire herd of 33 cattle was looted by Arabs. So many isolated police posts were destroyed that the police abandoned many of them and travelled about in over 100 armoured cars armed with machine guns.

July 1938 produced a series of major crimes in which 100 Arabs were killed outright by Jews and 27 Jews by Arabs. The two worst incidents were in Haifa, where on two occasions bombs were exploded in the Arab fruit market. In Jerusalem, 18 Arabs were killed and 60 wounded in bombing incidents in the Old City. In Tel Aviv, a bomb placed in an unattended motorcar injured 23 Jews.

More military reinforcements arrived from Egypt and patrolling was intensified. Land mines appeared on agricultural tracks. Kidnapping of Arabs by Arabs began; 50 were forcibly abducted. Barclays Bank at Hebron was robbed of £P 5000. In Jaffa a time bomb exploded in the crowded vegetable market, killing 24 Arabs and wounding 35. Beersheba was raided by a large Arab gang and the British police sergeant was killed, large quantities of arms and ammunition were stolen and everything in the town was destroyed.

The railway was sabotaged and trains derailed so often that movement had to be restricted to daylight hours. Trains were now preceded by armoured trucks and in front of each truck an iron rod was pushed out and connected to two wheels on which a small platform was fixed. A couple of Arabs taken from the villages through whose lands the line ran were seated on the platform so that if mines were placed on the line they would get blown up first. This stopped that particular type of crime.

My Bethlehem offices, within 70 yards of the Church of the Nativity, were burnt out. I moved all the registers from the Ramallah offices and two days later armed men came and stole the typewriters. The Arab bands had established their own 'courts' and people were brought up for summary trials.

District officers were at the end of their resources. They were unable to go out as there were no forces for their protection. Our own intelligence service was practically nil, as our agents were being steadily 'bumped off'. That of the Arab forces was well organized, properly directed and backed up by public opinion.

The Arab police could not be trusted. The military forces and the British police were inadequate in numbers to give protection even to such vital things as wireless stations, communications and water supplies. Lawlessness was paramount.

The Storm

Captain Orde Wingate of the Royal Artillery, small, unorthodox, wiry and dour, an imaginative Scottish soldier with deep-seated blue eyes who spoke with a nervous stutter, was put in charge of pipeline protection. He trained night squads of British soldiers and Jews to use guerrilla tactics to move about more quickly than the enemy, and thus routed Arab marauders. He was brought up as a member of the Plymouth Brethren and spoke Hebrew; 'Fear of the Lord' was the only fear that Colonel George Wingate had taught his son. He had the gift of pungent expression and combined mule and donkey transport with radio equipment.

The Jews were on the whole showing patience under alarming adversity. They continually asked the questions: 'Can government and won't? Or will government and can't?'

The high commissioner surrendered his powers, including control of the police, to the GOC and approved the appointment of military commanders to take over the particular powers of district commissioners under the defence regulations, and Major-General Richard O'Connor was appointed to Jerusalem. I acted as his political adviser. Mac-Michael never regained control.

The Old City had become the rallying point of bandits, so troops surrounded the walls and reoccupied it after loosing off some thousands of rounds of ammunition during the night. I entered the Muslim sanctuary and, at the top of the Antonia Tower,[9] picked up some recently-fired brass cartridge cases, one of which had been used to kill a British soldier.

For all practical purposes, military law was established. But I still had many unpleasant duties. As sheriff, I personally had to attend all executions.

The public had always accepted the judgments of the civil courts as *kismet*. But now things were different. Laws had been promulgated prescribing the death penalty for people found in possession of arms. Military courts had been set up to try such cases. Many convictions were made and sentences passed, and the GOC had confirmed 54 death sentences. The Arabs were revolted. Men were being killed, as the

9. A surviving section of an ancient fortress north of the Temple Mount, strengthened at one point by Herod and named in honour of the Roman commander Mark Antony.

Arabs put it, by the government for defending their homes and preventing Jewish aggression.

The central prison was housed in a most unsuitable building, the Russian Orthodox Church pilgrim hostel, which had been adapted for the purpose in 1918. The straggling one-storey building of large vaulted rooms was in the centre of a large compound, which was open to the public. The Russian cathedral was opposite the main gates. Two other buildings, in front, accommodated the government hospital and the law courts.

Hanging in this makeshift building was a pretty open business. Every inmate knew the actual minute it was taking place. So all the Arab prisoners, of whom there were generally about 300, took care to ensure that executions were made as unpleasant and difficult as possible for the officials.

As I drove across the compound to the prison gates there would be a press of people weeping and keening, for, according to law, the relatives could claim the body. I have known a convict's wife and children rush to me, tearing their hair and screaming for the man's life. That ordeal passed, once I was inside the main gate, a signal would be passed round the prisoners and they would begin to beat on the prison bars, shouting and screaming to the condemned man and being answered back. This was the accompaniment to my receiving evidence from two witnesses that the prisoner was the man actually sentenced in court and of my reading to him the death warrant, the walk to the scaffold chamber while the wretched man protested his innocence, and then the final scene.

One week, at hourly intervals, there were three executions one day, two the next and three on the third, and I wished that some of those more directly concerned with giving the sentences or approving them were in my shoes. The irony of the whole process was that not a single execution made the slightest difference to public security, to Arab opinion, to Arab fears, to Arab respect for law, or to Arab action. As I left the prison one day I reflected that, although I had seen scores of people die, I had never yet seen a man die a natural death.

Although it is customary for the British to talk with pride of the administration of justice, and a dishonest judge is rare, the courts in Palestine never won the approval or the heart of the people. Possibly the fundamental cause was that no British judge ever took the trouble to become competent in a local language, but invariably trusted to translators. Bedu law, based on the tribal and collective idea that knows no punishment qua punishment, but concerns itself solely with retribution and restitution, had been fixed among the nomadic tribesmen long before the creeds of Judaism, Christianity and Islam were formulated, and had gradually been carried into the settled areas. Whenever a man was murdered, and the average was four weekly, after the law courts had finished with the case, the whole matter would be retried among the Arabs themselves, and responsibility fixed irrespective of the findings of the courts. Blood had been spilled and the *diya*, blood money, had to be fixed and paid over to the relatives of the dead person.

It was a question of an eye for an eye or a tooth for a tooth; whose eye or whose tooth did not matter. It was therefore part of my duty when murders did occur to take measures to stop the matter getting out of hand and retaliation following.

I would first impose an *atwa* or truce, which held good for a year. Arbitrators were sought, men of good repute whose opinions carried weight. Once chosen and having got to work, they were customarily well fed to ensure the goodwill necessary for the proper settlement of the case, so essential to the peace of the village or quarter of the town.

With the award made known, the day of settlement would arrive. In the case of a village, I would drive to somewhere nearby and then walk up to the village preceded by the sheep and goats that were to be slaughtered for the feast of peace-making.

At the entrance to the village I would be met by the headman and stopped while a strip of cloth was tied to a stick and then knotted 33 times. Each knot represented £P 10, £P 330 at that time being the customary amount payable for a man's death. The arbitrators would remove the twisted headrope from the accused or his representative's head and place it round his neck. He would take the stick and hold it aloft and, as we entered the village, I greeted them with the words: 'Peace be upon you. Do you want to forgo your rights and make peace?' The injured party answered: 'We do, *subhana 'llah* [praise God].' The arbitrators then asked the murdered man's father to show mercy. This meant that he should consent to a reduction of the *diya* by £P 80, the figure previously agreed to. He proceeded to untie eight knots — 'This is for the Prophet, this for the Pasha,' and so forth. As he did so there was fervent clapping. At the pressing insistence of the arbitrators the father allowed more knots to be untied to cover the costs of the award and the expenses of the feast. The amount to be paid was left to the father's conscience and it was painful to watch. Eventually seven more knots were untied. He had waived all but £P 180 for his son.

The money was paid over and the father kissed the cheeks of his adversaries and they his beard.

Then began the final preparations for the feast. All but the meat had been made ready in advance. The sheep were led away and slaughtered and we lounged on cushions under the trees. Eventually my patience was rewarded. Great plated copper trays were brought forward. On some, sheep roasted whole looked at us with baleful eyes as they lay upon rice piled as high as it would go, the mound glowing with hot butter. Each of us was given a large flat round of coarse bread. Turning back my cuffs, with a '*Bism'illah*' ('In the name of God'), I plunged my hand into the hot rice, grasped a handful, moulded it into a ball and, in theory, gave a flick of the fingers and it had disappeared. The father tore a great piece of meat from the sheep and gave it to me. I dipped the flesh into the rich sauces and bowls of sour milk. Chickens split down the centre and stews made from spinach and *bamiyah* (okra) gave a spur to jaded appetites. Mutton grilled on skewers, kebab and marrows stuffed with rice, *kusa*, followed. I finished by eating the deep red heart of a watermelon.

With comfortable belchings and murmuring, '*El hamd l'Illah*' ('Praise be to God'), I moved away and gave place to others. My host brought a brass pitcher full of water and someone else produced a brass bowl and water was poured upon my hands until they were clean. In a corner of the guest room was an aged man with a white beard sitting beside a charcoal fire. He stretched out a hand behind him and into it was placed a massive iron spoon with a copper ladle attached to it by a chain. My host gave a nod to his son, who got a bag from the corner, opened it and counted out the requisite number of coffee beans and handed them to the coffee-maker, who dropped them into the iron spoon for which he had raked out a hole in the ashes. Some more charcoal was added to the fire and we sat or reclined in silence while the berries roasted. From time to time they were turned over by the copper ladle. Once they were sufficiently browned they were removed and placed in a large wooden mortar and pounded with a wooden pestle.

With perfect rhythm, the general metre was altered from time to time by a resounding whack against the side of the wooden vessel. The berries were placed in a pot and boiling water was poured upon them. Three times they were brought to the boil before handleless cups were brought and were carefully washed by the coffee-maker before they were filled with a minute drop of coffee, which was handed to me and replaced three times. When I had taken my portion and drained the cup to the last drop, the remainder of the guests were served. The idea of three servings was to make us prolong our stay. But Arabs do not linger long after a meal. I and the others got up and, after praising God and our hosts, not forgetting the women in the kitchen, we took our departure. Blood had been shed. Blood had been requited.

With such customs being at the very heart of Arab opinion it was not to be wondered at that, at the height of the disturbances and the imposition of the death sentences for persons carrying rifles, military court judgments had little effect upon Arab opinion.

Still more troops arrived and we had 18 battalions, armoured cars, cavalry and horse artillery. Yet the new airport at Lydda was destroyed by fire and 32 meteorological stations were sabotaged. Hundreds of miles of telegraph and telephone wires were destroyed. It was clear that British training and tactics were quite unable to cope with a whole nation at war. In the numerous engagements the British civil police bore the real brunt of battle. They were always first in and last to retire.

The report of the Partition Commission was published and His Majesty's Government stated that the political, administrative and financial difficulties were so great that partition was impracticable Arabs from Palestine and neighbouring states and also representatives from the Jewish Agency were invited to confer in London.

The Muslims expected the rejection of partition because they had always said that it was impracticable. After 30 months of struggle and sacrifice, they said, 'The pregnant mountain has given birth to a little mouse.' The Jews were deeply indignant at the inadequate understanding on the part of the Partition Commission of the problem and of the rights of the Jews. They had an impression that HMG dropped partition owing to the campaign of violence.

In July I had left for England for a few weeks' leave to see my wife, and the day I got back to Jerusalem I received a telegram to say that she had died. She had devoted her talents to Palestine. For years she had kept open house on Thursdays, and persons of every nationality and faith, pausing awhile from political strife, had found refreshment. Priest and Muslim, Arab and Jew, official and merchant, Orthodox rabbi and Druze initiate, once inside her drawing room had to abandon their differences. Strangely assorted persons would be seen on either side of her, drinking tea from the locally famous gold tea service.

The delegates went to London to confer with the secretary of state. There had been more changes. The minister was now Mr Malcolm MacDonald. Discussions were conducted by him at St James's Palace on the principles of Box and Cox, as the Arabs refused to meet the Jews round the table.

The conference concluded without agreement, so a further statement of policy by HMG was presented to Parliament, stating that:

> If immigration is continued up to the economic absorptive capacity, regardless of other considerations, such as Arab fear of indefinite Jewish immigration, a fatal enmity between the two people will be perpetuated. There would be a limit of 75,000 during the next five years, plus a special grant of certificates for 25,000 more to cope with the Jewish refugee problem. After five years, no further Jewish immigration would be permitted, unless the Arabs of Palestine agree. The objective is self-government where Arabs and Jews share authority.

Stern action by military and police continued. They never knew from day to day from where the next stab in the back was coming. Murder was still rife. Hold-ups by Arabs were frequent; communications were being destroyed; military and police were still being fired at and killed. In the Hebron hills, the rebel Julani, who had received fresh supplies of money, arms and ammunition, was of more account in the villagers' eyes than the military forces. The senior military officer was shot at and several district officials were killed.

The Arabs were getting tired themselves. The bands were being no longer referred to as fighters in a holy war (*mujahideen*), but as rebels (*thowar*). Arabs were hoping for peace. The Jewish community was tired also and most embittered by the policy. It too had made murderous attacks and thrown bombs in cafés and places where Arabs congregated. In Jerusalem city, Arab terrorism had been stamped out, but murderous attacks were made by Jews in three Jewish quarters. Jews now started attacking government servants. An extremely ingenious time bomb, worked by acid and touched off by the hour hand of a watch, was pushed into the letter box of the new main hall of the General Post Office, completely wrecking the lovely green marble walls and counter. The British armourer sergeant was sent for to examine another bomb, which had failed to explode. It went off and he was blown to bits. I saw his brains scattered over the ceiling while his lacerated body lay all over the floor.

With great ingenuity a bomb was carried into Broadcasting House and inserted into the main electrical machinery. It exploded and killed two officers. The police knew the Jew who committed the crime, but they had not enough evidence to bring him to justice. The migration offices in Jerusalem were bombed and other offices in Tel Aviv were destroyed. At mass meetings Jews took oaths to spare no sacrifice to frustrate and defeat government policy. The Ashkenazi chief rabbi dramatically tore up the parliamentary White Paper before the assembled congregation in his synagogue. Civil disobedience was proclaimed. A mine buried in the ground near my office was attached to a long electric wire and touched off by a bell push. I saw the mutilated bodies of two British police inspectors being picked up in baskets. This diabolically planned murder shocked everyone.

A score of vessels had been chartered by Jewish organizations for transporting Jewish refugees and landing them illicitly. Two ships, the *Patria* and the *Tiger Hill*, were run ashore and beached at Tel Aviv, carrying about 1400 passportless Jews. Over 11,000 immigrants had been landed up and down on the shores during the summer months. The defeat of the immigration restrictions would be at the forefront of the programme at the Zionist Congress, which was to open in Geneva in August.

Many persons had criticized our policy and our actions, and had offered suggestions, but perhaps the most self-assured of these was Dr

Buchman,[10] who arrived, fresh from Sweden, with his Oxford-Group team and was prepared, on a whirlwind tour, to capture the Holy City with his advice, and gave us his solution to all our problems. He and his associates were astonished to find that there was little or no response; one might say there was indifference. At the inaugural luncheon at the best hotel — not a single one of the little group who had started and kept the Oxford group alive in the city was invited — the doctor, after pointing out the previous and varied occupations of 'the team', from East Ender to coal-mine owner, plus an ex-vicereine of India, told me that he had spent three days in Egypt and that, as a result of his talk with the minister of education, that individual had been completely changed. 'A completely different man, Governor.' As I happened to know the old reprobate who was responsible for the youth of Egypt and also knew that the only two languages he understood were French and Arabic, neither of which Buchman spoke fluently, if at all, I discreetly enquired in what language the miracle had been performed, but I received no clue!

10. Dr Frank Nathan Daniel Buchman (1878–1961), US Christian evangelist. Founder of the Oxford Group at Oxford in 1921. In 1938 he launched in London the Moral Rearmament movement.

16

No Common Ground

Into this maelstrom the declaration of war against Germany came as a soft refreshing balm to a harassed land. Dr Weizmann pledged that the Jews would stand by Great Britain and would fight on the side of the democracies and place themselves under the co-ordinating direction of the British government.

Ragheb Bey Nashashibi, ex-mayor of Jerusalem, and Suleiman Bey Tuqan, mayor of Nablus, who a long time before had broken away from the Arab Higher Committee, told the high commissioner that they stood by and would support Great Britain with all their power and would suspend for the duration of the war, all political activities to enable Great Britain to concentrate on the war effort.

A couple of days before war was declared, hundreds of Arabs, fed with German money, had come down and destroyed 47 miles of railway line between Gaza and Rafah, so the line to Egypt was closed for a week and the service had to be cut by half for six months. By similar action the Lydda-Jerusalem line was closed for four months.

Arab states declared themselves in support of Great Britain. Emir Abdullah ranged himself on the side of Britain; and however varying our fortunes, he was unswerving in his conviction and his courage.

The Jewish Agency opened registration offices and appealed to Jewish men and women to volunteer — in its own words, 'for the maintenance and consolidation of the Jewish economy in all its branches, the defence of the Jewish population and assistance to the British Army in Palestine, if called for'. Within a week, 57,000 people walked about wearing a tag on which 'enlisted' was written in Hebrew.

Lastly, the Egyptian gentlemen who supplied Palestine with sugar and controlled the monopoly, our only source in wartime, trebled the price of that commodity, delivered by rail at Kantara.

There was an immediate run on the banks, where liquid deposits had reached nearly £P 20 million. Nearly a quarter was withdrawn.

There was an unfounded fear of a *gaz*, or paraffin, shortage; cart drivers going from house to house selling the fuel from barrels had to be guarded by supernumerary police because they were chased by men, women and children, creating the most ludicrous scenes: an Orthodox Jew turning on the tap, an Arab woman kicking his ankles as she tried to get her tin underneath, somebody else beating the cart driver, a couple of girls holding onto the ears of the mule and three boys being kicked off by the animal as they struggled with its tail.

Both Arabs and Jews started spending their last mils buying up and storing foodstuffs and other commodities. A neighbour told me, with pride, that he had bought two years' supply of toilet paper.

The year was also marked by an astonishing archaeological 'find'. Two young Englishwomen digging at Bethlehem within a slingshot of Our Lord's birthplace uncovered the skull of an unknown animal and two pairs of mammoth tusks. I saw the finds lying in an excellent state of preservation.

Many troops had been withdrawn for the Libyan desert. Major-General O'Connor had left with the staff of the Seventh Division and Major-General Montgomery had gone to England.

There was a remarkable absence of bitter feeling. Jews still disliked Arabs and Arabs hated Jews, but the forces of circumstances were beyond local influence. There was a feeling of truce.

Early in October an Italian aeroplane appeared high in the heavens above Haifa; it soared down and out stepped Philippa Barnard Massey, the girl who had cheered up my wife and me 27 years before in Manchester. We were married at Christ Church within the walls of the Holy City. Life became enriched and subsequently gave us Christabel Eve and Philip D'Aubigny. Although we thought our marriage would be quite quiet, we had a wonderful gathering. The high commissioner and representatives from every community came, from the Druzes to the ultra-Orthodox Jews and dancing *dervish*es, and the whole of the consular corps. We drove back to our house in a gaily decorated car with a police escort, where our beaming servants were waiting to welcome us. Home life began again with tea under the enormous jasmine in full blossom.

In October, the military authorities made a first call for volunteers in the auxiliary services. The Jewish authorities considered that Jewish military units, when formed, should serve only in Palestine, for, if able-bodied young Jews were withdrawn, Jewish morale and physical strength would be considerably weakened. There was a demand for a Jewish army, presumably paid for by the British taxpayer, which would fight under its own flag. By the end of the year 799 Jews and 313 Arabs had enlisted in the various units of the British Army.

Palestine had never grown enough grain to provide for its urban population. It relied on imports from Transjordan, the Hawran and Syria. Modern requirements were 70,000 tons annually. Our food situation was more than precarious. So we started to engage in propaganda and, in addition, the government produced a million vegetable seedlings, which were distributed gratis. As the weeks passed, Palestine saw her orange crop, about 15 million cases, left rotting on the trees for want of ships.

The physical strength of the Arabs had been undermined by constant calls to provide bandits with food, lodging and supplies, and by military and police searches. The olive crop had failed. Arab villagers constantly came in asking for more road construction, agricultural loans and the postponement of the collection of rural property taxes. The townsmen had no tourists to tap; Christian missionary money was dwindling.

The Jewish community was harder hit, owing to the damage done to its farms and stock, to the contraction of credit and to its partial reliance on funds from abroad, particularly Poland. The merchants were in a precarious condition. Many individual Jews came to me saying that they were virtually starving; businessmen had no orders. Some 16,405 Jewish immigrants had been registered during the year. Nearly 30,000 Jews in and around Tel Aviv were in receipt of some form of relief provided by the government and there were 20,000 unemployed Arabs in Jaffa. The Jews pressed for public works and for direct relief to assist their unemployed.

Pinchas Rutenberg was elected president of the Jewish National Council. He was a driving force. He issued an appeal and the Jewish emergency tax was established with the object of dealing with unemployment, encouraging production and strengthening the *yishuv*.[1] More British troops were withdrawn, so the police force was brought up to 5000 in the regular force and 4000 auxiliaries, mainly Jews, were enlisted.

The year ended with the spectre of general unemployment. Slight thought was then given to the benefits that great armies bring: the large contracts for military works, the growing demand for labour and increasing wages. Few realized that there would be no compulsion to contribute one penny to the mandatory power towards the cost of the war or that the thousands of men to be given employment in Jewish settlement police work would be paid for by the British taxpayer.

Little did the people of Palestine in 1939 realize that a gold mine would accrue both to them and to Egypt through the blood, the sweat, the wealth, the anguish, the heroism of Britain.

At New Year the high commissioner announced that the government would provide £P 750,000 for relief and public works. Little of it was used because a few days afterwards the advance party of the First Australian Division arrived and military contracts for hutting, road construction and supplies were given out. By the middle of the year unemployment had come to an end.

Further highly organized arrangements were made to defeat the immigration ordinance and 3200 Jews were landed from three ships.

Government regulations prohibiting and restricting transfers of land were published. Mr Ussishkin declared them to be an attempt to confine the Jews in a pale of settlements in their homeland. Countrywide demonstrations lasted a week. There were bombs in Jerusalem and attempts to set fire to the law courts in Haifa, where 91 Jews were

---

1. *Yishuv* means literally 'ingathering' or 'settlement' and was the word used by Zionists to describe the Jewish community in Palestine.

slightly injured in a baton charge by the police. There was arson and there was sabotage against Jewish farmers employing Arabs. The immediate Arab reaction, except among those who wanted to sell land, was joy at a political victory.

Because there was Jewish opposition to the Jewish Emergency Fund taxes, sand was placed in the engines (or bombs in the bodies) of cars belonging to Jews who refused to pay the arbitrarily-imposed taxes. Professor Zondek,[2] the distinguished gynaecologist, was one of the victims.

Our work of pacification went quietly on. Hundreds of cases of blood feuds among Arabs, arising out of the revolution, were outstanding. In one village, we settled 32 by arbitration. The erection of 77 police stations and posts recommended by Tegart was finished. So we started tax-collecting. A citrus control board was established but there was l neither wood for boxes nor ships for transport. From now on the groves were kept alive by government grants for maintenance.

Mr Ben Ami of Netanya village had a brainwave. He helped a couple of Antwerp Jewish diamond-cutters start their trade. Within a couple of years, over £P 2 million-worth of cut industrial stones were exported. Output became restricted as a result of numerous strikes. Wages were enormous. Little long-curled Orthodox lads were leaving the *yeshivah*s (religious schools) and, after a few months of experience, were being paid up to £P 40 a month.

The collapse of France shook Palestine but there was no panic.

Now seemed the time for the government, led by the high commissioner, to rally the whole country to work together. But the opportunity was lost. Arabs, like Jews, disliked the prospect of serving abroad, even in neighbouring states. Arabs feared the ex-*mufti*'s displeasure, or suspected that when all was over they might find that after all they had only been fighting for the Jewish national home. Thousands of Arab labourers were finding work. There was complete apathy among their young intelligentsia; I do not know of one Palestinian Arab of the educated classes having offered his services in a military capacity throughout the war. By the end of the year, 2337 Arabs and 4226 Jews had joined the army. Haifa had a couple of air raids, with 55 killed. Seven weeks later Tel Aviv had a raid with 120 killed.

---

2.   Bernhard Zondek (1891–1966), endocrinologist and gynaecologist.

Mr Rutenberg had been to London and come back greatly impressed by the unity and single-mindedness in England. He described Palestine's faction-ridden Jewry as a 'fool's paradise'. It presented such a melancholy spectacle of disorganization and party rivalries, of intrigue and terrorism, that he resigned from the Jewish National Council, ostensibly on the grounds of ill health. The Hebrew press was very outspoken. It said: 'Mr Rutenberg's noble approach failed; it lacked the cold political calculation of the sorrowful condition of our public life.'

Vladimir Jabotinsky, leader of the Revisionists, died. Flouted and feared in life by the majority of Jews, he reached almost Leninesque immortality after death. Numbers now thought that the policy of the Revisionists was right and waverers became worshippers. Paying tribute to his memory, Dr Weizmann stated: 'Dissatisfaction was an important factor in Jewish life and every Jew ought to carry the spark of it in his soul.'

In the autumn, the chartering of special ships to bring illegal immigrants began again. Three ships were intercepted. The government requisitioned the *Patria*, a vessel of 11,000 tons, to take the people to Mauritius. Nearly 2000 were aboard when, with the help of people ashore, this valuable British ship was sabotaged in Haifa harbour and sank — 268 persons were drowned or unaccounted for.

Only 278 people were murdered this year, half the number of the year before.

While these events were happening, the Arabs' medieval life was going on almost untouched. Thousands were flocking to Kafr Yasif, near Acre, by car, camel and donkey, to visit and touch a little Christian Orthodox girl who was declared to be seeing visions and to have been granted the gift of healing. Many returned feeling they had wasted their money fruitlessly.

In November, just as I was about to leave to kick off at a football match in aid of the Red Cross and St John fund, the senior naval officer in Haifa came in and handed me a telegram from the Admiralty announcing that my son's submarine was missing. Martin had been an exhibitioner at Winchester and when he took the special entry for the fighting services, he was top of England in Latin, general knowledge and English. He had gained his five ones, the naval prize for engineering and ship construction, and later the Admiralty gold medal for naval history. He had been awarded a DSC early in the war. HM submarine *Triad* has never been heard of again.

By 1941 Palestine was becoming mindful of war, if not war-minded. All sorts of odd trades had gone. One flourishing business had disappeared entirely. Arab men, from towns, from villages or from desert, liked wearing European overcoats. But Western men's garments hung like slops over their slender shoulders. Discerning Oriental Jews had found out that European women's coats fitted Arabs to perfection. Discarded coats could be purchased in Europe and sold cheaply. Moreover the buttons closing from right to left were ideal for Arabs, so thousands of second-hand ones were imported annually. I would often meet in council half a dozen bearded village elders with rich velvet eyes and high, sharp hooked noses crowned with flowing *keffiyeh*s and black goat-hair *ighal*s. Smart tailor-made, three-quarter-length ladies' coats with velvet on collars and cuffs hid somewhat coquettishly their embroidered waistcoats and flowing skirts.

Income tax was introduced and a war supply board was appointed. Controllers were set up to deal with agricultural production, food, fuel, manpower, prices and transport. The importation of cereals became a government monopoly. A Jewish scientific advisory committee was constituted under Dr Magnes[3] of the Hebrew University, and it rendered valuable service. Jews began breeding carp in artificially made ponds and lakes in the Jordan valley, which brought a welcome change of diet.

A remarkable Jewish industrial effort began. Hundreds of little factories were started. The range of articles was extraordinary, from pumps to boots, from mines to wire, from optical instruments to textiles-a valuable contribution to the fighting forces.

3. Judah Leon Magnes (1877–1948) was a US rabbi who was chancellor of the Hebrew University of Jerusalem from 1925 to 1935 and its first president from 1935 to his death in 1948.

Police work against Arab terrorists had been going on unobtrusively. In the Hebron area alone, out of 240 wanted persons, all but 16 had been arrested and interrogated. Some *mukhtar*s (headmen), village elders and near relatives of certain terrorists at large made history by voluntarily signing a document absolving from any blood-feud liabilities all who, while assisting the police, might kill the wanted men. Haj Amin, the deposed *mufti*, left Iraq for Germany and became a satellite of Hitler.

Soon after the civil administration had started, a countrywide underground semi-military Jewish organization, the Haganah, had been created by responsible Jewish leaders for self-defence in outlying settlements. Training in the use of military weapons had gone on ever since. Such ideas have a way of spreading. Jabotinsky's Revisionist Party, not content with the more sober outlook of the Haganah, had set up its own military organization. From this a band of desperate criminals led by Stern[4] was to emerge. Demands for money from Jews for the Revisionist organization were enforced by bomb-throwing, abduction and even torture.

I could not spend all my time at work. My wife and I found the *corps consulaire* very good company. Many of them became personal friends. The *de carrière* officers would have nothing to do with the honorary variety and were openly rude to them. Of course the majority, beyond signing a few passports, had little to do except write voluminous reports to their secretaries of state, so they had to have other distractions. France and Italy were keen about the Holy Places — France to try to regain her old position as defender of Western Christianity and Italy to obtain some fresh hold. Others specialized in archaeology and some in picnics or in golf. The Americans, with the help of a British judge, founded the Sodom and Gomorrah Golf Club at the Dead Sea and I was its first president. But all of them gave most excellent dinners, which I

---

4. Avraham Stern (1907–42) was active in the Irgun Zeva'i Le'ummi, a military group formed in 1931 by Haganah commanders who broke away in protest against its defensive character. Stern stayed in the Irgun when it split in 1937 and half its 3000 members rejoined the Haganah. Stern was imprisoned from 1939 to 1940 and, while he was in jail, his opposition to the suspension of attacks on British targets for the duration of the Second World War caused a new split in the Irgun. Those who followed Stern became known after his death as the Lohamei Herut Israel or the Stern Group. Stern was killed in a police raid in 1942.

much enjoyed. Each expressed something of his own country's tastes in the menu. The Americans gave chicken Maryland with rice; the Austrians saw that one was welcomed with light beer and whatever wine went with the dinner; a heavier beer finished the meal. The French offered a good brand of champagne and the Romanians always had a rich goulash.

The year 1942 was notorious for trial and error and trials and terrors. For the ordinary man and housewife life was becoming more of a struggle. Controllers were more active and no appeal tribunal was set up to hear complaints. Controllers did not welcome district commissioners' investigations, so a safety valve was cut off.

Food rationing was begun but was a comparative failure. The Arabs ignored it and the Jews evaded it. But it kept a large number of clerks happy counting dots. The government had never got the ear of the public and failed to exercise price control or prevent inflation of wages. The black market raged openly. Discontent was growing and, in a case before the High Court, the judge criticized one wartime department in language of uncompromising severity.

I had received enthusiastic and effectual help from the Jewish community in air-raid precautions in Jerusalem. It gave me over 2000 wardens; British residents provided a few. Arab help was fatalistic and negligible. Up to the battle of El Alamein, district commissioners had had to carry out air-raid precautions with little money. After Rommel's defeat, despite our advice to the contrary, scores of thousands of pounds were squandered on arrangements introduced by an enthusiastic and well-meaning gentleman from England. He had come from Bomb Alley, Kent. Again the British taxpayers paid. The height of absurdity was reached when this earnest man solemnly proposed that nine full-time wardens with trailer pumps should be posted permanently to Jericho in case German planes, foiled in their efforts to bomb the potash works at the Dead Sea, might unlimber their bombs over Jericho. Jericho consisted of a convent, two hotels and a few mud and reed huts! His proposals for earthworks at Hebron were ruthlessly set aside by the Muslims, who refused to work and who stated that Abraham, *Khalil* (the Friend of God), would never allow the city to be touched. The Stern Gang had carried out several hold-ups and robberies to provide the group with money. It now resorted to murder. Two of the gang were arrested by the police, so others of them set a trap, and the Jewish superintendent of police at Tel Aviv and his assistant were blown to pieces. The organization issued a pamphlet announcing that these two police officers had been sentenced to death because the police had tortured their comrades.

The police got really busy and four of the gang were arrested. Two of them, including Stern, were shot 'while being arrested' by a British inspector. The killing of Stern led eventually to the murder of Lord Moyne, a British minister of state in Cairo. At his trial in Cairo, the murderer denounced Lord Moyne for having refused to launch an enquiry into Stern's death when he had been the colonial secretary of state. The prisoner accused the police inspector of Stern's murder. Though 20 members of this group were arrested, a year later, through skilful planning, they all got away from the detention camp by an underground trench. The gang got bolder and bolder as the years passed and, after many crimes and raids, attempted to murder Sir Harold MacMichael. They also blew up the King David Hotel, killing 70 government officers.

Flying the Panama flag, the ship *Struma* had 769 Jews on board, intending to come without permits to Palestine. She was in Turkish waters, badly overcrowded, and considerable repairs were necessary. As admittance to Palestine was refused, the Turks decided to send the vessel back to the Black Sea. There was an explosion near the Bosphorus and only three survivors were picked up. There was bitter denunciation of anti-Jewish bias in the administration. Streams of pamphlets against the high commissioner were distributed. One had his photograph and underneath the words:

MURDER
Sir Harold MacMichael
known as High Commissioner.
Wanted for Murder of 800 refugees
in the Black Sea.

There were a good many troops stationed in Jerusalem and hundreds used to come on leave or for hospitalization. The Australian troops

behaved very well when visiting the Holy City. I had only one difference of opinion with the British military authorities, when they hired
the old Hensman's Hotel in the centre of the new city and established a
brothel there, with periodical medical inspections of the prostitutes.

I sent for the divisional commander and told him that it must be
closed. The weight of medical evidence given before the war had
proved that, however well and often prostitutes were examined, this
was no safeguard against venereal disease and I would not tolerate its
establishment.

The general argued that the military could do what it liked on military property, whether owned or leased. I replied that possibly he was
right, but if the brothel was not closed within 48 hours, either he or I
would go, and I did not much care who, but I was sure that the matter
would not stay there. Within two days Zeinab and her motley crew
were sent off elsewhere, outside my district.

The Armenian patriarch died and, amidst the cacophony of noise, of
shootings and bomb throwing, Father Cyril was voted onto a list of
three candidates and finally elected patriarch by a secret vote. As he
was not yet a bishop he had to set forth for Echmiadzin in Armenia,
now part of the Soviet Union, to be consecrated bishop by the Supreme
Catholicos, supreme in matters of doctrine and ecclesiastical discipline.

Before being received into the Cathedral of St James and enthroned,
he had to be granted the high *berat*. I had seen many Turkish *berat*s
signed by sultans.

They were written on papyrus, vellum or silk. All were illuminated in
gold and colour, carried the imperial cypher and, without exception,
were rolled upon wooden rollers. They gave the patriarch extensive
powers, including the right to shave off the beards of priests deserving
punishment and, in accordance with custom *ab antiquo*, no policeman
might stand against his sceptre, his horse and his servitors and none of
his followers might be converted to Islam without his consent. The
British high *berat*s, printed on white paper, seemed rather dull
compared with these ancient scripts, especially the one four feet long,
except that ours was signed by His Majesty, in the king's own hand. It
was presented to the patriarch with ceremony in a scarlet silk bag made

by my typist. The Armenians now had the distinction of owning, for the first time in history, documents signed by the king, recognizing and approving the appointment of a patriarch of an Eastern Church.

As our forces in the western desert retreated to El Alamein, there were the wildest rumours ranging from 'King Farouk has left for Khartoum' to 'Churchill has gone to America for the safety of his life'. A whispering campaign was started among groups of Muslims that once the Germans were here, the share of loot for each Arab would be one Jewish house and one shop. The Jews were naturally apprehensive. The flight from Egypt of 1500 evacuees holding British passports did nothing to increase British prestige. Our wives were standing fast and so were the Jews. Our food situation was most serious. At one time we had only one week's supply of flour left in Jerusalem.

The War Supplies Board was working hard but it had a heavy task. The Jewish workmen did not consider that the War Supplies Board had any right to fix basic wages, even in the industries that had accepted registration for war work on those terms. They said it was an attempt to freeze wages at a time when prices were rising. No sooner had some little industry started on war work than up came a demand for higher wages and up went the price to the army. 'We want the worker to be an active and not a passive factor in Jewish industry,' said Mr Ben-Gurion.[5] 'We want him to guard his standard of living and to have a part in the benefits that have resulted from the war.'

5. David Ben-Gurion (1886–1973) was born in Plonsk, then in Russian Poland, the son of a legal adviser whose house was a centre of Zionist activity in the town. After early involvement in Zionist youth groups he settled in Palestine in 1906 and became an agricultural worker and watchman in Lower Galilee, which left him with a lasting conviction that settlement of the land was of central importance to Zionism. He began to write and eventually studied law in Constantinople. Ben-Gurion and Ben-Zvi were exiled to Egypt in 1915 and later that year they went to New York. In 1918 Ben-Gurion returned to Egypt with the Jewish Legion. During the 1920s he played a leading role in the development of the Jewish Labour movement and the establishment of its links with, among others, the British Labour Party. He became a member of the Jewish Agency executive in 1933 and was elected its chairman in 1935. From then until 1948, together with Chaim Weizmann, he directed all Zionist affairs. Ben-Gurion spent some of the Second World War in the United States, directing a political and propaganda campaign,

Thousands upon thousands of people from both communities who were without work in 1939 were now, after 1940, being paid wages three and a half times higher than the 1939 rate.

Most of the retail traders of all communities, Spinneys general stores being a notable exception, had started skyrocketing their prices upon goods purchased at pre-war costs and villagers had followed suit with vegetables.

Despite the infiltration of people with new ideas and new ideals, begging was still big business. Wartime gave it fresh stimulus. It was carried on by Christians and Jews to an extent that can hardly be realized. The Muslims alone stood aside, except for repairs to the *Haram al-Sherif*, but even they were the indirect beneficiaries of the golden stream that the names of Jerusalem, Bethlehem, Nazareth and Eretz Israel attract.

One day I was in Safad post office, about three weeks before the Day of Atonement, when an old Jew walked in and placed six packets of letters on the counter, saying in Arabic: 'These represent my year's work.' Interested, I learned that, except on the Sabbath and holy days, he wrote at least ten letters a day and addressed them to the United States, obtaining addresses from a firm in Jerusalem that supplied them at so much per hundred. He had kept them until now so that they would reach America at a time when Jewish hearts were most likely to be softened and to look favourably towards the holy city of Safad. If only 10 per cent sent him a dollar his livelihood was assured and he could devote himself to religious practices and the procreation of children. His hands were as perfect as those of a woman of leisure.

which called for the opening of Palestine to Jewish immigration and settlement and the establishment of what he called 'a Jewish commonwealth integrated in the structure of the democratic world'. Relations with the British grew increasingly strained and Ben-Gurion was prominent in the political struggle against them and the armed struggle against the Arabs. When the Mandate was terminated in 1948 and the State of Israel was established, Ben-Gurion became prime minister and minister of defence. He resigned from this dual role in 1953, but was recalled to it in 1955 and continued in office until 1963, when he again resigned.

In Jerusalem and Tiberias there were colonies of *halukka*[6] Jews who existed entirely on monies sent them for praying by the charitably minded.

Christian communities gathered in large amounts of money. The Jerusalem and East Mission of the Anglican Church collected monies from special offertories made on Good Fridays in a large number of its churches all over the world. It was devoted to maintaining its clergy and various, establishments, and to maintaining schools in which the fees for education were kept far below the actual cost. The Church Missionary Society also ran missions and schools. The Franciscans collected large sums from all over the world-on average £P 50,000 a year. The *custos* told me that they distributed free about 15,000 loaves daily. If Roman Catholics sent in their rosaries with a suitable fee, they could have them placed on the holy sites and returned with a certificate granting papal indulgences. Provided the candidate was suitable, orders might be obtained in the Order of the Holy Sepulchre, awarded in the grade accorded to the value of the donation. Other orders of monks and nuns doing admirable work were maintained by subscriptions from abroad.

The Jerusalem YMCA had been built at a cost of £P 170,000 given by an American and required £P 6000 a year from the United States to keep it up.

The Hebrew University had to go begging annually to maintain its obligations, of which only £P 3500 a year was found in Palestine, to meet a bill of £P 130,000.

That excellent organization, the Jewish Hadassah Hospital collected the necessary money to keep afloat. Out of a total sum of nearly £P 3 million, only one sixth was collected from patients' fees.

But of course in the fine art of collecting money, mainly paid over to Arabs for land purchases, the Jewish National Fund, the Keren Kayemeth, had collected £P 7 million in 21 years. The Jewish Foundation Fund, Keren Hayesod, had collected nearly £P 10 million, of which £P 270,801 came from within Palestine.

Well administered, an orphanage could be as profitable as bee-keeping. In one orphanage known to me a staff of six tended the girls,

6. *Halukka* means financial support for inhabitants of biblical Israel from Jews of the Diaspora.

but 11 clerks and a manager earned a good living in the office collecting the funds.

There were various other steady streams of begging. Lest any of my
readers should think that I exaggerate, a searching test was made and
during 19 days, no less than 150,000 separate begging letters were
despatched abroad through the Jerusalem General Post Office.

Bishop Graham-Brown was killed in a railway accident. Remarkable
tributes were paid to him for his belief that man was made for noble
things. It was certainly the first time in history that the Samaritan high
priest had attended a Christian service in Jerusalem.

Four days of mourning were kept by the Jews to protest against the
extermination of Jewry by the Nazis. The Bukharan community[7] had a
public service and prayed that Hitler might be anathematized. At a
public meeting, Mr Ben-Zvi, the chairman, said: 'We have assembled
not only to protest against the atrocities, but to accuse the United
Nations that a heavy guilt rests upon them because for years they
remained indifferent to the fate of our people and we accuse them of
standing aloof and of locking the gates of the only remaining salvation.'

How was this great moral issue being faced by Arabs and Jews?
What was the national home offering of her own blood and treasure?
The armed forces had been calling for recruits for three years. Fewer
than 20,000 Jewish men and women had joined. In addition, 7000 Jews
were employed on full-time paid work as settlement police. Great Britain met the expense. The Arabs had remained apathetic. Labour, mainly
Arab, had been provided at high wages for the construction and maintenance of airfields and bases. Valuable work was being done in
factories and industries, mainly Jewish, to supply the forces. But many
commodities were being manufactured to save shipping space almost
without regard to price. The country during five years had drawn £11
million out of the British taxpayer by way of grants in aid. Millions of
pounds had been spent by His Majesty's Government in a spate of
orders. Enormous sums had been spent by the troops.

---

7. Jews originating from the central Asian khanate of Bukhara, now known as
Uzbekistan.

The response to an appeal for the public to take up war bonds of 3 per cent guaranteed by the British government had been £100,000. Donations to a spitfire fund came to £33,000.

Palestine had had not only free defence but an unprecedented circulation of money directly from the war. She was incurring no war debt and the war had stimulated activity, for which the British people paid.

Dr Magnes, addressing the Hebrew University, was very scathing. 'It is simple to give the profiteer free rein for the accumulation of his economic and political power. Whence are those profits amassed? Out of the war against Hitler, out of the blood and misery of millions of our brothers and sisters and there is no shame. We are at ease in Zion.'

A still more urgent call came from the army for more recruits. I addressed a good many meetings in what, I hoped at the time, were eloquent addresses in Arabic or Hebrew. The creation of a Palestine regiment of the British Army consisting of separate Jewish and Arab infantry battalions was announced. The decision was just three years too late. There were complaints that rates of pay on the 'Malta scale' were insufficient. So half a million pounds was collected by Jews for a Jewish War Needs Fund, of which £P 180,000 was spent on relief for soldiers' families and others. The rest, £P 300,000, was earmarked for defence of settlements, guards and other internal security measures.

Moshe Shertock of the Jewish Agency inspired the Jewish effort and gave the driving power. He laid down the rules. But undoubtedly in a number of cases there was improper pressure, and a conflict with the government on the methods employed ensued. The Arabs took no interest in British units and, although the Transjordan Frontier Force got some recruits, a company of them failed when called upon to fight in Syria. The unit had no Arab tradition and there had been a constant change of British officers. On the other hand, Emir Abdullah's Arab Legion, which had had two remarkable commanding officers, Peake[8] and now Glubb,[9] had no difficulty in finding recruits and the force was now greatly enlarged. When called upon by Glubb to fight against

8. Peake Pasha was an army officer who commanded the Arab Legion in Transjordan.

9. Major-General John Glubb served in the First World War, became an administrative inspector in the Iraq government and transferred to Transjordan in 1930. He became the officer commanding the desert area in 1932 and was officer commanding the Arab Legion from 1939 to 1956.

Rashid Ali's forces in Iraq, although like every Arab they were convinced that Great Britain was finished, they responded to this bonny fighter's call and fought well.

Ben-Gurion was proving to be a man of fire and enthusiasm. Rugged, uncouth, determined, single-minded, simple in his habits, he could talk for hours and sway his audiences with hard logic and forceful utterances. He worked all day and almost all night. He stood out above his colleagues and all of them feared and followed him. He had but one ideal and one aim, the creation of a Jewish national home in Palestine controlled by a Jewish government.

Haj Amin, the *mufti*, was alert, shrewd and crafty. Wherever his hideout might be, he played upon religion to the nth degree and used every device to hold Arab opinion. He had visited Jewish death camps and was involved in the establishment of fascist units in Yugoslavia. He did his utmost by propaganda in the press and on the radio to get Great Britain and her allies beaten.

The Jews, inconsiderate towards Arabs, were morbidly hypersensitive with regard to themselves. This self-deception was almost pathological and they never admitted that the reason for Arab hostility might be because of faults in the Jews themselves. This lack of psychological honesty destroyed any chance of *rapprochement*, even had the Arabs been willing to meet. For them, who had left their all in Europe to come to Palestine, there could be no holding back, no half measures. They were all Revisionists at heart and determined to hold on to all that they had obtained and press for more. A life of opportunity, hard and deficient though it might be, was in many ways a life of freedom in which they could achieve their own salvation and that of their children, who would be born and brought up free men and women.

Of course it was sad to see the lives of a pastoral people changed by the course of events. But one had only to look at the state of health of the country to appreciate that it was not only the Jews who had benefited from the national home policy. Travelling in neighbouring countries confirmed how superior in every way the conditions of our own people were. In the end, it was pride and self-assurance in their own ability to defeat the enemy and drive it out that caused subsequent Arab misery.

Now was the time for inspired leadership from the head of the government: not intellect, nor judgement, nor political wisdom, but the flame of enthusiasm. Something more than character was wanted, some talent that would bind people together. A demand that would compel men to give just that 10 per cent more power, more energy, more will that no money can buy. The call had come. Alas! there was no Plumer.

MacMichael, after a brilliant university career, had joined the Sudan Political Service and had spent his first three years living a lonely life at Bara, in Kordofan Province. The habits he formed there never left him. In Darfur, where he had been deputy provincial governor and my immediate superior, I had seen him only once for half a day. Later on, when he was married, it made no difference. His administrative ability, his strength of character and firmness of purpose were almost unknown. He shut himself up in Government House and dealt with everyone through his chief secretary. He contented himself with reading of official papers and, as a relaxation, read crime novels. Although a tower of strength, he remained practically unknown to the public. During six years, I saw him alone in his office three times. The Arabs called him 'the Man of the Palace' and the *corps consulaire* referred to him as 'that cold fish'. Others called him 'Simon Stylites', the latter being the leader of a school of ascetics that sought holiness by living upon the summit of pillars and who himself occupied this pious but isolated position for 30 years in the fifth century. In a broadcast MacMichael had once incautiously referred to some of the people as being like that historical character and had unwittingly expressed his own character. Mindful of the recommendations of the Royal Commission, he had handed over control of the police to the army early in the riots and, while it says much for the common sense of all concerned that it worked harmoniously, there was an obvious loss of powers and influence of the high commissioner. Throughout the war he never regained his former statutory powers. He was and remained a civilian enigma to the people. Yet he was a delightful man to go for a drive with and his knowledge of Sudanese Arab history was profound.

This isolation and lack of attempts by the government to get both sides to meet in a debating chamber became more and more serious. The legislative council had been much enlarged. I used to look round during discussions when bills vital to their interests were being debated, but never the voice of a Jew or an Arab was heard. Mutual confidence did not exist. We had little knowledge of what was going on. The Criminal Investigation Department was always outflanked by Arabs and Jews. With the exception of Miller and Champion, who spoke and wrote Arabic fluently, and one or two others, no one in the administration, police or department had ever passed the higher standard Arabic or Hebrew examinations. Once the first three chief secretaries had left, not one was ever able to speak with a Palestinian in his own tongue. Not a single British judge was competent to hold a court in a local language or to examine a document without a translator. Few immigrants knew English and the majority were entirely cut off from personal contact. So the government was severed from the governed. All parties thought their own thoughts and went about their own affairs and the cleavage became almost complete.

Although, before the war, both houses of parliament had considered that the establishment of an elected legislative assembly was premature, circumstances were different now. A consultative council should, and undoubtedly could, have been formed. I kept a mixed municipal council going in Jerusalem under both Jewish and Arab mayors. When difficult problems arose I used to go and sit with the members during discussions and many differences were smoothed over. Co-operation was a flame, like a charcoal fire, that needed fanning.

The fundamental differences were that the Jews were absorbed in the problem of putting, cost what it might, political theory into practice and looked upon the Arabs as an encumbrance upon the ground, their Jewish ground. The Arabs nourished their implacable hatred of Jews, yet sold Arab land and took Jewish money and, with prime conceit in themselves, believed the day would come when they would defeat the Jews and drive them out. And the mandatory was interested primarily in holding the reins, keeping the peace and in the technique of government. There was no common ground and no inspired British leader was found to change public opinion and bring the races together.

With the defeat of the Germans in North Africa, orders for the manufacture of army stores started to go down and Palestine, except as an air base for planes going to the Far East, became less important to the war effort. Instead of a bold policy and rallying Jews and Arabs to the forces, we had given way grudgingly a little at a time. Some Arabs and Jews had gallantly laid down their lives. Those Jews who fought did so in the knowledge that, if taken prisoner by Hitler's hordes, they might be put in chains, as many of them were. Several won distinction. An Arab officer of the Transjordan Frontier Force won the George Cross on special service. Arab Jaffa boatmen, enlisted as pioneers, had done fine work at Tobruk. By the end of the war about 40,000 Jews had enlisted in the army and police and a brigade of them had fought in Europe wearing the Shield of David. About a quarter of this number of Arabs had joined up, mainly in the Legion.

Emir Abdullah had been steadfast. Ragheb Bey and Suleiman Tuqan had kept their word. The Jews, sorely tried by the horrors of Nazi extermination of their people, gave their aid to Britain in accordance with their pledge.

Britain, battered and torn, had received much help, but she had had to pay in treasure, as well as pour forth her blood.

The deprivations from which Palestine had suffered sank into insignificance in comparison with what Palestine had been spared.

17

Farewell

Illness compelled my retirement. For nine years I had suffered from periodical spasms of asthma. They were becoming so frequent and continuous that I found it almost impossible to walk up the office stairs, and when I got to my table I would spend half an hour fighting for breath. So it seemed to me in the public interest that I should leave, after my third extension of service. It was a difficult decision to take and when I had taken it I realized what a privilege I had enjoyed in serving so long in the Holy City. In Turkish times, pashas of Jerusalem had come and gone with rapidity. From such records as existed, it appeared that I had held office longer than any of them.

It was hard to say goodbye. I had had many kindnesses shown me, but I was overwhelmed by the sympathy I received from Muslim, Jew and Christian. Reuters telegraphed that I was 'affectionately known as the Pasha among all sections of Jerusalem's heterogeneous population'. Receptions and farewells followed one after the other; from the Supreme Muslim Council and Jewish Agency to the Hebrew University; from the three patriarchs to my colleagues in government. From the apostolic delegate. From the police, who gave me a silver ashtray inscribed, 'TO THE PASHA IN AFFECTIONATE REGARD FROM THE OFFICERS OF THE FORCE.' I received special blessings from the two chief rabbis and many religious orders. The Carmelite nuns and the Poor Sisters of Clare gave my wife and myself interviews from behind the black curtains and double grilles. The villagers, both Arab and Jew, made speeches and danced, or fired shots in the air and showed off their prowess by wild galloping, or else they showed us their lovely cows and young forests. Haifa Municipality named a road after me, a road that I had had built up Carmel. The Jerusalem Municipal Council endowed and named a bed after me in the Hospital for Crippled Children, which served all creeds. On the day the name plaque was placed above the bed, it was occupied by a little Jerusalem-born Sephardi Jewish girl, who spoke to me in all three official languages.

The 31 March 1943 arrived, my fifty-eighth birthday. I was received *ad portas* by the warden of the Hospital of St John of Jerusalem, robed in his black mantle with the eight-pointed white cross and chain of office, and by the matron in her scarlet gown; afterwards some 300 of my colleagues, headed by the officer administering the government and the chief justice, gave a reception to my wife and me at the King David Hotel and expressed their good wishes in a beautiful bouquet to Philippa.

In my pocket I had a letter from the high commissioner expressing in generous terms His Excellency's

> great appreciation of the devoted and distinguished services and altruistic counsel which you have rendered to the Government and people of this country during the past twenty-three years. Your unflagging interest in, and care for, their welfare is reflected in the affection, respect and regard in which you are held by all sections of the population.

I took a final sunset walk from Olivet. I left the Dead Sea, shimmering like molten silver, behind me and started down the stony track to Gethsemane, which wanders through scattered patches of cultivation, dotted with old, old olive trees, and past a sheltered nook where fig trees had secured a holding.

Turrets, minarets and spires stood out for brief moments, like a train of camels on the skyline. The coppered domes of the Russian Church in the garden reflected the setting sun. The bells crashed out and died away; others replied from across the valley. A *muezzin* called to prayer from the *Haram al-Sherif*. A shepherd boy passed, playing his pipe. Children called. Camel bells sounded melodiously.

Having crossed over Kedron I entered the city by the Gate of Sitna Miriam, Our Lady Mary. In the arched gateway of the sombre Via Dolorosa an old man rocked a child to sleep. An oil lamp flickered.

I turned into the Temple area. There was a sense of space and calm.

Some of the faithful were saying their evening prayers: 'There is no God but God and Mohammed is the Apostle of God.' Little groups of women were at worship. A wee Muslim child was heard repeating the wisdom of his fathers: '*Allahu Akbar*. God is greatest.'

Leaving the Dome of the Rock, I entered the vaulted building overlooking the Wailing Wall, seen through barred windows, in deep shadows. A chorus of lamentations beat the air, like the wave roar of a distant sea, but from time to time a staccato voice carried a sound of throbbing, poignant sorrow. 'Therefore will I wail and howl,' spake Micah the Morasthite, 'I will make a wailing like the dragons and mourning as the owls.' As one's eyes became accustomed to the growing darkness, figures of individual worshippers gradually stood out from the swaying groups. Orthodox Jews with twisted sidelocks, dressed in velvet gaberdines and fur-trimmed hats, or non-Orthodox in lounge suits and caps, rocked their bodies to and fro, and from side to side, shaking themselves in obedience to the psalm: 'All my bones shall say, "Lord, Who is like unto Thee?" ' as they fervently prayed to God. 'For the Temple that is destroyed we sit in solitude and mourn.'

In David Street restaurants and coffee shops were closing; desert Arabs in camel-hair cloaks worked with gold, and *imam*s — the teachers of Islam — trim of beard and wearing neatly rolled white turbans round red fezzes, sat side by side. An Arabic song from a gramophone struck harshly on the ear. A richly saddled donkey stood across the path, waiting to take his master home. Men squatting on low coffee stools exchanged gossip.

Near the entrance to the courtyard of the Holy Sepulchre, a tailor was working late, finishing a coat for the early morning, and a heavy iron sizzled on damp cloth. A blind man came slowly along, tapping the timeworn stones. The courtyard was almost deserted; the great doors of the basilica were about to be closed. In the darkness a lamp flickered over the Stone of Unction. Franciscan friars, bearded Greeks and hooded Armenians were preparing for their night offices. Calvary was flooded with light from candles offered by the faithful. Little groups stood chanting the *Kyrie Eleison*, 'Lord, have mercy upon us.' Before the holy tomb, outlined by olive-oil lamps, a penitent said his prayers.

The vivid day was succeeded by the beauty of the night. From a distant cavalry camp on the Field of Rephaim a trumpet sounded.

These unceasing devotions gave the meaning of the city's pangs and pageantry; gave the reason why, in this little city of great things, each faith had jealously guarded rights and rites in sanctuaries and shrines through famine, siege and battle; for Moslem, Jew and Christian were maintaining in their own ways, and by customs hallowed through the centuries, man's relationship with God. 'Mankind comes to God along many roads, but by whatever road men come, on that road, He welcomes them, for all roads are His.'

Thus my memory leaves her, in the peace of eventide; still the Holy City — the Holy City still.

Index

Aaron, 63
Abbas 1, 178
Abbasid, 122
Abdullah, Emir, 70n, 71n, 89, 96, 99, 165, 186, 186n, 187, 190, 205, 220, 224
Abraham, 62, 73, 118, 124, 213
Abyssinian(s), 153, 161, 162, 168
Acre, 110, 145, 210
Addis, Sir Charles, 15
Aden, 20
Affuleh, 83
Africa(ns), xiv, xv, 40, 43, 90, 133, 195
Agudat Israel, 85, 114, 120
Aid for Prisoners of War, 40n
Ain Herod, 83
Al Azhar University, 94–5
al-Aqsa mosque, 118, 123
Albanian, 161, 178n
Aleppo, 68
Alexandria, 32–4, 59, 194
Ali, ex-king of Iraq, 165, 166
Ali, Rashid, 221
Allen, Charles, xv
Allenby, General Edmund, 53n, 67, 68, 69, 89, 187
Allenby Bridge, 175
America(n), 69, 95, 115, 121, 129,

137–8, 142, 149, 162, 167, 172–3, 212–13, 216–18; *see also* USA
Amery, Leopold, 66, 117
Amharic, 168
Ami, Ben, 209
Amin, Haj; *see* Husseini
Amman, 99, 104, 175, 176
Ammonite, 175
Andrews, Mr, 190
Anglican(s), 14, 78–9, 124, 154–5, 168, 188, 218
Anglo-Egyptian Sudan, xvii
anti-Semitism, 63, 85, 96
Antonia Tower, 197
Apollo Bunder, 21
Aqaba, Gulf of, 177
Arab Higher Committee, 111n, 183, 184, 186, 190, 205
Arab horses, 33, 69, 169
Arab Legion, 220, 224
Arabia, 19
Arabia, 37
Arabic, xvii, 35, 39n, 40, 42, 59, 69, 75, 77, 80, 81, 86, 87, 105, 111, 113, 115, 140, 144, 172, 204, 217, 220, 223, 227
Aramaic, 153
Arlosoroff, Chaim, 139, 140

229

Armenia/Armenian(s), 54, 75, 78,
  111, 112, 153–4, 158–9, 164,
  168, 215–16, 227
Aragon, 31
Ashbee, C. R., 54, 75, 78
Ashkenazi, 78, 79n, 80, 101, 119,
  140, 168, 188, 203
Asia Minor, 180
Asquith, Herbert, 65, 92n
Assemblies of God, Church of the,
  172
Assyrian, 57
Aswan, 35, 51
Atbara, 51
Augustine, 156
Aurelian, Emperor, 180
Australia(n), 24, 130n, 189, 190
  First Australian Division, 208
  soldiers/troops, 34, 51, 214
Austria(n), 117, 185, 213
  Austrian Empire, 40n
  Austrian Red Cross, 40n
Bab, tomb of the, 160
Back Bay, 25
Baden-Powell, Lord, 151
Badul, 176
Baghdad, 90, 165
Baha'is, 160
Bahr al Ghazal Province, 46
Bailey, Morris, 185
Baldock's stables, 24, 27
Balfour, Arthur James, 65, 66–7,
  147
Balfour Declaration, xviii, 64n, 65,
  67n, 70, 87, 96
Bandra, 24
Bank Clerks' Union/Bank
  Officers' Guild, 16
Bank of England, 17, 115

Barclays Bank, 196
Barnard, Violet Oliva (author's
  first wife), 12, 18, 19, 28–9, 31,
  41, 49–50, 77, 82, 101, 102, 113,
  134, 175–7, 194, 201, 206
Barnum and Bailey's Circus, 6
Basingstoke, 11–12, 14
Bassa, 194
Battershill, Chief Secretary, 190
Battir, 52, 177
Bay of Biscay, 32
BBC, 186
Bedu, 56, 60, 62, 68, 85, 99, 138,
  150n, 175–6, 180, 199
Beersheba, 96, 196
Beirut, 190
Beit Laham, 59
Belgium, 145
Ben-Gurion, David, 83n, 216,
  217n, 221
Ben-Zvi, Itzhak, 83, 216n, 219
Bentwich, Norman, 74
Berbereens, 35
Beringiah, 47
Berlin, 64, 65, 83n, 130n, 188
Berlitz School of Languages, 59
Bethlehem, 57, 61–2, 93–4, 102,
  105, 156, 158–9, 170, 189, 196,
  206, 217
Bexhill, 14
Birdwood, 33
Birmingham Municipality, 101
Bisharin tribe, 41, 49
Bishop Gobat school, 79
Black and Tans, 88
Black Sea, 214
Black Watch, 130n, 131, 132
Blake, William, 52, 103
Bodley, 54

Bols, Major-General Sir Louis, 53, 70, 72

Bombay, xvii, 19, 21–4, 27, 29, 38
—Light Horse, 24, 27, 29, 34
—Port Trust, 23

Bosphorus, 214

Bowman, Humphrey, 75

Bowman, Mrs Humphrey, 94

Boyce, Mr, 38

Brahmins, 22

Brandrick, Sergeant-Major, 31

Breasted, Professor, 103

Brighton, 11, 14, 100

Bristol, 2, 4

Britain/Great Britain, xiv, xvi, xviii, 55, 64n, 65n, 66, 68–9, 72, 88n, 90, 92n, 93, 108, 136, 140n, 189, 205, 208, 219, 221, 224

British Agency, 53n

British, xviii, 22–3, 37–8, 49, 54n, 59, 66n, 71n, 79n, 80n, 85, 87, 98, 111n, 112, 117, 137, 140n, 145n, 149, 150n, 172, 186n, 189, 192, 198, 201, 207–8, 210, 212, 213–16, 216n, 217n, 219–20, 223
—Army/military/soldiers/troops, 40, 51, 64n, 74n, 117n, 130n, 131, 187, 194, 197, 203, 205, 207–8, 215, 220
—embassy, 178, 188
—empire, xiv, xix
—gendarmerie/police, 88, 89n, 98, 119, 124, 136, 187, 190, 192, 196, 201, 203
—government, 39n, 66–7, 71, 73, 85, 115, 124, 127–9, 142, 146, 166, 186, 190–1, 205, 220
—Mandate, xviii, 54n
—officers, 42, 58, 62, 81, 123, 183, 187, 220
—officials, 41, 81, 85, 150, 187

Broadcasting House, 203

Buchman, Dr, 204

Buckingham Gate, 17

Bukhara, 219n

Bukharan community, 219

Bunney, 4

Burberrys, 12

Cairo, 30, 34, 49, 51, 53, 55, 74, 78, 88, 94, 105, 144, 155n, 178, 181, 214

Calais, 19

Calcutta, 191

Calthrop, Lord, 13

Calvary, 58, 152, 227

Cambridge, 2, 39n, 53n

Campbell, Beatrice Stella (Mrs Patrick), 15

Campbell, James, 15

Campbell, Revd R. J., 14

Canaan/Canaanites, 63

Canada/Canadian, 95, 115, 175, 179

Canterbury, Archbishop of, 7, 79, 154

Carmel, 134, 160, 189, 226

Carmelite(s), 105, 225

Casson, Lewis, 92

Cenacle, 116

Central Europe, xviii

Ceylon, 23, 90

Champion, Mr, 223

Chancellor, Lady, 121

Chancellor, Sir John, 121, 124, 129, 194

Chandlers Ford, 5, 6

Chapel of the Reparatrice Sisters, 159

Charlottenburg, 64n
Charterhouse School, 55
Chelsea barracks, 31
Chicago, 169
Chile, 29
Chipping Campden, 55
Christ Church, 158, 206
Christian Street, 58
Church Lads' Brigade, 14
Church Missionary Society, 155n, 218
Church of England, 14, 74
Church of the Nativity, 156, 159, 196
Churchill, Mrs, 89
Churchill, Winston, 88–91, 92n, 93, 96, 115, 131, 216
circumcision, 40
Cistercian(s), 106, 160
Citadel, 53, 69
Clapham, 18
Clayton, Sir Gilbert, 89
Clifton Downs, 2
Clifton, 2
Cockin, Canon, 2
Colonial Office, xiv, 74n, 88, 90–1, 100, 135, 166
Colonial Service, xvi, xviii, 90
Committee of Imperial Defence, 121n, 194
Constantinople, 140n, 154, 188, 216n
Cope, Sir Anthony, 13
Copenhagen, 65
Copts/Coptic, 112, 153, 161, 171
Cornes, Jerry, 192
Cornwall, 29
Corsair, 154
Cotswold, 2, 5, 58

Coupland, Professor Reginald, 188
Cresswell, Captain Archie, 71
Crimea, 159
Croome, Thomas Clutterbuck, 2
Crosbie, Harold, 132
Crosbie Hall, 18
Crusader(s), 137, 145
Crusades, 62
Cunard Line, 19, 31
Cunliffe Lister, Sir Philip, 146, 184
Curzon, Lord, 67, 68, 88
Cyprus, xix, 54n, 100, 134, 148
Cyrenaica, Emir of, 102
Cyril, Father, 215
D'Aubigny, Philip (crusader), 58
Dajani family, 116
Damascus Gate, 54, 71, 160
Damascus, 56, 61, 68, 74, 89, 168, 179
Damianos, Patriarch, 156
Dan, 96
Darfur, xvii, 36, 38, 39, 40, 45, 222
Darmstadt, 64n
Daubeney family, 2, 58
David Street, 55, 155, 227
David, King, 161
  Shield of David, 224
Davidson, Bishop (later Archbishop) Randall, 7, 154
Day of Atonement, 119, 124, 159, 217
Dead Sea, 53, 60, 126, 128, 135, 177, 212, 213, 226
Deedes, Brigadier Wyndham, 74, 75–6, 87, 89
Deedes, Rosie, 74
Delhi, 27

Derbyshire, 39n
Devonshire, Duke of, 11
Devonshire Park, 11
Diaspora, 63, 66, 218n
Dill, Lieutenant-General J. G.,
    186, 187
Dinar, Sultan Ali, 38–9, 46–7
Dobbie, Brigadier, 123, 124
Dome of the Rock, 118, 123, 227
Dominican father(s), 105, 160
Downing Street, 90, 92, 165
Druze, 96, 201, 206
Duke of Wellington's Regiment,
    71
Dunkley, George, 137
Dutch, 80, 113
dysentery, 33
Earls Court, 10
East Africa, 64, 65
 Joint East African Board, 39n
East India Company, 2
Eastbourne, 11, 14
Eastern District, 39
Eastern Europe(an), 80, 81, 101,
    126, 150
Eastern Telegraph Company, 37
Eastleigh, 6, 7, 9
Echmiadzin, 215
Eder, Dr Montague David, 54, 95,
    151
Edicule, 58, 152, 153
Egypt, xvii, 30, 34–6, 53, 55, 59,
    67, 74, 75, 89n, 96, 112, 123,
    135, 145, 153, 155n, 161n, 178,
    180–1, 194, 196, 204, 205, 208,
    216
Egyptian, 34–6, 40n, 51, 53n, 74n,
    103, 161, 178, 181, 205, 178
—Army, 34, 36, 89n, 126

—Expeditionary Force, 31, 67n
El Alamein, 193n, 213, 216
El Arish, 177, 178
El Fasher, 38, 46
El Obeid, 38, 45, 50
El Quweira, 176
Elias, Bishop, 171
Emeq Zevulun, 115
Emmaus, 159
England, xvii, 12, 14, 23, 28,
    34, 50, 66, 70, 95, 104, 108, 121,
    127, 129, 132, 134, 140, 146,
    150n, 156, 167, 185, 188, 190–1,
    194, 195, 201, 206, 210, 213
Eretz Israel, 125, 190, 217
Es Sik, 176
Esdraelon, plain of, 60, 83
Essex, 11
Essex House Press, 54
Essex Regiment, 189
Eton College, 74n, 98n, 117
Eurasian, 22, 26
Evil Council, hill of, 102–3
Ezekiel (prophet), 119
Faisal, Emir (king of Iraq), 70, 71,
    165–6
Farouk, King, 178n, 216
Farrell, Jerome, 75
father (of Edward Keith-Roach),
    xvii, 2, 4–8
First World War, xvii, 40n, 53n,
    65n, 67n, 68n, 74n, 79n, 80n,
    89n, 92n, 98n, 117n, 120n, 130n,
    140n, 186n, 187n, 193n, 220n
Foot, H. M., 136
Foreign Office, 88, 90–1, 165
Four Square Gospel Church, 104
France, 63, 64n, 66, 72, 88n, 111,
    117n, 132, 187n, 209, 212

French, 4, 14, 33, 56, 59, 69, 71, 75, 80, 90, 111, 113, 168, 186n, 204, 213

French Equatorial Africa, 45, 49

Franciscan(s), 78, 105, 116, 153, 155, 157, 159, 218, 227

Franconia, 31

Freiburg, 64n

Freud, Sigmund, 54n

Furowi(s), 42, 43, 45, 49

Galilee, 60, 127, 132–3, 135, 140, 216n

Sea of Galilee, 77, 84, 134

Gallipoli, 30, 31, 33, 74

Garstang, Professor, 103

Gaster, Moses, 66

Gaza, 51, 94, 177, 205

Ge'z, 153

Geneva, 64n, 203

George Cross, 223

George of Saxony, Revd Prince, 134

George V, 116n, 166

George VI, 187

Germany/German(s), 32, 53, 54, 58–61, 69, 76, 78, 87, 100, 105, 112, 117n, 134, 141n, 142, 150, 193n, 205, 212, 213, 216

German Hospice, 53, 76, 78

German Templar community, 59

Gezira Sporting Club, 181

Ghazi, king of Iraq, 166

Gibraltar, 32

Gladstone, Noel, 119

Glasgow, 178

Gloucestershire, 2, 12

Glubb, Major-General John, 220

Goanese, 19, 22

Gokaldas Tejpal Hospital, 26

Gordon College, 40

Gordon, General Charles, 40

Government House, xiv, 78, 82, 99, 102, 121, 130, 132, 191, 195, 222

Graham-Brown, Bishop, 124, 194, 219

Grant Road, 26

Great Synagogue, 159

Greece, 128

Greek(s), 4, 33, 57, 76, 78, 79, 143, 148, 153, 157, 169–70, 175, 227

Greig, Robert, 192

Grey, Sir Edward, 66

Greyhound Hotel, 8

Grindelwald, 28

Guild of Handicraft, 54

Habima, 142

Hadassah, 94

Hadassah Hospital, 218

Haganah, 212

Haifa, 59, 60, 61, 83–4, 87, 93, 100, 115, 133–6, 139, 144, 145n, 147, 149, 165–6, 169, 173, 183–4, 186–9, 196, 206, 208–10, 226

Haining, Lieutenant-General R., 193

Hall, Hathorne, 91

Halley's comet, 26

Halstead, 11

halukka, 218

Hama, 68

Hamilton, Ian, 33

Hampshire Downs, 4

Hampshire, 3, 11

Hankin, Yehoshua, 70

Haram al-Sherif (Noble

Sanctuary), 53, 104, 117–18, 124, 125, 160, 167, 217, 226
Harbour Department, 136
Harewood, Lord, 117
Harrison, Austen, 102–3
Hartley Wintney, 13
Hastings, 14
Hausa, 45
Hawran, 207
Hazely Down, 3
Hebrew University, 64n, 74n, 211, 211n, 218, 220, 225
Hebrew, xviii, 60, 66n, 69, 75, 77, 80, 81, 83, 86, 87, 94, 113, 122, 141, 150, 159, 162, 168, 197, 205, 210, 220, 223
Hebron, 78, 122–4, 192, 196, 202, 212–13
Hefher, valley of, 115
Heinnemier, Miss, 14
Hejaz, the, 36, 67, 68, 96
Hensman's Hotel, 215
Herod the Great, 118, 197n
Heron, Colonel George, 75
Hertz, Dr, 67
Hertzl, Theodor, 64
Highlanders, 130n, 165
Hillel the Elder, 159
Hindu/Hindus, 22, 25, 26, 164
Hitler, Adolf/Hitlerism, xviii, 60, 149, 212, 219–20, 223
Hitler Youth, 148
Holy Places, 69, 78, 108, 123, 125, 152, 156, 212
Holy Sepulchre, 55, 58, 71, 79, 104, 112, 152, 155, 158, 161, 171, 218, 227
Homs, 68
Hong Kong and Shanghai Bank, 15

Hong Kong, 23
Hooker, Fanny, 4
Horsham, 10
Hospital for Crippled Children, 226
House of Commons, 65, 92, 128, 130, 184, 194
Houston, 137
Hove, 14, 15
Hove Lawns, 100
Howard-Williams, Colonel, 11
Huberman, Bronislaw, 141
Huddlestone Bey, 39
Hudson, William, 75
Hughes, Robert, 59
Huleh (Lake), 80, 148, 191
Husseini, Haj Amin el, 71, 94, 183, 185, 190, 212, 221
Ibrahim Pasha, 178
Imperial Airways, 134
India, xv, xvii, 28, 75, 109, 134, 188, 193–4, 204
Indian, 17, 22–3, 25, 78, 124, 193
—civil service, 2, 20
—medical service, 26
—police, 75, 191
India Office, 91
Indian Ocean, 175
Iraq, 70n, 72, 75, 96, 113, 153, 165–6, 184, 186–7, 212, 221
Iraq Petroleum Company, 137, 139, 185, 193
Ireland, 2, 88, 98n, 130n, 165
Irish, 91, 165
Northern Ireland, 131
Isaac, 118
Isis, Temple of, 161
Islam(ic), 68, 78, 79, 115, 122–3,

125, 150, 160, 176, 199, 215, 227
Ismail, khedive of Egypt, 40n
Ismailiya, 34
Italian(s), 33, 69, 75, 159, 189,
  193, 206
consul general, 116
firms, 136
Italy, 55, 64n, 98n, 116, 136, 157,
  212
Izzed Din al-Qassim, Sheikh, 145
Jabotinsky, Vladimir, 71, 114,
  139, 210, 212
Jacobites, 153, 164; *see also*
  Syrian Orthodox
Jaffa, 59, 61, 77, 79n, 82, 86–7,
  95, 123, 128, 132, 145, 185, 196,
  208, 224
Jaffa Gate, 53, 69, 121, 123, 169
Japanese, 31, 193n
Jarvis Bey, 126
Jericho, 130, 213
Jerusalem Municipal Council, 110,
  226
Jerusalem Sports Club, 100, 149
Jewish Agency, 83n, 114, 117,
  129, 139, 140n, 150, 205, 216,
  220, 225
Jewish Colonial Association
  (JCA), 80
Jewish Foundation Fund (Keren
  Hayesod), 87, 114, 218
Jewish Labour Federation, 83
Jewish National Council (Va'ad
  Le'ummi), 83, 95, 208, 210
Jewish National Fund (Keren
  Kayemeth Leisrael), 83, 114, 115,
  127, 150, 170, 218
Jewish Territorialist Organization,
  54n

Jewish War Needs Fund, 220
Jiddah, 36
Jordan
—river, 94, 114, 135, 148, 175,
  177, 187
—valley, 60, 70, 157, 160, 171,
  211
Joshua, 63
Judaea, 54n, 60
Judaean hills, 52, 160, 177
Justinian, 118
Kadria, Princess, 177, 178
Kafr Yasif, 210
Kantara, 178, 206
Karachi, xvii, 27
Karrieme, 149, 159
Kauwakji, Fawzi el-, 186, 187,
  188
Kedron, 226
Keith-Roach, Anthony (author's
  son), 31, 134
Keith-Roach, Christabel Eve
  (author's daughter), 206
Keith-Roach, Martin (author's
  son), 29, 82, 134, 210
Keith-Roach, Philip D'Aubigny
  (author's son), 206
Kelly Pasha, 39, 46
Kelmscott Press, 55
Kensington, 10
Kent, 213
Kerrari, 36
Kew Gardens, xvi, 8
Khalidi, Mustapha, 111
Khartoum, 34, 36, 38, 39, 40, 41,
  44, 47, 49, 51, 216
Khedivial University, Cairo, 55
King David Hotel, 214, 226
Kipling, Rudyard, xvii, 20, 37

Kirkuk oilfields, 137
Kisch, Colonel, 117, 120, 139
Kisselov, Jacob, 192
Kitchener, Lord, 38
Kitzbühel, 185
Knights of St John, 103, 116
Koran, 43, 125, 160
Kordofan Province, 38, 40, 42, 195, 222
Kuk, Chief Rabbi Abraham Isaac, 79, 80, 140
Kurdish porters, 55, 169
Labour Party, 114, 139, 140
—, British, 128n, 216n
Lachish, 192
Ladino, 80
Lag Ba'Omer, (feast of), 159
Lajjun, 173
Lambeth Palace, 7
Lancashire Fusiliers, 29
Lancashire, 7, 30
Lancastrian Prince, 137
Landau, Annie, 81
Lang, Cosmo Gordon, 154, 155, 156
Law Society, 81
Lawrence, T. E., xvii, 68, 88–9, 91
League of Nations, xviii, 121, 185
Lebanon, 149
Mount Lebanon, 150n
Lefgren, Mr Jules, 124
Ley, Major, 75
Libyan, 35, 206
Lincoln, 12
Lion Gate, 8, 10
Littlehampton, 14
Liverpool, 65n, 167
Lloyd George, David, 64, 65, 67, 87–8

Local Government Board, 66
London, xvii, 6, 8, 10, 13, 15–19, 22–4, 28–9, 52, 54n, 59, 65–6, 79n, 89, 92n, 102n, 115, 155n, 184, 188, 201–2, 210
London and County Bank, 8, 15
London and South Western Railway, 6, 52
London Mission to the Jews, 59
Lucerne, 145, 146
Luke, Henry Charles, 117, 120, 121, 122
Luxor, 35, 51
Lydda, 61, 82, 89, 104, 177, 191, 201, 205
Ma'an, 176
MacDonald, Malcolm, 202
MacDonald, Ramsay, 128, 129, 130
Macedonian, 175
MacInnes, Bishop, 155, 156
MacMichael, Sir Harold, 39, 195, 197, 214, 222
Madda Theatre Norwich Players, 11
Madrid, 188
Magnes, Dr, 211, 220
Malabar Hill, 21
malaria, 61, 80, 83, 94, 148
Malaya, 39n, 75, 90
Malta, 39n, 74n, 98n, 123, 124n, 184, 220
Manchester, 28–31, 64, 65, 92, 206
Mar Hanna, 103
Mar Saba convent, 157, 171
Mardin, 153
Markham, Miss, 5
Marlborough, 2

Marseilles, 19
Marsh, Eddie, 92
Masefield, Mr and Mrs John, 102
Massey (B & S Ltd), 28
Massey, Philippa Barnard
 (author's second wife), 28, 206,
 212, 225–6
Masters, John, xv
MCC, 100
McCarthy, Lillah, 102
McDonnell, Chief Justice, 185,
 189
McGeagh, William, 192
McMahon, Sir Henry, 67
McNeill, Brigadier Angus, 89
McPherson, Aimée Semple, 104
Meads, 11
Mecca, 42, 46, 50, 118, 152
 Sherif Hussein of, 36, 62, 68, 144,
 178, 186n
Medical Department, 124
Medina, 42
Mediterranean, 32, 126, 137, 175,
 191
 Mediterranean Fleet, 165
Megiddo, 67n, 177
Megone, Norfolk, 11
Meir, Chief Rabbi Jacob, 79, 80,
 168
Meiron, 159
Meirum, 80
Melchett, Lord, 120
Melchite, 169
Mercantile Bank of India, xvii, 15
Mesopotamia, 72, 96, 130n; *see
 also* Iraq
Middle East Conference, 88
Middle East Department, 88, 91
Miller, Mr, 223

Mills, Eric, 127
Minchinhampton, Rector of, 2
Moab, hills of, 82, 103
Mohammed, the Prophet, 58, 118,
 123, 125, 227
Mohammed Ahmed Ibn Sayid
 Abdullah, 40n
Monck, Nugent, 11
Montagu, Edwin, 66
Monte Carlo, 154
Montgomery, Major-General
 Bernard, 193, 194–5, 206
Morestead, 3
Morgan, Pierpont, 154
Moroccan(s), 70, 118–19, 125
Morris, Jan, xv
Morris, William, 55
Moses, 47, 94, 160
mother (of Edward Keith-Roach),
 1, 2, 4–5, 7, 29, 58
Mott, Dr, 115
Mount Gerizim, 162
Mount of Olives, 52, 76, 104, 105,
 115, 159, 170
Mount Scopus, 53, 54
Mount Thabor, 159
Mount Zion, 76
Moyne, Lord, 214
Mudeiris, Abu, 82
mufti of Jerusalem, 71n, 94–5,
 102, 115, 122, 144, 145, 160,
 185, 209, 212, 221
Musa, 48
 Nebi Musa, 161
 Wadi Musa, 175
Musa, Dr and Mrs, 167–9
Muslim(s), 22, 25 6, 40, 45, 47,
 54–5, 57, 63, 68, 70–1, 73–4, 76,
 78–9, 81, 95–7, 99, 101, 104,

111, 113, 115, 117–20, 122,
124–5, 127, 146, 149–50,152–3,
158, 160–2, 164–6, 173, 180,
185, 190, 197, 201, 213, 216–17,
227–8
Supreme Muslim Council, 71n,
95, 120, 160, 165, 225
Mussolini, Benito, 116, 136
Muza Kazim Pasha, 79
Nabatean(s), 175–7, 180
Nablus, 104, 122, 162, 183, 191,
205
Nahalal, 83
Nashashibi, Ragheb Bey, 54, 79,
173, 205
Nazarenes, Church of the, 111
Nazareth, 190, 217
Nazi(s), 60, 74n, 141n, 219, 224
128n
Nebuchadnezzar, 118
Netanya, 209
New York, 84, 120, 169, 216n
New Zealand, 130n
Nicanor, Cave of, 170
Nigeria(n), 37, 42, 45
Nile, 35, 36, 46, 51, 61, 177, 178,
179, 181
Nimr, Abu, 82
Noble Sanctuary, *see Haram al-
Sherif*
Nordau, Max, 68
North Africa, 193, 223
Novomeysky, Moshe, 128, 149
O'Connor, Major-General
Richard, 193, 197, 206
O'Leary, General, 32
Odenathus, 180
Odessa, 63, 140
OETA (Occupied Enemy Territory

Administration), 49, 53, 74, 75
Olivet, 53, 226
Omar, Caliph, 152
Omayyad, 122
Omdurman campaign, 36
Order of St John of Jerusalem,
103, 159
hospital, 94, 226
St John fund, 210
Order of the Rafidain, 166
Ormsby-Gore, William, 184, 191
Orpen, SirWilliam, 155
Orr-Ewing, Dr, 124, 179
Ottoman, 65, 115
—army, 178n
—Empire, 78
—Turks, 53n, 54n, 61, 68n, 73
Owlesbury, 3–5
Owlesbury House, 3
Oxford, 65n
Oxford Group, 117, 188, 203
P & O, 19
Painswick, 2
Palestine Economic Society, 112,
Palestine Police, 88
Palmer, Mr, 136
Palmer's Gate, 137
Palmer, Sir Frederick, 93
Palmyra, 150n, 151, 179, 180
Panama, 214
Parsee, 20–2, 25, 164
Partition Commission, 201
Passover, 63, 158, 162
Patria, 203, 209
Peake, Commanding Officer, 220
Peel, Lord, 188
pelota, 33
Penang, 23
Pentateuch, 159

Perowne, Stewart, 102
Persia/Persian, 44, 167, 168, 175, 179
Persian Gulf, 33, 180
Pestonjee, 24
Petah Tiqvah, 183
Petra, 175, 177, 180
Pharaoh(s), 63, 94, 153
Philae ruins, 35
Philoxinos, Bishop, 170–1
Phoenicia, 133
Pilgrim Hostel, 198
Pinero, Sir Arthur Wing, 11, 15n
Pinsker, Leon, 63, 170
Plumer, Field Marshal Lord, 98, 99–104, 116–17, 193, 222
Plumer, Lady, 99, 121
Plymouth Brethren, 197
Plymouth, 31
pogrom, 63
Poland, 63n, 86, 188, 207, 216
Poles, 78, 86
Poor Sisters of Clare, 105, 225
Port Said, 20
Port Sudan, 36–8
Port Sudan Club, 37
Portsmouth, 194
Prince Line, 137
Princess Royal, 116, 137
Pro-Jerusalem Society, 55
Protestant(s), 125, 126, 169
Prussia
Franco-Prussian war, 61
king of, 79
public custodian of enemy property, xvii, 53, 58, 76
Punjab, 130
Putney, 18
Qiryat Anavim, 83

Quetta, 194
Rabbath-Ammon, 175
Rafah, 205
Railway Administration, 37
Ramallah, 82, 177, 196
Ramla, 104
Red Cross, 40n, 112, 210
Red Sea, 63
Red Sea Club, 37
Red Sea Province, 37
Refugees Settlement Commission, 128
Rehovot, 64n
Rendal, Mr, 136
Repton, 2, 130n
Revisionist, 114, 139–40, 210, 212, 221
Rhodes, 55, 116
Rhodesia, 54n, 121n
Richmond, 8, 10
Richmond, Ernest, 76
Ridler, Miss Hilda, 84
Rifle Brigade, 74
Riot Commission, 151
Rishon, 80
Rochdale, Colonel Lord, 32
Rockefeller Foundation, 94
Rockefeller, John D., 103
Roman, 53, 63, 144, 175, 180, 197n
—empire, 180
—legions, 138
Roman Catholic, 14, 57, 66, 125–6, 149, 153, 218
Roman Church, 154
Romanian(s), 66, 213
Rome, 126, 180
Rommel, Field Marshal Erwin, 213

Rosh Pinna, 84
Rothschild, Baron Edmund James de, 61, 66, 67, 80, 147
Rotterdam, 80n
Rotunda, 58, 152, 153, 158
Roulstone, Sister, 185
Royal Air Force (RAF), 68n, 88, 89, 178
Royal Army Service Corps, 84
Royal Artillery, 183, 197
Royal Exchange, 18
Royal Fusiliers, 98
Rumbold, Sir Horace, 188
Ruppin, Dr Arthur, 83
Russia(n), 56–7, 63–4, 76, 78, 83, 86, 93, 128, 150, 153, 159, 187, 198, 216n
Russian Orthodox Church, 153, 198, 226
Rutbah Wells, 138
Rutenberg, Pinchas, 93, 149, 208, 210
Rye, 14
Saad el Din, 123
Sacher, Harry, 80
Sadlier, Sister, 185
Safad, 84, 110, 123, 217
Sahara, 38, 48
St Bartholomew's Church, 14
St Charles of Borromeo convent, 134
St George's Cathedral, 99, 103
St George's school, 79
St Helena' s chapel, 153, 161
St James, Cathedral of, 215
St James's Palace, 166, 202
St John's, Cambridge, 2
St Leonards, 14
St Mark, Church of, 158, 170

St Matthew, 58
St Paul's Convent, 54
St Peter's, Rome, 126
St Thomas's Hospital, 28
Saladin, 103
Salford, 29
Salonica, 80
Salt, 104
Samakh, 84, 184
Samaria, 60, 115, 133, 146–7, 150
Samaritan(s), 162, 219
Samuel, Lady, 81, 87, 96
Samuel, Sir Herbert, 65, 72–5, 77–8, 81, 87–8, 93, 96–7, 98–100, 136
San Remo, xviii, 72
Sarona, 58
Sassoon, xvii
Saunders, Major Alan, 59
Scarborough, Lord, 103
Scind Club, 27
Scotland/Scottish, 16, 17, 197
Church of Scotland, 158
London Scottish volunteers, 17, 24, 29
Scottish Mission Hospital, 135
Scott, C. P., 64
Scott, Paul, xv
Seaforth Highlanders, 137
Semitic, 153
Sephardi, 66, 78, 80, 101–2, 120, 168, 226
Seychelles, 111n
Shafaat, 102
Shakespeare, William, 4
Shakespearean, 121
Shallal, 35, 51
Sharett, Moshe; *see* Shertock, Moshe

Sharon, plain of, 60, 115
Shaw, George Bernard, 15, 92
Shawford, 3
 Shawford Park, 3
Shefa Amr, 82
Shemen Soap & Oil Factory, 83
Sherifian Party (Ashraf), 122
Shertock, Moshe, 140, 220
Shoreham, 14
Shrubb (tobacconist and athlete),
 10
Shuckburgh, John, 91, 92
Sierra Leone, 117
Simpson, Sir John Hope, 128
Sinai, 51, 61, 64, 126, 156, 177,
 178
Sirhad, Abu, 82
Slatin, Baron Rudolph Carl von,
 40
Sodom and Gomorrah Golf Club,
 212
Sokolow, Nahum, 66
Soloman, Colonel, 84
Solomon, 118, 177
 Solomon's pools, 61
 Temple of, 125
South Africa(n), 7, 14, 31, 142
South American, 29
South Western Railway, 6, 52
Southampton, 6
Southport, 31
Soviet Union, 215
Spain, 80, 120
Spinneys, 217
Staff College, 121n, 193, 194
Stanhope, Lady Hester, 150
Starkey, John Llewelyn, 192
Stavsky, Abraham, 140
Stern, Avraham, 212, 214

Stern Gang, 39n, 214
Stern Group, 212n
Stone of Unction, 58, 152, 227
Storrs, Sir Ronald, xvii, xix, 53–5,
 70, 75, 100–1, 108, 117–19, 156
Strathearn, Dr John, 94, 124, 185
Struma, 214
Stuart, Dr, 124
Stuckey, Mr, 137, 139
Suakin, 37
Sudan, xvii, 36–38, 39, 40, 41, 45,
 62, 89n, 91, 98n, 155n, 178, 195,
 222
 Sudan Political Service, 39n, 222
Suez Canal, 20, 34, 51, 178
Sunni, 78
Supreme Catholicos, 215
Supreme Muslim Council, 71n,
 95, 160, 165, 190, 225
Survey Department, 44
Sussex (cruiser), 183
Sussex, 10, 14
Sweden, 124, 203
 Swedish, 112
Swiss, 59, 64n, 165
Switzerland, 165
Sykes, Sir Mark, 66, 68
Syria/Syrian, 33, 68, 71, 72, 83,
 93, 96, 111, 145, 153–4, 169,
 170, 184, 186n, 187, 207, 220
 Syrian Orthodox, 153, 158, 164,
 167, 170
Tabgha, 84
Tadmur, 180
Talmud, 113, 159
Tanganyika, 39n, 195
Tangier, 63
Taranto harbour, 134
Tasmania, 189

Tegart, Sir Charles, 191, 192, 209
Tel Aviv, 61, 83, 86, 87, 114, 139,
  142, 196, 203, 207, 209, 214
Temple area, Jerusalem, 53, 70,
  117–18, 227
Temple of the Sun, 180
Territorials, 30
Terry, Mr, 9
Texas, 137, 138
Thomas, Jimmy, 92
Thorndike, Sybil, 92
Thornycrofts, 12
Tiberias, 134–6, 218
Tiger Hill, 203
Timotheos, Archbishop, 156
Titus, 118
Tod & MacGregor, 178
Torrance, Dr Herbert, 135
Toscanini, Arturo, 141
Trajan, Emperor, 180
Transjordan, 70n, 71, 89, 96,
  98–9, 104, 126, 165, 175, 178,
  186, 207, 220n
—Frontier Force, 98, 220, 223
Trappist monks/monastery, 42,
  106, 160
Triad, HM submarine, 211
Tripoli, 112
Tritton, Mr, 136
Troad (blacksmith), 5
Trusted, Harry, 189
Tryon, Major, 31
Tulkarm, 183, 195
Tuqan, Jamal Beq, 192
Tuqan, Suleiman Bey, 205, 224
Turkey, 38, 115
Turkish, 36, 54n, 66, 68, 74, 76,
  79, 80, 99, 100, 128, 140n, 160,
  161, 188, 214, 215, 225

Turkish Agricultural Bank, 59
Turkish army, 74, 186n
Turks, 32, 36–7, 53n, 60, 67, 68n,
  69, 73, 76, 83n, 85, 94, 152, 160,
  214
Turton, 30
Twyford, 3, 6
typhoid fever, 12, 33
Tyre, 169
Ukraine, 70n, 83n, 93n, 139n,
  140n
Umberto, Crown Prince, 116
Umm Keddada, 39, 49
United Nations, 64n, 219
USA, 64n, 66, 83n, 84, 90, 92n,
  94n, 114, 169, 173, 211n, 216n,
  217–18; *see also* America(n)
Ussishkin, Menahem, 83, 115,
  170, 208
Va'ad Le'ummi; *see* Jewish
  National Council
Valhalla, 177
Vatican, 79, 126
venereal disease, 34, 215
Vienna/Viennese, 64, 117
Vriesland, Siegfried Adolf van, 80
Wadi Araba, 177
Wadi Halfa, 36, 51
Wadi Rum, 177
Wailing Wall, 53, 70, 117–18, 121
  4, 167–8, 227
Wales, 60
Welsh, 59
Wallis, Mr, 6
War Office, 31, 88, 194
War Supplies Board, 216
Warburg, Felix, 129
Waterloo, 18
Wauchope, Major-General Arthur,

130, 131–3, 143–5, 184–6,
190–1, 195
Wavell, Major-General Archie,
187, 193
Weizmann, Dr Chaim, 54n, 64, 65,
66, 70, 87, 96, 117n, 118, 129,
205, 210
Wellington, 2
Wells, H. G., xvii, 89
West African, 42
Western Command Chester, 29
Whitechapel, 55
Wilhelm, Kaiser, 69
Wilhelmina, 59
Wiltshire, 2
Winchester, 3–6, 134, 210
Wingate, Captain Orde, 193, 197
Wingate, Colonel George, 197
Wingate, General, 37, 49, 51
Woodruff, Philip, xv
Worthing, 14
Yacub, (priest), 171
Yiddish, 86, 87
YMCA, 149, 162, 218

Young, Mark, 91
Yugoslavia, 221
Zangwill, Israel, 54n
Zarqa, 176
Zenobia, 180
Zerubbalal's Temple, 118
Zion, 190, 220
Zion Square, 110
Zionism, 63–4, 67, 68n, 74, 114,
117, 216n
Zionist Commission, 54, 64n,
69–71, 81, 83n, 114, 120
Zionist Congress, 83, 145–6, 203
Zionist Executive, 54n, 65, 66,
80n, 83, 95, 117n
Zionist Organization, 64, 69, 82,
114, 118
Women's, 94n
World, 64n, 66n
Zondek, Professor Bernhard, 209,
209n
Zonnenfeld, Rabbi, 120
Zoroastrian, 21